Through a Vegan Studies Lens

CULTURAL ECOLOGIES OF FOOD IN THE 21ST CENTURY

Series Editors: Tom Hertweck (University of Nevada, Reno) and Iker Arranz (University of California, Santa Barbara)

As we move deeper into the 21st century, people around the globe have become increasingly aware of the way their food choices produce ecologies of effects, environmentally and otherwise. *Cultural Ecologies of Food in the 21st Century* invites manuscripts that, using a truly interdisciplinary framework, parse the complexities of contemporary food culture. Encompassing any characteristics of food and drink, from their agricultural or technological production to their traditional or market-based consumption, and including their systems of waste and the cultures of thought that surround them, works in the series will uncover how humanity's daily eating is constellated within and among diverse bodies of knowledge. *Cultural Ecologies* encourages the work of specialists who are eager to relate their learned understanding of eating to those outside their own discipline. From the politics, economics, and scientific practices of agriculture at any scale, to the systems of promotion, distribution, and consumption that make food salable, to the representational economies of value that tell us what is good to eat and when: any transdisciplinary approach that brings food into focus will be considered.

Of particular interest are those manuscripts that include deep place-based perspectives or the environmental effects of how we eat as part of their investigations, including those that attempt either to pose well the questions food scholars and real-world eaters must face as well as to answer the extant dilemmas of our time. The series also welcomes projects that tackle the global reach of food systems and comparative studies of producing, eating, and food thought, as well as those studies that attempt to ground their work in the historical systems that inform our present moment.

Through a Vegan Studies Lens

Textual Ethics and Lived Activism

Edited by Laura Wright

UNIVERSITY OF NEVADA PRESS *Reno & Las Vegas*

University of Nevada Press | Reno, Nevada 89557 USA
www.unpress.nevada.edu
Copyright © 2019 by University of Nevada Press
All rights reserved
Cover art by Tristanbm, dreamstime.com
Cover design by Matt Strelecki

LIBRARY OF CONGRESS CATALOGING-IN-PUBLICATION DATA
Names: Wright, Laura, 1970- author.
Title: Through a vegan studies lens : textual ethics and lived activism / Laura Wright.
Other titles: Cultural ecologies of food in the 21st century.
Description: Reno ; Las Vegas : University of Nevada Press, [2019] | Series:
   Cultural ecologies of food in the 21st century
Identifiers: LCCN 2018041482 (print) | LCCN 2018045689 (ebook) | ISBN
   9781948908108 (pbk. : alk. paper) | ISBN 9781948908092 (cloth : alk.
   paper) | ISBN 9781948908115 (ebook)
Subjects: LCSH: Veganism--Philosophy. | Vegetarianism in literature. |
   Ecocriticism. | Veganism--Social aspects. | Vegetarianism--Social aspects.
   | Food habits in literature. | Humane education.
Classification: LCC TX392 .W75 2019 (print) | LCC TX392 (ebook) | DDC
   641.3/03--dc23
LC record available at https://lccn.loc.gov/2018041482

FIRST PRINTING

Manufactured in the United States of America

Contents

Doing Vegan Studies: An Introduction

Laura Wright

In "Animal Worlds in Modern Fiction," the introduction to his 2014 edited special issue of *Modern Fiction Studies*, David Herman begins with an analysis of Jonathan Lethem's 2014 short story "Pending Vegan." Herman notes that "the story, focalized through [Paul] Espeseth, explores how two days after going off his medication the protagonist finds himself in a fragile, fearful psychological state, slowed in his progression from pending to actual vegan" (422). Paul's position of being stuck in between omnivorous present and herbivorous future occurs from a combination of laziness and a sense of shame at the possibility of admitting to being vegan as well as a kind of dread of being held accountable to some higher power for failing to become vegan. Veganism as a possible identity embarrasses Paul, but not embracing veganism, he fears, endangers his soul. Further, Herman notes that in an interview in the *New Yorker*, Lethem traces the origin of the story to a class that he was teaching on "Animals and Literature," for which he prepared by purchasing (but not reading in their entirety) numerous vegan and animal rights manifestos. In the interview, Lethem says, "What would it be to think you've gone about halfway, or not even halfway, down some irreversible ethical path, then got stuck there?" (qtd. in Herman 422). I mention this anecdote as Herman situates it in his own work as a way of engaging the "remarkably divided sensibility, a profoundly double vision" (422) that often characterizes animal studies more broadly: in the realm of animal studies approaches, as scholars, we can write about, theorize about—and care about—animals, even as we might continue to instrumentalize, ingest, and exploit them.

But I also mention Lethem's story because it effectively illustrates the place from which a specifically vegan studies approach emerges and differentiates itself from more familiar conceptions of "animal studies," an umbrella term for a three-pronged field that gained prominence in the late 1990s and early 2000s, consisting of critical animal studies, human animal studies, and posthumanism. While veganism is certainly a consideration of these modes of inquiry, it is also a distinctly different entity, an ethical delineator that for many scholars marks a complicated boundary between theoretical pursuit and lived experience. From the perspectives of many of us working to make veganism "fit" as scholarly endeavor and deeply held identity category, animal studies had "gone about halfway [and] then got[ten] stuck," often unsure of what to do with veganism and vegan scholars, whether to embrace veganism, treat it as an overly emotional and quixotic response to an environmental and dietary paradox, or to mediate its presumed extremity via a discourse of "ethically sourced" animal products.

For vegan studies scholars, for animal studies to matter, the work that is done in its name necessarily has to be in the service of animals—and the work of feminist animal studies scholars (and more specifically ecofeminist animal studies scholars)—is work that actively asks the question, as Greta Gaard does, "has the growth of animal studies been good *for animals*?" (520, my emphasis). A vegan studies approach is theoretical, but it engages a lived politics of listening, care, emotion, and the empathetic imagination. As Stephanie Jenkins says, for vegans, "our ethics are not just a theory but a way of life" (507), and this reality is what distinguishes a specifically vegan studies mode of inquiry from animal studies more generally. Further, if vegan studies is about listening (rather than speaking for), then we must be willing to listen to perspectives that may challenge our conceptions of "theory" in favor of work that is more activist, potentially experimental, and less bounded by the strictures of academic writing. This is not to say that vegan studies should be anti-theory, but that it should be theoretically *different*: informed by theory, driven by theoretical inquiry, but also fully engaged in activist praxis, dedicated to establishing a conversation that crosses boundaries and expands both knowledge and social engagement beyond the confines of the academy—and to my mind, this difference is what makes vegan studies so exciting.

In this introduction, I briefly trace the field of vegan studies, its origins and importance, and I discuss the difficulties of the truly intersectional approach required by the vegan theorist, as this approach often forces the scholar to engage with incredibly difficult—and often traumatic—subject matter. Further, by centering this discussion on the deaths of seventy-one refugees who were abandoned by human smugglers who left them to die, as Sophia Jones of *The Huffington Post* notes, "stuffed like cattle" in a meat truck left on the side of a road in Austria in August of 2015, I want to extend the reach of vegan studies beyond the West to look at how the discourse with regard to the status of displaced peoples renders their individual identities absent referents[1] subsumed by the terms "immigrant" or "refugee." My focus will be on what a vegan reading of this incident reveals about the tacit linkages between the Syrian refugee crisis, the rhetoric of climate change, and the rhetoric of meat in the construction of a political narrative about the displacement of bodies, both animal and human.

Civil war in Syria began in March of 2012; as of July 2017, around half a million people had died in the fighting, and nearly twelve million people had been displaced ("Syria's Civil War"). Much of the coverage of the crisis traces the roots of the conflict to the 2011 events of the so-called Arab Spring and the subsequent suppression of protestors by President Bashar-al-Asad and the rise of the rebel group, the Free Syrian Army. The primary narrative is one of a revolt against economic insecurity and lack of personal freedoms. ISIS, known for its hardline brutality, entered into the conflict in 2013. It has also become increasingly clear that the severe drought that crippled Syria from 2006–2010 played a role in setting the stage for conflict:

> Starting in 2006, Syria suffered its worst drought in 900 years; it ruined farms, forced as many as 1.5 million rural denizens to crowd into cities alongside Iraqi refugees and decimated the country's livestock. Water became scarce and food expensive. The suffering and social chaos caused by the drought were important drivers of the initial unrest. (Mansharamani)

Scientists have argued that climate change played a role in the severity of the drought and that the changes to weather patterns are likely permanent, so even if the conflict is resolved, the underlying environmental stressors will remain. Further, in 2014, the Pentagon noted climate change a "threat multiplier" that could lead to increasingly violent conflict, causing increased instability "by impairing access to food and water, damaging infrastructure, spreading disease, uprooting and displacing large numbers of people, compelling mass migration, interrupting commercial activity, or restricting electricity availability" (qtd. in Mansharamani). When discussing the refugee crisis that resulted from the unrest in Syria from a vegan studies standpoint, it is important to note that the enmeshed and reinforcing nature of increasingly volatile environmental instability (resulting, in large part, from the West's disproportionate historical dependence upon fossil fuels), violent extremism, and the dehumanization of refugees underscore the slippage that ultimately constitutes their dead bodies as "meat" in a series of rhetorical maneuvers that also render animals utterly absent.

On August 27, 2015, police discovered the bodies of seventy-one people from Syria, Iran, Iraq, and Afghanistan locked in a truck on the side of a highway in Austria. Simon Tomlinson and Darren Boyle reported, "Many of the bodies had decomposed, suggesting they had been dead for several days in the back of the air-tight refrigerated lorry that usually carried frozen chicken," and images of the truck, which was formerly owned by Hyza, a Slovakian chicken company, appeared in print and online. Beside the truck, which is covered in images of Hyza products, people in hazmat suits prepared to open the back doors, upon one of which appears a photographic image of a chicken's head with eyes seemingly staring directly at the lock. This image is the only one on the truck that depicts a living animal and not the meat made after it is killed. In the news coverage that followed the discovery, the people who died in the truck were referred to, almost interchangeably, as migrants or refugees—sometimes in the same article. For example, in a May 4, 2017 article in *The New York Times* titled "Hungary Indicts 11 in Truck Suffocation Deaths of 71 *Refugees*" (my emphasis), Alison Smale writes, "the discovery of the bodies in the truck, in the sweltering heat . . . became a turning point in the European Union's disorganized response to the waves of *migrants* flooding into the Continent to escape war and deprivation in the Middle East and elsewhere" (my emphasis).

While the distinction between "migrant" and "refugee" may seem minor, it nonetheless has rhetorical consequences in terms of how readers view the people who died: the assumption is that "migrants" choose to leave their homeland for another, while "refugees" are forced to leave in order to flee violence, starvation, or other horrific circumstances that endanger their lives. And increasingly, the rhetoric of "immigration" reform from many Western countries, including the US and those of the European Union, has focused on curbing immigration by associating immigrants with crime. For example, during his 2016 presidential campaign, Donald Trump referred to Mexican immigrants as rapists and criminals,[2] and his various attempts at a so-called "Muslim ban" restrict entry into the US by citizens of six predominantly Muslim countries, including Syria. Further, one of the main reasons that British citizens voted to leave the European Union was because of immigration. According to Josh Lowe, "Britons who voted for Brexit . . . did so largely because of prejudice against immigrants, while those who had got to know foreigners were more likely to vote remain." The narrative that continually posits that immigrants are dangerous criminals works to depersonalize and stereotype individuals who cross borders. The term "immigrant" places people into a homogenizing category that renders them faceless—and onto which can be projected fear and hatred. And once they have been depersonalized, it becomes much easier to dehumanize them. For example, at a recent rally in Ohio, Trump referred to immigrants not only as criminals but also as animals:

> And you've seen the stories about some of these animals. They don't want to use guns, because it's too fast and it's not painful enough. So they'll take a young, beautiful girl, 16, 15, and others, and they slice them and dice them with a knife, because they want them to go through excruciating pain before they die. And these are the animals that we've been protecting for so long. Well, they're not being protected any longer, folks. (qtd. in Murphy)

Trump clearly thinks that animals are of less ethical concern than humans—he is the first modern American president not to have a pet, and one of his favorite go-to expressions when angered by a woman is to call her a dog. Rendering groups of humans as animals allows Trump and other politicians throughout history to do rhetorical harm that often precedes physical harm.[3]

The three rhetorical moves that take us from individual "person" to homogenizing "immigrant" to "criminal" to "animal" work to remove personhood and humanity from the humans who are seeking asylum. The effective erasure of the term "refugee" serves to situate all migrants as immigrants, people leaving their homelands by choice—and that choice is then associated with a conscious decision to commit crime in the country to which they migrate. In a 2015 *Sun* article, Katie Hopkins referred to migrants attempting to cross the Mediterranean as cockroaches and called for sending out gunboats instead of rescue vessels (Finch 231), clearly demonstrating this rhetorical elision. And viewing immigrants as a homogenous group rather than as individuals with life stories enables their subsequent dehumanization and brutalization. According to Tim Finch, "an appropriate response to a person fleeing for their life should be a display of human warmth. But under the pressure of high numbers of asylum applications over many years, and other increases in migration, Europe hardened its heart against those seeking a safe haven" (234). Even more recently, in July of 2017, ten people died in an unventilated truck in San Antonio. The driver, James M. Bradley, claimed not to have known that he was transporting human cargo and only became aware of that fact when "he was knocked down by fleeing immigrants and said 'he then noticed bodies just lying on the floor *like meat*,' according to the criminal complaint" (Pérez-Peña and Montgomery, my emphasis). In this statement, we clearly see a fourth rhetorical shift. From "person" to "migrant" to "criminal" to "animal," a dead human becomes a commodity that results from the killing of nonhuman animals: "meat." And for the people who smuggle them across borders, these people are commodities, items in an exchange economy, regardless of whether they live or die.

I want to recognize the danger inherent in invoking the position that human beings are treated like animals in specific circumstances (therefore, animals are treated like humans in others) in order to make the case for veganism. Indeed, the danger of such comparisons is that they fail to recognize the beingness of the humans that are used in the service of the analogy while arguing for the beingness of the animals that are suffering. We are better served when we acknowledge that certain groups of people have historically been treated in the ways that we have also historically treated animals and that this treatment in either circumstance—animal or human—is wrong. For example, comparing enslaved black people to animals (a familiar false analogy) as a means of gaining converts to veganism fails to acknowledge that the struggle for human rights for black people in the West and elsewhere is still very much a contemporary struggle, one that requires black people to unfairly have to assert their humanity in societal systems that consistently deny humanity to them. Similarly, it is my hope that my rhetorical analysis of the linguistic shifts that situated the refugees who died in the Hyza meat truck as animals is done in the service of illuminating the ways that removing the identities and agencies of individual refugees eliminated them from a broader discussion of rights and ethical treatment. If we dehumanize groups of people in order to treat them *like animals*, we do so because we do not deem nonhuman animals worthy of the same rights as humans.

At the time of this writing, all but one of the seventy-one people who died in Austria in August 2015 have been identified, and we know that fifty-nine were men, eight were women, and four were children from Syria, Iraq, Iran, and Afghanistan. In May of 2017, eleven people were indicted in their deaths (Smale). The process of identification of the victims turns migrants back into individual people, as did the iconic photo of tiny Aylan Kurdi's lifeless body washed ashore on a Turkish beach, which was published a few days later in early September of 2015. Also in September, less than a month after the police made their horrific discovery in Austria, a German theater invited participants to engage in a partial reenactment of what had transpired. Seventy-one people got into a truck the same size as the Hyza meat truck in which the refugees died, figuratively embodying the dead and bearing witness within the space that rendered the refugees meat ("German Theater"). As Carol J. Adams has famously noted, nonhuman animals as embodied beings become absent referents in the discourse of meat, which rhetorically removes them from consideration; we are pre-sented with "steak" instead of "cow," "ham" instead of "pig." Similarly, human animals become absent as individuals when they are rhetor-ically homogenized as "migrants," a move from which it becomes increasingly easy to deny them their humanity and consider them ani-mals, then commodity: meat. The people who are fleeing terror have already been dehumanized by the people from whom they are fleeing; in Syria and elsewhere, they have been othered and consumed, often literally, by ISIS—a refugee named George told a reporter, "I knew I had to find a way to leave Aleppo, when my five-year-old son saw an ISIS fighter kill a man in the street and eat him" (Southam)—only to be recommodified and rendered absent when they flee.

But these moments, the deaths of the seventy-one refugees and the image of Aylan Kurdi, shifted Europe's stance with regard to the refu-gee crisis. According to Tim Finch,

> once the refugee crisis produced its iconic image of *individual* suf-fering, the emotional response changed. . . . "Refugees Welcome" banners weren't just paraded at protest marches by the usual liberal suspects, but were unfurled on the terraces of football grounds. . . . "Mother Merkel" effectively threw open Germany's borders to any migrant who wanted and was able to come, and even David Cameron announced a much enhanced Syrian refugee resettlement program. (231, my emphasis)

It is, of course, unfortunate and telling that people had to die horrific and avoidable deaths before the response shifted, and it is tragic that these people's individual identities and their very humanity were restored to them only after dying. The images that shifted the narrative are indeed powerful; the body of a small child lying on a beach and investigators in hazmat suits standing ready to open a meat truck, ostensibly being watched by the chicken emblazoned on the door, call us to recognize the individuals who died fleeing violence and uncertainty from a civil war that has already displaced millions of people. The image of the unopened truck makes manifest the horror of treating humans like nonhuman animals that are rendered absent in order to become meat, but a vegan studies reading requires that we recognize in that image that the animals killed and processed by the Hyza meat company were individuals as well, beings who suffered, were commodified, and then made absent. The face of a lone chicken on the truck, watching as investigators prepare to unpack the human cargo within, displaced by war brought on in part by climate change, is an entreaty, a plea to be seen, to have those who unlock the door also look the animal in the eye even in the moment before they face the horror within. And a vegan reading requires that we see the enmeshed oppressions—of the land, the animals, and the people—as necessarily inherently linked and mutually reinforcing.

When I published *The Vegan Studies Project* in 2015, it was such linkages that I hoped to expose and explore through the lens of ethical veganism, and my goal was to examine the formation and dissemination of the current contradictory social discourse surrounding vegan identity, particularly as that identity has shifted to be constituted in specific ways in the twenty-first century US. Further, my book worked to expose the reasons for this discourse and to reconcile such presentations with those positive, healing, and personally productive aspects of vegan identity that were, during the first decade of the twenty-first century, cast in shadow in the glare of what constituted a marked backlash against such an identity position that began taking shape in the wake of the September 11, 2001 attacks on the US. As a postcolonial ecocritic, writing such a text was, in many ways, different from anything else I had ever written: a cultural studies analysis of the ways that veganism and vegans were depicted and characterized in the post-9/11 US, this work appears to be a radical departure from postcolonial studies, my primary area of specialization. But it is instead a decidedly ecofeminist work that constituted a culmination of my scholarly and pedagogical foci on enmeshed and reinforcing oppressions, of displaced and oppressed peoples, of animals, and of the environment, as I hope is clear in my discussion of the meat truck as microcosm for a larger world engaged in environmental destruction, animal exploitation, and violent human displacement.

I worked to posit the field of vegan studies as a field that exists as a product of the discourse of vegan representation as it is situated within and outside of the three-pronged field of animal studies (critical animal studies, human-animal studies, and posthumanism), animal welfare/ rights/liberation, and ecofeminism, and I worked to unpack the tension between the dietary practice of veganism and veganism as an identity category that is at once created by vegans and simultaneously interpreted and reconstituted by and within contemporary media and art. I worked to show how vegan studies and vegan theory provide a new lens for ecocritical textual analysis. A vegan studies approach examines texts (broadly speaking) via an intersectional lens of veganism as practice, identity category, and theoretical perspective in order to complicate our understandings of, our relationships with, and our access to food, animals, the environment, and other humans. Like contributor Carol J. Adams's foundational 1990 text *The Sexual Politics of Meat*, *The Vegan Studies Project* constitutes a cultural studies analysis, but my work examines the mainstream discourse surrounding and connecting animal rights to (or omitting animal rights from) veganism, with specific attention to the construction and depiction of the post-9/11 US vegan body—both male and female—as a contested cite manifest in contemporary works of literature, popular cultural representations, advertising, and news media. The vegan body and vegan identity, as created by vegans and non-vegans and as depicted in art, literature, and pop culture media, constitute a performative project and an entity in a state of perpetual transformation and alteration, and our understanding of veganism is in many ways based on various assumptions that seek to limit veganism's complexity and situate it as either one thing or another.

To be vegan is, quite simply, to abstain from all animal products as food or clothing.[4] A 2006 estimate placed the number of vegans in the US somewhere around 1.7 million, and with "vegan movement organizations counting their membership in the tens of thousands, there are arguably more practicing vegans in the USA than there are members of vegan organizations" (Cherry 156). Furthermore, since 2006, the number of vegans in the UK has risen by 360 percent (Quinn). As an identity category and a lifestyle, veganism constitutes a subject position that allows for environmentally responsible consumer choices that are viewed, particularly in the West, as oppositional to and disruptive of a capitalist system that is largely dependent upon big agriculture. Furthermore, veganism has become increasingly visible via celebrity endorsements and universally acknowledged health benefits, and veganism and vegan characters (as well as tacit vegan politics[5]) are increasingly present in works of art and literature in ways that insist upon their recognition as worthy of critical inquiry.

There are many reasons why people choose to become vegan, and there are reasons why others choose not to be—and there are certainly socioeconomic and structural hindrances that keep veganism from being a viable option for many others, a reality upheld by racist and classist food systems, particularly as food is commodified and distributed in places like the US. Veganism continues to be a largely white, upper-middle-class identity; it is often depicted as an elitist endeavor, and it is gendered as a female undertaking and, therefore, often dismissed as naively emotionally motived—or characterized as disordered consumption.[6] That the ability to eat well and to be vegan remains unattainable to so many people is indicative of systemic food insecurity resulting from income inequality and underlying structural racism. A 2014 study in the *Journal of the American Medical Association Internal Medicine* found that "socioeconomic status was associated strongly with dietary quality, and the gaps in dietary quality between higher and lower SES [socioeconomic status] widened over time" (qtd. in Ferdman), and in an article that they wrote for the Hunter College New York City Food Policy Center, Nicholas Freudenberg and Diana Johnson note that

> the inequitable distribution of food—and education, housing, health care employment and safe environments—is not an accident but rather a consequence of systems of political and economic stratification. One such system is structural racism—a pattern of policies and institutional practices that produce barriers to opportunity for people of color.

In many ways, it is accurate to assert that the inability of certain populations to afford or even access healthy food is in and of itself the product of racist and classist institutional policies that disenfranchise specific populations.

Despite the existence of the Vegan Society, which was founded in England in 1944, vegans tend *not* to constitute a unified group in possession of a cohesive ideological mandate; they tend *not* to be joiners, but they do have "a propensity towards alternativism in other areas of life . . . and eschewing the use of all animal products represents a change that necessarily involves all areas of life" (McDonald 2, emphasis in original). As an ideology, veganism tends to be marked by conscious individual actions that are directly oppositional and confrontational to the consumer mandates of capitalism. For this reason, the actions of individual vegans pose tangible threats to such a paradigm; furthermore, whether one is vegan for ethical reasons, for health reasons, or because of religious mandates, adopting a vegan diet constitutes environmental activism, whether or not the vegan intends such activism. In the study "Analysis and Valuation of the Health and Climate Change Cobenefits of Dietary Change," published in *Proceedings of the National Academy of Sciences* journal in 2016, the authors conclude that

> transitioning toward more plant-based diets that are in line with standard dietary guidelines could reduce global mortality by 6–10 percent and food-related greenhouse gas emissions by 29–70 percent compared with a reference scenario in 2050. We find that the monetized value of the improvements in health would be comparable with, or exceed, the value of the environmental benefits although the exact valuation method used considerably affects the estimated amounts. (Springmann et al.)

Because of these findings, as well as because of the obvious linkages between veganism and animal welfare/rights, lived and literary representations of veganism are deserving of rigorous theoretical analyses informed by but distinct from other theoretical approaches. Further, a vegan theoretical analysis also works to draw attention to absences and silencings—of animals and of humans—in texts that ostensibly may have nothing to do with veganism (like the narrative of the seventy-one refugees who were left to die in a meat truck in 2015); in this way, a vegan studies approach can illuminate underlying and invisible linkages that are often overlooked in more traditional deconstructive analyses of power and oppression.

༄

The essays in *Through a Vegan Studies Lens* are informed by my previous work, but they are also engaged with texts and spaces—historical, social, and global—well beyond its previous boundaries, and they are very much engaged with doing theory *differently*. The text is divided into four sections, the first of which, "Vegan Studies: Expanding Ecocriticism(s)," includes essays by Kathryn Kirkpatrick, John Yunker, and Alexa Weik von Mossner. These essays take a vegan studies approach to expand and extend more traditional ecocritical readings. Weik von Mossner's essay works to link vegan studies and cognitive ecocriticism by examining texts at two ends of what she calls the "affective spectrum": texts that promote veganism via what Suzanne Keen has called *authorial strategic empathizing* and vegan cookbooks, food blogs, and guides that focus on *positive emotions*. Kirkpatrick's essay focuses on "extending ecocriticism" by looking at the often-belittling representations of vegans in locavore literature, texts privileging local food culture that often includes locally produced animal products. Yunker's essay asserts that environmental literature must evolve to engage with environments that it has historically ignored, those that Yunker claims "vegans experience everyday."

The second section, "Vegan Studies in the United States," considers US textual analyses that span the twentieth century. The first essay by Carol Adams, whose foundational work *The Sexual Politics of Meat* (1990) effectively underscores any conception of vegan studies as a field of inquiry, explores "The Sexual Politics of Meat in the Trump Era," via an analysis of such policies as ag-gag laws, which criminalize the dissemination of information about the treatment of livestock animals, Trump's tendency to label women he dislikes as "pigs," "cows," and "dogs," and Trump's nomination of Andy Puzder, the CEO of CKE Restaurants (the parent company of the Carl's Jr. and Hardee's burger chains), as Secretary of Labor. In "A Vegan Approach to Upton Sinclair's *The Jungle*," Ryan Phillips applies a vegan rhetorical materialist approach to Upton Sinclair's 1906 novel *The Jungle*, allowing for a nuanced reading of a text that has long been examined in terms of that work's instigation of the USDA's Federal Meat Inspection Act of 1906. Tom Hertweck offers a joint reading of the 1973 science fiction film *Soylent Green* and the contemporary meal replacer called Soylent in order to show how a vegan studies approach provides a new way of considering our relationship to food ethics in consumer culture.

Finally, Chris Kocela examines what he calls "scarecrow veganism," a term based on a moniker used to describe a Buddhist character in Richard Powers's 2006 novel *The Echo Maker* who becomes dangerously thin and mentally unstable. The trope is repeated in Jonathan Franzen's 2015 novel *Purity*, and Kocela claims that such characters present a straw man argument about the relationship between veganism, environmental activism, and Buddhism that effectively neutralizes the political and ethical potential of vegan subjectivity.

"Vegan Studies Beyond the West," the third section, includes essays that move vegan studies beyond the US and the UK Caitlin Stobie offers a reading of the situational ethics of South African-Scottish writer Zoë Wicomb's 2014 novel *October*, in which Stobie considers the novel's postcolonial positioning in a reading that is informed by the idea that there is merit in "reading for" an inclusive vegan theory by considering how novels such as *October* treat human *and* nonhuman life. Kadri Aavik examines, via an intersectional feminist lens, vegan identities in the post-socialist space of Estonia, a Baltic country where animal rights and veganism are relatively novel concepts, having emerged in the last decade. Margarita Carretero-González offers a vegan studies reading of South Korean novelist Han Kang's *The Vegetarian*, first published in 2007 and later translated into English and published in the UK in 2015 and the US in 2016. Carretero-González focuses on Kang's focalization choices (the novel is told from the perspectives of three characters, none of which is the vegetarian of the title) as narrative strategy that reveals both understanding and misinterpretation of vegetarianism, gender, and the material body. Finally, Shanti Chu's "Nonviolence through Veganism: An Anti-Racist Postcolonial Strategy for Healing, Agency, and Respecting Life" situates plant-based diets within pre- and postcolonial non-Western history, and her work engages with veganism as a mode of postcolonial resistance. Chu mediates the seemingly oppositional philosophical positions of Frantz Fanon and Mahatma Gandhi by placing their work in conversation with that of A. Breeze Harper's focus on veganism as an act of radical nonviolent resistance on behalf of both human and animal oppression.

The fourth section, "Hypocrites and Hipsters; Meat and Meatlessness," contains essays that examine negative reactions to and assumptions about veganism as well as the hypocrisy that often accompanies nature writing's tendency to omit the plight of nonhuman animals from its scope. Alex Lockwood examines such hypocrisy in an essay that explores what it means to read pro-environmental contemporary nature writing through a vegan lens. His essay, "H Is for Hypocrite," looks in particular at Helen Macdonald's *H Is for Hawk* (2014) and Charles Foster's *Being a Beast* (2016) and the ways that both works fail to address the structural causes of the devastation to nonhuman bodies that they argue pro-environmental behavior will protect. In "The Best Little Slaughterhouse in Portland: Hipsters and The Rhetoric of Meat," D. Gilson takes on US "hipster" culture via an examination of the Portland Meat Collective and Jonathon Safran Foer's *Eating Animals* (2009) in order to explore how hipsters eat meat expressively, self-fashioning themselves as victims of a system that ironically leads them to the ultimate form of privilege: the privilege not only to consume nonhuman animals, but to mark some animal consumption—that available to those of a lower socioeconomic status—as bad, in contrast to their own as *humane*, and thus good. Finally, in "Meatless Mondays?: A Vegan Studies Approach to Resistance in the College Classroom," Natalie M. Dorfeld examines her students' resistance to Meatless Mondays as evidence of the demonization of vegetarianism and veganism that is created by several factors including upbringing, the popular media, and high school and college coaches who often view non-normative diets as potentially detrimental to student athletes' performance.

I conclude the volume with a discussion of the ways that vegan studies constitutes an "enmeshed" discourse, one that engages with multiple forms of interconnected oppressions simultaneously. Via a brief reading of Mike White and Miguel Arteta's 2017 *Beatriz at Dinner*, a film that engages very explicitly with veganism, immigration, ecofeminism, and toxic Western masculinity, I return to my earlier discussion of human and animal commodification in terms of increasingly troubling international responses to refugees and displaced peoples, and I ponder how we move forward—beyond the conflation of criminality, commodification, and meat—as we head into the third decade of the twenty-first century. The works in this collection provide specifically vegan readings of texts and contexts, politics, careers, and locations; offer challenges to conceptions of environmental writing and animal studies; offer an enmeshed and interconnected framework for analysis, aligned with intersectionality but also respectful of the challenges that the inclusion of animal lives represents to that framework; and in many ways refuse to remain firmly rooted in the theoretical spaces of academic writing and life, seeking instead to engage a more holistic audience of vegan activist thinkers across a variety of identity categories. This collection contains essays from established and emerging writers from around the world who are doing vegan theory, a compendium of activist scholars, affiliated with the academy and doing work beyond it—a distinction that I hope marks vegan studies as a pedagogy and scholarly venue that is not exclusive and that owes its existence to lived animal rights activism.

WORKS CITED

Adams, Carol J. *The Sexual Politics of Meat: A Feminist-Vegetarian Critical Theory*. New York: Continuum, 1990.

Cherry, Elizabeth. "Veganism as a Cultural Movement: A Relational Approach." *Social Movement Studies* 5, no. 2 (2006):155–70.

"Definition of Veganism." *The Vegan Society*, December 6, 2018 *https://www.vegansociety.com/go-vegan/definition-veganism*.

Ferdman, Roberto A. "America's Growing Food Inequality Problem." *Washington Post*, September 2, 2017. https://www.washingtonpost.com/news/wonk/wp/2014/09/02/americas-growing-food-inequality-problem/?utm_term=.c05413eab2ba.

Fernandez, Manny, and Richard Pérez-Peña. "In San Antonio Smuggling Case, a Fatal Journey in a Packed and Sweltering Truck." *The New York Times*, July 24, 2017, *https://www.nytimes.com/2017/07/24/us/san-antonio-truck-trafficking.html*.

Finch, Tim. "Love and Management: Reflections on the 2015 Refugee Crisis. *Juncture* 22, no. 3 (2015): 230–34.

Freudenberg, Nicholas, and Diana Johnson. "Race, Racism, and Food Justice: Reflections." Hunter College New York City Food Policy Center, March 12, 2015. http://www.nycfoodpolicy.org/race-racism-and-food-justice/.

Gaard, Greta. "Speaking of Animal Bodies." *Hypatia* 27, no. 3 (2012): 520–26.

"German Theater Revives Tragedy of 71 Asylum Seekers Found Dead in Austrian Truck." RT, September 3, 2015. https://www.rt.com/news/314243-theater-austria-refugee-truck/.

Herman, David. "Animal Worlds in Modern Fiction: An Introduction." *MFS* 60, no. 3 (2014): 421–43.

Jenkins, Stephanie. "Returning the Ethical and Political to Animal Studies." *Hypatia* 27, no. 3 (2012): 504–09.

Jones, Sophia. "71 Refugees Suffocate in Back of Truck in Austria." *The Huffington Post*, August 27, 2017, http://www.huffingtonpost.com/entry/refugees-suffocate-dead-truck-austria_us_55defe14e4b08dc094867ca8.

Letham, Jonathan. "Pending Vegan." *New Yorker*, April 7, 2014. https://www.newyorker.com/magazine/2014/04/07/pending-vegan.

Lowe, Josh. "Why Did Brexit Happen? Hatred of Immigrants Drove the British Vote, Study Says." *Newsweek*, June 22, 2017. http://www.newsweek.com/brexit-eu-referendum-vote-prejudice-immigration-628353.

Lonergan, Kenneth, dir. *Manchester by the Sea*. Performances by Casey Affleck, Michelle Williams, Lucas Hedges, Kyle Chandler, and Gretchen Mol, Santa Monica: Amazon Studios, 2017.

Mansharamani, Vikram. "A Major Contributor to the Syrian Conflict? Climate Change." *PBS NewsHour*, March 17, 2016. http://www.pbs.org/newshour/making-sense/a-major-contributor-to-the-syrian-conflict-climate-change/.

McDonald, Barbara. "'Once You Know Something, You Can't Not Know It': An Empirical Look at Becoming Vegan." *Society & Animals* 8, no. 1, (2000): 1–23.

Murphy, Tim. "What Happened in Ohio Proves that Trump Is Only Going to Get Worse." *Mother Jones*, July 26, 2017. http://www.motherjones.com/politics/2017/07/what-happened-in-ohio-proves-that-trump-is-only-going-to-get-worse/.

O'Grady, Siobhán. "Rwandan Who Called Tutsis 'Cockroaches' in 1992 Gets Life Sentence." *Foreign Policy*, April 15, 2016. http://foreignpolicy.com/2016/04/15/rwandan-who-called-tutsis-cockroaches-in-1992-gets-life-sentence/.

Parker, Alison R. "Trump calls Immigrants 'Animals' who 'Slice and Dice' Young Girls at Unhinged Rally in Ohio." Shareblue Media, July 25, 2017. http://shareblue.com/trump-calls-immigrants-animals-who-slice-and-dice-young-girls-at-unhinged-rally-in-ohio/.

Quinn, Sue. "Number of Vegans in Britain Rises by 360 Percent in 10 Years." *Telegraph*, May 18, 2016. http://www.telegraph.co.uk/food-and-drink/news/number-of-vegans-in-britain-rises-by-360-in-10-years/.

Ross, Janell. "From Mexican Rapists to Bad Hombres, the Trump Campaign in Two Moments." *Washington Post*, October 20, 2016. https://www.washington-post.com/news/the-fix/wp/2016/10/20/from-mexican-rapists-to-bad-hombres-the-trump-campaign-in-two-moments.

Smale, Alison. "Hungary Indicts 11 in Truck Suffocation of 71 Refugees." *The New York Times*, May 4, 2017. https://www.nytimes.com/2017/05/04/world/europe/hungary-indicts-11-in-truck-suffocation-of-71-refugees.html.

Southam, Hazel. "How Austria Has Become Central to Europe's Migration Crisis." *Guradian*, August 28, 2015. https://www.theguardian.com/world/2015/aug/27/austria-western-europes-migration-crisis-starts-here.

Springmann, Marco et al. "Analysis and Valuation of the Health and Climate Change Cobenefits of Dietary Change." *PNAS* 113, no. 13(2016): 4146–51. doi: 10.1073/pnas.1523119113.

Sullivan, Katherine. "*Beatriz at Dinner*: Another Mike White Film, Another Touching Ode to Animals." *PETA*, June 9, 2017. https://www.peta.org/blog/mike-white-beatriz-at-dinner-animal-rights-messaging/.

"Syria's Civil War Explained from the Beginning." *Al Jazeera,* July 18, 2017. http://www.aljazeera.com/news/2016/05/syria-civil-war-explained-160505084119966.html.

Tomlinson, Simon, and Darren Boyle. "Austrian Migrant Lorry Death Toll Rises to 71 as New Details Emerge." *Daily Mail*, August 28, 2015. http://www.dailymail.co.uk/news/article-3213858/Migrant-death-toll-chicken-meat-truck-rises-70.html.

Vidal, John. "The Tribes Paying the Brutal Price of Conservation." *Guardian*, August 28, 2016. https://www.theguardian.com/global-development/2016/aug/28/exiles-human-cost-of-conservation-indigenous-peoples-eco-tourism.

Welch, Craig. "Climate Change Helped Spark Syrian War, Study Says." *National Geographic*, March 2, 2015. http://news.nationalgeographic.com/news/2015/03/150302-syria-war-climate-change-drought/.

Wright, Laura. *The Vegan Studies Project: Food, Animals, and Gender in the Age of Terror*. Athens: University of Georgia Press, 2015.

END NOTES

1. The "absent referent," as defined by Carol J. Adams, "is that which separates the meat eater from the animal and the animal from the end product. The function of the absent referent is to keep our 'meat' separated from any idea that she or he was once an animal," and just as animals are absent referents in the rhetoric of meat, "they also become the absent referent in images of women butchered, fragmented, or consumable" (xxiv-xxv).

2. In a 2016 *Washington Post* article about Trump's rhetoric with regard to Mexican immigrants, Janell Ross notes that Trump "has never, ever backed away from his promise to govern by way of group assessments and, with this, make America great."

3. For example, "in 1992, Leon Mugesera, a senior politician in Rwanda's then-ruling Hutu party, told a crowd of supporters at a rally in the town of Kabaya that members of the country's minority Tutsi population were 'cockroaches' who should go back to Ethiopia, the birthplace of the East African ethnic group" (O'Grady).

4. The full definition provided by the Vegan Society is "A philosophy and way of living which seeks to exclude—as far as is possible and practicable—all forms of exploitation of, and cruelty to, animals for food, clothing or any other purpose; and by extension, promotes the development and use of animal-free alternatives for the benefit of humans, animals and the environment. In dietary terms it denotes the practice of dispensing with all products derived wholly or partly from animals." ("Definition")

5. A very recent example of such tacit politics occurs in Kenneth Lonergan's 2016 film *Manchester by the Sea*. Patrick (Lucas Hedges) opens a freezer to find something to eat, and frozen meat falls out. Patrick begins to panic, picking up the meat and putting it back in the freezer only to have it fall out again. His father Joe (Kyle Chandler) has recently died and because his death occurred in the winter in New England, his body must be refrigerated until the spring thaw. In this scene, for the first time since his father's death, we see Patrick's sublimated grief manifest in his identification of the frozen meat with the refrigerated body of his father. Also notable are the packages of Gardein products—vegan meat alternatives—that are positioned in the freezer door, fully visible and secure, throughout the scene. Casey Affleck, who stars as Patrick's Uncle Lee, is an outspoken ethical vegan, so the placement of the vegan "meat" in juxtaposition to the frozen *real* meat is clearly intentional, as is the linkage between the body of the man and the body of the dead animal.

6. I have written extensively about the ways that veganism is problematized by race, gender, and socioeconomic status in *The Vegan Studies Project*, so I will not replicate that work here except to point out that I am very aware of the complexity and often impossibility of veganism.

PART I

VEGAN STUDIES,
EXPANDING ECOCRITICISM(S)

CHAPTER 1

Vegans in Locavore Literature

Kathryn Kirkpatrick

Several years ago, I attended an evening reading by a locavore writer my university had brought in as convocation speaker. Her morning talk had subjected us to a slide of the heads of the two pigs she had raised and taken for slaughter. Although she had not been present at the killings and admitted their bruised bodies afterward suggested that their deaths had not been particularly painless or easy, she nonetheless said that the expressions on their postmortem faces encouraged her to feel they had died happy. This "humane death" trope is central to the discourse of locavorism, because like vegans, locavores are motivated in part by concerns about the suffering of animals. So the very different solutions to this problem constitute a key area of contention between the two groups and one in which many locavore writers resort to ad hominem attacks on vegans, tapping stereotypes and prejudices that disparage and belittle vegans, much as they degrade the animals that locavores are preparing to kill. My locavore writer is a case in point. Introducing her talk that evening, she characterized the vegan activists working for ordinances against backyard slaughter in her inner-city neighborhood as "pasty-skinned people who look like they crawled out from under rocks." Making use of a hierarchy in which reptiles and insects are devalued, this writer was suggesting that when humans do not eat meat, the result is something inhuman—the bloodless undead.

"Vegans," Carol Adams has observed, "are the locavore's Other."[1] To Other is to project unacknowledged, unwanted, and unintegrated sides of the self onto another group that is thereby demonized. Locavore literature uses vegans to reassure other meat-eaters that despite the UN climate report citing animal agriculture as one of the leading causes of climate change, it is vegans who indulge in what Michael Pollan dismisses as "dreams of innocence" which depend on "a denial of reality." Even though locavore meat-eating practices might well be described as a form of niche pastoralism available to gentlefolk farmers in First World nations rather than a viable way to feed the world, locavore writers project the impracticality of their own vision onto vegans, who in their texts appear as utopian, unrealistic, and obsessed with purity. In Michael Pollan's *The Omnivore's Dilemma* (2006), Barbara Kingsolver's *Animal, Vegetable, Miracle* (2007), and Novella Carpenter's *Farm City* (2009), vegans are consistently represented as naïve, uninformed, and out of step with human evolution. In *The Vegan Studies Project*, Laura Wright identifies post-9/11 US culture as generating a backlash against all and any outlying cultural practices. Allison Carruth in *Global Appetites* locates the rising popularity of the locavore diet in the same period. The locavore project therefore needed to situate itself in a comfortable and unthreatening liberal center, and to create that center, it needed to generate an Other to balance the horrors of factory farming. So locavores looked under stones and found vegans, their walking dead.

In the discussions of locavore texts that follow, I focus on close readings of the rhetorical strategies these writers employ to cast vegans as misguided in their own responses to the abuses of the industrial food system. In taking a vegan studies approach to the politics of representation in locavore writing, I do not intend to discount the important cultural work these locavore texts do in educating readers about the pesticide toxicities, soil depletion, corporate overreach, and animal abuse of industrial agriculture. Rather, I suggest that the negative representation of the vegan these narratives rely on supports a similarly rigid and mystified discourse about local food, a discourse of pastoral nostalgia that reverberates in the white rural nationalism of the Trump era. As Carruth observes, "the locavore desire to restore agricultural and culinary practices elides the histories of empire, territorial war, and slavery that define food in the era before American agribusiness and that . . . continue to in the era since" (159). By understanding better the ways vegans are represented in locavore texts, we might disentangle the affirmational support for local organic farmers from the pastoral nostalgia that obscures the sexism, racism, and speciesism of locavorism's agrarian roots.

LOCAVORE WRITING AND GENRE

Emily Lind Johnston locates Pollan's *The Omnivore's Dilemma*, along with Kingsolver's *Animal, Vegetable, Miracle* and Carpenter's *Farm City*, in the emerging genre of the "life narrative of alternative food" (10), a genre that combines elements of the conversion story, shtick lit, immersion journalism, and the adventure tale to produce "a narrative of discovery in which the narrator pursues a path of foodie enlightenment" (13). Johnston charges that locavore writing's autobiographical mode employs selective remembering of an idealized and static agrarian past "that never was" (11), and that the ways such distorted retrievals reproduce "the inequitable social and economic order of neoliberalism remains largely unexplored terrain for literary studies" (11–12). I want to add to Johnston's collection of generic influences the bildungsroman, the novel of formation.

Bildung is the German word for education, and the bildungsroman emerged at the end of the eighteenth century as a coming-of-age genre that fashions the Enlightenment subject to the requirements of modernity. Having charted the protagonist's psychological and moral development through experience, the bildungsroman integrates a transformed main character into an existing social structure with a reconciled sense of his or her role in the larger world. In some ways, the genre has much in common with autobiography as "a distinct Enlightenment-era formation that privileges the autonomous, self-interested individual who gives a biographical account of himself *[sic]*" (Johnston 12). But for my analysis of the locavore text, the bildungsroman's emphasis on the intersections of private and public narratives is key. N. Nardini observes that "the work performed by the Bildungsroman is always, in an important sense, political. From its earliest examples, the Bildungsroman has been just as concerned with the emergence of communities as with the emergence of individuals" (160). Laura Wright argues that veganism has been put under pressure by national narratives of identity, particularly after 9/11 when the non-WASP Other came under scrutiny as un-American—a term that readily included such a non-normative practice as veganism (23). At the same time, the locavore project needed to represent itself as essentially mainstream and meat-friendly—carnist.

Psychologist Melanie Joy coined the term *carnism* in *Why We Love Dogs, Eat Pigs, and Wear Cows* (2009) in order to name the pervasive ideology that eating animals is "normal, natural, necessary, and nice."

Her work also addresses the defense mechanisms—denial and justification—that those who ascribe to this worldview, carnists, use to ward off the cognitive dissonance involved in eating animals. In an extension of Joy's work, psychologist Hank Rothgerber found that the cognitive dissonance inherent in the practice of meat-eating is heightened and defended against more vigorously in the presence of vegetarians or vegetarian ideas (33). Drawing on the ideology of carnism, locavore life-writing inscribes meat-eating as essential to being human. The killing of another animal therefore becomes a significant rite of passage. The bildungsroman is structured by obstacles whose overcoming will forge the new self. In the carnist bildungsroman, the vegan is necessary as the significant antagonist: indeed, he or she must be continually evoked in order to be banished, for the vegan presents the alternative view that another animal need not be killed in order to eat sustainably and well. The carnist bildungsroman therefore deploys rhetorical strategies that defend against the unsettling of the human that the vegan represents.

The Omnivore's Dilemma (2006)

In the introduction to *The Omnivore's Dilemma*, Michael Pollan suggests that one of the many choices confronting the human omnivore is whether or not to eat other animals: "Shall I be a carnivore or a vegetarian? And if a vegetarian, a lacto-vegetarian or a vegan?" (5). Yet this stated choice among diets sits undigested within an opening that everywhere works to naturalize meat-eating.Indeed, the next sentence reinscribes the eating of animals as the only real choice:

> Like the hunter-gatherer picking a novel mushroom off the forest floor and consulting his sense memory to determine its edibility, we pick up the package in the supermarket and, no longer so confident of our senses, scrutinize the label, scratching our heads over the meaning of phrases like "heart healthy," "no transfats," "cage-free" or "range fed." (5)

Here, even as he acknowledges the array of diets on offer for late twentieth century eaters in the US, Pollan immediately reminds readers of our "*hunter*-gatherer" history and the carno-normative diet in which "cage-free" and "range fed" are operative. Having named vegetarian and vegan diets as apparently legitimate in his opening, he addresses his readers as carnists: everywhere the assumption is made that to be human is to eat meat.

Pollan kills two animals as individuals in his narrative, and those kill-ings are in close proximity to vegetarians and vegans. The first killing, of a chicken, is under the tutelage of celebrity locavore farmer Joel Salatin at Polyface Farms, a figure who emerges as the first of Pollan's significant guide figures in this carnist bildungsroman. The chapter, "Slaughter: In a Glass Abattoir," opens with the symmetry of the "food chain" standing in for natural law: "the sun fed the grass, the grass the cattle, the cattle the chickens, and the chickens us" (226). Pollan is taught to collect five chickens in one hand, holding them by the feet, an action that renders them collectively as a thing, and a cheerleader's thing at that: "I had five chicken legs and a giant white pom-pom of feathers in my right hand" (228). This objectification of the chickens is the prelude to a feeling of meat-eater's authenticity, manifested in his willingness to do the deed himself: "It seemed to me not too much to ask of a meat eater, which I was then and still am, that at least once in his life he take some direct respon-sibility for the killing on which his meat-eating depends" (231). Though Pollan meets the eye of the first bird he ever kills, he renders his chicken an object who does not return his gaze: "I looked into the black eye of the chicken and, thankfully, saw nothing, not a flicker of fear" (254). Unlike Derrida's cat, Pollan's chicken does not respond, though the "thankfully" here suggests that Pollan is most interested in protecting himself from his response to her death. In what might be read as a moment of visual denial, his own gaze is obscured by the killing: in the process of cutting her throat, "an errant droplet spattered the lens of my glasses" (254). She is the only individual chicken he even partially sees. After killing "a dozen or so," he acknowledges his own numbness: "the most morally troubling thing about killing chickens is that after a while it is no longer morally troubling" (233). If it is morally troubling that killing a lot of chickens is not morally troubling, one has to wonder why killing the first was so easy. In a chapter that might have been called "The Making of an Absent Referent," the chicken bodies have their feathers spun off, and "they emerge as naked as supermarket broilers. This is the moment the chickens passed over from looking like dead animals to looking like food" (233).

At the table when Pollan serves his Polyface chicken is a vegetar-ian: "Matthew, who's fifteen and currently a vegetarian (he confined himself to the corn), had many more questions about killing chickens than I thought it wise to answer at the dinner table" (271). Indeed, yes. Matthew might have raised morally troubling issues. And Pollan admits that enjoying his meal and protecting that enjoyment relies on obscur-ing and mystifying the process not only for others at the table but for himself. "Thankfully all of that, the killing cones, too, had retreated to the mental background for me, chased by the smokey-sweet aromas of the meal, which I found myself able to thoroughly enjoy" (271).

Having tried to established a discourse of meat-eating as so physically and culturally embedded in our humanness as to be practically unassailable, Pollan feels able to adopt a tone of respectful regret toward the animals he has killed while also appearing wise and mature in his embrace of what amounts to being human. Key here is that the counter to his argument that humans can not only survive on vegetarian and indeed vegan diets but also thrive appears marginal and unthreatening. Matthew is only fifteen, and so he is represented as going through an adolescent developmental phase on the way to adulthood. He is "currently a vegetarian" because his status is likely to change, not least, perhaps, because it's clear that vegetarianism, among unaccommodating carnists, is a diet of scarcity. No apparent attention has been given to his dietary needs, so he is left to eat what he can. Matthew is a questioning, non-conforming type—the vegetarian teenager going through a phase. He has not yet, as has Pollan, mastered the art of transforming his chickens and the site of their slaughter into absent referents.

Pollan's second killing of an animal, a boar, is coupled with a more intense and challenging encounter with the figure of the vegan in the form of Peter Singer's text, *Animal Liberation*. When Pollan wins a concession from Singer through email over whether or not a chicken or a cow might have "a sense of its own existence over time, and have preferences about its own future" (327), Pollan returns to his inherent conviction that "What's wrong with eating animals is the practice, not the principle" (328). That is, having satisfied himself that the leading contemporary male vegan could be answered, Pollan is confirmed in his decision to kill the boar as a rite of passage. In *The Aesthetics of Care: On the Literary Treatment of Animals*, Josephine Donovan observes, "The rite of animal sacrifice may be seen as encompassed in the developmental process of 'becoming men.' Intimately connected to or derived from male bonding rituals, animal sacrifice enables a distancing from the feminized abjection the victim represents" (167). Accordingly, Pollan will need to seek out a male guide for his nostalgic pastoral: Angelo Garro is an Italian emigrant intent on recapturing a lost pastoral, "the flavors and foodways of his childhood" (283). Extravagantly praised by Angelo for his "first pig," Pollan admits a "powerful upwelling of pride" (353). Although this feeling is later replaced by disgust as he struggles to help clean the dead body, Pollan has clearly succeeded in passing through the central initiation rite of his carnist bildungsroman: "I had actually done this thing I'd set out to do, had successfully shot a pig. I felt a flood of relief, too, that the deed was done, thank God, and didn't need to be done again" (353). Pollan thus presents the killings narrated in *The Omnivore's Dilemma* as having earned him, and by symbolic proxy his readers, the right to eat other animals. Dismissing the vegan antagonist has been central to that project.

ANIMAL, VEGETABLE, MIRACLE (2007)

Although Barbara Kingsolver's locavore memoir is significantly different from Pollan's, not least in its multivoiced narrating of her family's year of growing and eating local food, it nonetheless features the generic conventions of the carnist bildungsroman I have been charting. Kingsolver's gender identity makes of her volume a familial adventure, and so the animal killing and confrontation with vegan antagonists is familial too, with her husband, Stephen Hopp, and her daughters, Camille and Lily, sharing the protagonist role communally. Moreover, Kingsolver, a feminist, must wrestle with the re-domestication of women in the kitchen as she confronts the radically increased domestic labor involved in the family's production of much of its own food.

Because Kingsolver's carnist bildungsroman is shared, she is able to transfer the ethical questions around killing and eating animals to her daughters. For Kingsolver herself, the questions have largely been answered offstage. After a long period of vegetarianism, the family is returned to meat-eating because the problem of animal suffering inherent in factory farming has been solved for her by the locavore diet her volume promulgates: "In '97, when our family gave up meat from CAFOs (concentrated animal feeding operations), that choice was synonymous with becoming a vegetarian. No real alternatives existed. Now they do" (228). Since the carnist bildungsroman enacts for readers the initiation that the protagonists are shown to be themselves in the process of achieving, *Animal, Vegetable, Miracle* becomes a demonstration of how ethical vegetarians can return to eating animals.

Kingsolver turns an ethical question into a developmental one through her youngest daughter, Lily, and thereby represents the vegan position as simply childish. The chapter in question is "The Birds and the Bees." This title, of course, evokes a parent's frank discussion of sex with a child, a preparation for the rite of passage that is puberty. But in this case, the birds are mail-order chicks for Lily's egg business and the bees for someone else's hives. The gravity of the mother/child exchange is not over sex but over the killing of animals, and by transposing the two subjects, Kingsolver suggests that accepting both are matters of maturation. Her own narrative voice is brisk and practical, more than a match we are encouraged to feel, for the "animal-rights groups that have tried to make an issue" of hatcheries sending chicks by mail: "Mail-order chicks from reputable hatcheries have virtually a 100 percent survival rate" (88). And that, end of paragraph, is that. Yet even though Kingsolver as narrator kindly poses instructive questions for her daughter, which lead Lily to separate the Partridge Rock chickens to be killed from the flock who will lay—"Pets are pets. Food is food" (96), the ethical questions around killing animals and eating them are relegated to childhood, and the narrative suggests that both Lily and later, Camille, make the mature choice.

As in Pollan's book, the most flagrant Othering of the vegan appears in close proximity to the killing of animals. In "You Can't Run Away on Harvest Day," winter is coming and with it the slaughter of the family's animals, all in harmony with nature's cycle. But in the carnist bildungsroman, before the animal can be killed, the vegan antagonist must be confronted. The preface that precedes her appearance in Kingsolver's text is crushing indeed:

> To envision a vegan version of civilization, start by erasing from all time the Three Little Pigs, the boy who cried wolf, *Charlotte's Web*, the golden calf, *Tess of the d'Urbervilles*. Next erase civilization, brought to you by the people who learned to domesticate animals. Finally, rewrite our evolutionary history, since *Homo sapiens* became the species we are by means of regular binges of carnivory. (222)

This passage—which is largely inaccurate—works to place the vegan outside human history, culture, and biology. While vegans might suggest that they would like to be human in a new way, Kingsolver maintains they are in denial about their true human nature. And then, as if to demonstrate how truly ridiculous a vegan might be, Kingsolver has her daughters serve up a magazine profile of "a famous young vegan movie star":

> What a life's work for the poor gal: traipsing about the farm in her strappy heels, weaving among the cow flops, bending gracefully to pick up eggs and stick them in an incubator where they would maddeningly *hatch*, and grow up bent on laying *more* eggs. It's dirty work, trying to save an endless chain of uneaten lives. Realistically, my kids observed, she'd hire somebody. (223)

Like Pollan, Kingsolver is intent on naturalizing the locavore return to the land, but her pastoral nostalgia is delivered through ongoing, and practically engaged, hard work. Her vegan antagonist isn't a respected philosopher; rather, Kingsolver's vegan is "super-rich" and her "moral superiority combines with billowing ignorance" (223). Vegans, that is, aren't to be taken seriously because they haven't got a clue. They live "at a remove from the actual workings of a farm," and as a result their fantasies of "farm liberation" pose practical problems "no thoughtful person really wants" (223). Casting herself as the expert on animal husbandry, Kingsolver patiently clears up "the modern cultural confusion about farm animals" (223) by naturalizing their capitalist commodification: "They're human property, not just legally but biologically. Over the millennia of our clever history, we created from wild progenitors whole new classes of beasts whose sole purpose was to feed us" (223). Thus, Kingsolver presents the protagonist's defeat of the vegan antagonist as a *fait accompli*: the relationship between humans and food animals is biologically determined, and no vegan can undo the instrumentalist "sole purpose" humans have literally "created" in farm animals. If the carnist bildungsroman initiates the protagonist morally and psychologically into the community of meat-eaters, Kingsolver presents herself as already the knowledgeable outcome of that process. Her firsthand knowledge of killing, and it is clear that this is the key to being an authentic locavore, allows her to "dispense with all delusions about who put the *live* in livestock, and who must take it away" (223).

Over half of this chapter, displaying the carnist bildungsroman convention of killing an animal, is devoted to Rothgerber's documented defenses against cognitive dissonance among omnivores: the denial of animal pain and the denial of animal mind. Kingsolver tells us that the family is careful not to see them as individuals, not to give them names. Accordingly, the first bird to die is "rooster #1." The chickens have been earlier described as having limited mental capacities when, released hungry from their mail-order box, they peck at the newsprint periods and commas onto which they are released rather than the feed scattered for them. Kingsolver opines, "Oh, well, we didn't grow them for their brains" (88). But why assume two-day-old chicks, with their just emerging specialized chicken sight, can immediately distinguish between newsprint and feed? Clearly, unnamed birds destined for slaughter do not get the benefit of empathy, which might open a window onto their particular ways of being in the world. Instead, right before the euphemistically named "harvest," they are reduced to "crops that blink their beady eyes" (223). Moreover, denial of their pain is enacted through the comments that "All sensation ends with that quick stroke," the killing does not "cause pain," and the flapping of the rooster's body as well as the opening and closing of the beak of the severed head are "only an explosion of massively firing neurons" (232).

Having banished the vegan's objections in her text, Kingsolver is left to reinstate as natural, necessary, and normal the killing of animals. On this particular day of killing, a family who has lost their son recently are present, and Kingsolver relegates to them the anthropocentric ordering of life and the human/animal binary: "Harvesting turkeys . . . was just another kind of work. A rendezvous with death, for them, was waking up each morning without their brother and son" (233). Lest readers forget Kingsolver's credentials as a progressive social critic in her writing and worry that she returns them to the same carnism that has given us industrial agriculture in the first place, we are reminded that Kingsolver had recently been featured in a right-wing list of "one hundred people who are Destroying America" (235). Vegans are thus allied to liberalism's enemies.

FARM CITY (2010)

Noelle Carpenter's urban locavore memoir *Farm City* has been praised for calling "into question the high-minded tone of books like *The Omnivore's Dilemma* and *Animal, Vegetable, Miracle*" (Carruth 162): "At stake in this information-age georgic . . . is not a restoration of the past but an experiment in cultivating possible food futures" (164). A former student of Michael Pollan, Carpenter pointedly rejects pastoral nostalgia, identifying it with the failed back-to-the-land adventure of her "hippy homesteader" mother in rural Idaho. But while the setting of *Farm City* in a multiracial community in a poor Oakland neighborhood could not be more different from the rural idylls of Pollan and Kingsolver, the conventions of the carnist bildungsroman are still very much in play.

Farm City is divided by section into the three species of animal Carpenter raises and kills during her "meat experiment": "Turkey," "Rabbit," and "Pig." Like Pollan, Carpenter takes readers through her first acts of killing, and despite the many vegetables she raises in her urban garden during the course of the book, the arrival of her first "meat birds" by mail sets the narrative in motion: "Meat birds. I felt a bit nuts, yes, but I also felt great. People move to California to reinvent themselves" (12). Making explicit that her personal transformation through the killing of another animal is what she's after, Carpenter also banishes the requisite vegan in her opening chapter; in order to begin her meat experiment, she must first relocate: "Because of inexperience and a housing shortage, Bill and I wound up sharing a ramshackle house in the Oakland hills with a pack of straight-edge vegan anarchists. They wore brown-black clothes, had earth names like Rotten, and liked to play violent computer games in large groups in the common room. Sober" (8). Like some of the animals she will later kill, Carpenter locates these vegans in the nature/culture binary with stereotypes of other animals: they don't have names, live in packs, home near the earth, associate with decomposition, follow inexplicable codes, and are given to random violence. Less threatening but no more positive a figure is Lana, a strict vegetarian. She is rendered unthreatening by her whimsical impracticality: she "love[s] all animals and refuse[s] to put out rat traps" (41); she keeps her guinea pig, Maya, loose in her home despite "tiny brown pellets" on the furniture; and she offers Harold, the turkey Carpenter raises, both a name and asylum as Thanksgiving approaches. Although Carpenter lived as a vegetarian earlier in her life, her representation of Lana fully participates in the trope of the naïve, uninformed vegan who "just hated the fact that animals die" (74) and believes "that animals were like little people wearing fur coats" (56). A reminder of a less informed phase of Carpenter's life, Lana need not be banished because she has already been trivialized.

Nonetheless, it is Lana's offer of asylum to Harold on slaughter day that opens chapter 10 where Carpenter's first intentional killing will take place. In the previous chapters she has linked Harold's approaching death with the necessary deaths of slugs who are eating her watermelon seedlings and an opossum who has poached a duck and a goose. This kind of conflation of all deaths as one way or another inevitable, a conflation we also see in Kingsolver's text, helps to rationalize the impending killing, as does the framing of it as natural and normal: "Harold and I, there in that squat lot, embodied the latest endpoint of centuries of mutual dependence" (91). Carpenter offers Rothgerber's familiar "pro-meat justifications" and "reduced perceived choice" as she readies herself for the killing: "I eat meat, I like eating meat, it is part of my culture and, some might argue, my heritage as a human being. While Harold had to die, I had to kill" (91). For Carpenter, meat is nice to eat, and according to a locavore moral code, she has no choice but to kill Harold if she is to indulge this appetite: "I don't think much of people who say they like to eat meat but go 'ick' at the sight of a bleeding animal" (89). Finally, Lana's vegan reasons for wanting to save Harold must be dismissed, Kingsolver fashion, through a hard-nosed practicality and realism: "I wasn't a hobbyist with a pet. I was a farmer with a turkey on my hands whose feed-to-weight ratio had reached a plateau" (89). This decidedly unempathetic language distances through its abstraction: Harold has begun the process of disappearing as an animal, becoming absent, and becoming meat. By chapter's end, the rite of passage central to the carnist bildungsroman is complete; it has "turned [Carpenter] into a farmer" (95). Like Pollan, she prepares Harold's flesh for the group whose purpose it is in part to witness and acknowledge the rite of passage, and she basks in her new status: "By meal's end I was uncommonly satisfied and full" (95). Later she acknowledges that killing has transformed her: "I had killed an opossum with a shovel and axed a turkey with my bare hands—did he understand what kind of crazy bitch he was dealing with?" (97). Although this language is partly a jest, it is also an assertion of power in the discourse of meat-eating: "Eating 'real,' 'natural' meat can be seen as a method of reconnecting with the natural world, as well as a statement about subjugating it" (Parry 248).

After the killing of Harold, Lana leaves for Mexico even though she has lived for years in the Oakland neighborhood, and though she demurs when Carpenter asks if her backyard slaughter operation has driven her away, the departure functions like the usual vegan banishment for this carnist bildungsroman. With Lana gone, Carpenter admits "my experiment in self-sufficiency . . . was going to be so much easier" (121). Lana's exit functions to fulfill the structural banishment of the vegan before another killing, this time of a rabbit, and Lana is sent out of the narrative with a familiar vegan stereotype: "She was like a child in her love of animals" (121). Carpenter now describes the killing of more of her meat birds, one duck killed graphically in the bathtub with tree pruners, and she observes, as Pollan did after the killing of a number of chickens: "The killing thing was starting to feel a bit routine" (159). She deploys the pruners again after knocking out the rabbit, and justifies the slaughter by saying she was hungry and in need of the meal. With the buying of pigs, Carpenter calls herself "complete, whole" (205). She takes the pigs to be killed at a slaughterhouse but is not allowed to watch. Shortly before this Carpenter ushers in another vegan to dismiss, a man who responds to her online farm blog by suggesting that she create a petting zoo for children or a sanctuary for farm animals rather than engage in backyard slaughter. The suggestion inspires her to imagine visitors who might "meet their meat."

By the time this carnist bildungsroman closes, Carpenter is both psychologically and socially formed. She has helped to create the community of locavores she wants to join: "I had finally figured out who I was, who my people were: they were folks who love and respect animals, who learn from them, draw sustenance from them directly" (269). And they are decidedly *not* vegans.

In *Ecocriticism and the Idea of Culture: Biology and the Bildungsroman*, Helene Feder observes that as a genre of formation, the bildungs-roman is "humanist culture's story about itself": "Explicitly the genre of the Bildungsroman is the story of the individual's coming into cul-ture ("coming of age"), . . . but it is fundamentally culture's story of coming out of and apart from nature" (101). Just so: by employing a vegan studies approach to locavore writing, I have found that these best-selling locavore narratives of the first decade of the twenty-first century participate in the making of the human through mastery, subjugation, and finally, the killing of other animals. By understand-ing better this violence at the origin of human identity as well as the tendency to scapegoat the efforts of vegans to change such a relation between humans and animals, we might identify and address the defenses widely deployed to address the cognitive dissonance created by carnism. We might retell the bildungsroman along with what it means to be human in something other than a carnist key.

WORKS CITED

Adams, Carol. *The Sexual Politics of Meat: A Feminist-Vegetarian Critical Theory*. Continuum, 1990.

———. *Living Among Meat Eaters: The Vegetarian's Survival Handbook*. Brooklyn: Lantern Books.

Carpenter, Novella. 2010. *Farm City: The Education of an Urban Farmer*. New York. Penguin, 2010.

Carruth, Allison. *Global Appetites*. New York. Cambridge University Press, 2013.

Donovan, Josephine. 2016. *The Aesthetics of Care: On the Literary Treatment of Animals*. New York: Bloomsbury Academic, 2016.

Feder, Helene. *Ecocriticism and the Idea of Culture: Biology and the Bildungsroman*. London: Routledge, 2014.

Johnston, Emily Lind. "Agrarian dreams and neoliberal futures in life writing of the alternative food movement." *Food and Foodways*. 24:1–2, 9–29, 2016.

Joy, Melanie. *Beyond Carnism*. Accessed May 18, 2017.

———. *Why We Love Dogs, Eat Pigs, and Wear Cows*. San Francisco: Conari Press, 2009.

Kingsolver, Barbara. 2007. *Animal, Vegetable, Miracle: A Year of Food Life*. New York: Harper-Collins, 2007.

Nardini, N. "A Fresh-Start Doctrine: The Marshall Plan, *The Adventures of Augie March*, and the Bildungsroman after Nationalism." *Arizona Quarterly: A Journal of American Literature, Culture, and Theory* 71, no. 2 (2015): 149–74. Project MUSE, doi:10.1353/arq.2015.0015.

Parry, Jovian. "*Oryx and Crake* and the New Nostalgia for Meat." *Society & Animals*, 17 (2009): 241–56.

Pollan, Michael. *The Omnivore's Dilemma: A Natural History of Four Meals*. London Penguin, 2007.

Rothgerber, Hank. "Efforts to overcome vegetarian-induced dissonance among meat eaters." *Appetite*. 79 (2014): 32–41.

Wright, Laura. *The Vegan Studies Project: Food, Animals, and Gender in the Age of Terror*. Athens: University of Georgia Press, 2015.

END NOTES

1. See, for example, Vasile Stanescu's "Why 'Loving' Animals Is Not Enough: A Response to Kathy Rudy, Locavorism, and the Marketing of 'Humane' Meat." *Journal of American Culture*, vol. 36, no. 2, June 2013, pp. 100-110. EBSCOhost, doi:10.1111/jacc.12017.

2. Carol Adams, personal communication.

3. Food and Agriculture Organization of the United Nations . Livestock's Long Shadow: Environmental Issues and Options. http://www.fao.org/docrep/010/a0701e/a0701e00.HTM Rome, 2006. PDF download.

4. For more on this subject, see Zackary Vernon's "The Problematic History and Recent Cultural Reappropriation of Southern Agrarianism," Isle: Interdisciplinary Studies in Literature and Environment, 2014 Spring; 21 (2): 337-352

5. See Carol Adams' discussion of this term in "War on Compassion" in The Carol Adams Reader (Bloomsbury Academic 2016), 3-22.

6. See Adams' classic work, *The Sexual Politics of Meat* (1990. Rpt. Bloomsbury Academic, 2010), for her full discussion of the absent referent.

7. For more on this subject, see *Adams' Living Among Meat Eaters: The Vegetarian's Survival Handbook* (Lantern Books, 2008).

8. Most historians agree that rather than meat, it was the growing of cereal crops that led to the development of the world's earliest civilizations—Mesopotamia, Egypt, the Indus valley, and China; see for example Yuval Noah Harari's Sapiens: A Brief History of Humankind (Harper Collins, 2015). See also K. Milton's "Hunter-gatherer diets—a different perspective (*American Journal of Clinical Nutrition*; March 2000; 71; 3; p665-p667) for a discussion of the problems with generalizing about the diets of our human ancestors.

CHAPTER 2

The New Environmental Literature: Perspectives of a Vegan Publisher

John Yunker

If you were to walk into a bookstore and ask for the "vegan literature" section, you would probably be met with a blank expression, or, after some degree of confusion, directed to the vegan cookbooks section. That doesn't mean that vegan literature doesn't exist, just that it's not easy to find. This degree of obscurity has proven a challenge not only to those who write vegan literature but to the publishers who produce such books for bookstore sections that don't yet exist. As one such publisher, we've learned a lot over the past six years about this emerging field, and in this article share our perspective on vegan studies, where we think vegan literature is headed, and how it is already influencing environmental literature.

VEGAN STUDIES IS ABOUT MUCH MORE THAN COOKBOOKS

Based purely on what one sees in a bookstore, it can be easy to assume that the vegan movement is largely centered around cooking plant-based meals. For example, a December 2017 query of Amazon's book catalog using the word "vegan" returned 9,466 results (out of a catalog that includes more than three million books). Approximately 90 percent of these books are cookbooks, with the rest comprised of nonfiction advocacy and how-to books.

Where are the fiction titles? They do exist, but not within any formally defined category, which is why vegan studies programs are essential—to helping bring clarity and definition where none exists. Vegan studies, by looking across genres and disciplines, identifies the emerging and established artistic works that are pushing veganism into mainstream culture around the world. As a publisher, we work to play a role in not just publishing books *for* vegans, but publishing books to expand the vegan audience, an audience that is still relatively small. A 2016 Harris Poll commissioned by the Vegetarian Resource Group found that 3.7 million US adults (less than two percent) are vegan ("How Many Adults").

VEGAN STUDIES IS ABOUT THE EMERGENCE OF A WORLDVIEW, NOT JUST A DIET

Though the number of vegans is vastly outweighed by the number of carnivores, that number is multiplying. As one indicator, the Veganuary movement (in which one commits to going vegan during the month of January) has grown from 3,300 participants in 2014 to an estimated 150,000 participants in 2018. Culturally, it appears that vegans are beginning to enjoy some time in the spotlight, as reflected in a recent BBC News headline: "Veganism: How a Maligned Movement Went Mainstream" (Lowbridge).

But like so many social movements, veganism is not emerging wholly formed nor singular. There are "ethical" vegans who do so for the animals while there are those who embrace veganism as a healthier way of life. There are those who are vegan periodically, such as on "Meatless Mondays." There are *pescatarians* and *flexitatarians* and there are those who resist the vegan label entirely, opting instead for "plant-based."

As authors and publishers, we are sensitive to how these labels are used and how they are evolving in society. Our prime focus is on redefining the "environmental literature" label to be more inclusive of vegan literature. And we're only just getting started.

THE ORIGINS OF A VEGAN PRESS

In 2008, I wrote a novel, *The Tourist Trail*, which tells the story of a vegan penguin researcher and her love affair with an anti-whaling activist (also vegan) who is on the run from the law. I found an agent to pitch the book to mainstream publishers, yet she was ultimately unable to find a home for the book. While the animal rights themes in the book made it a challenging sell, the larger challenge was one of categorization, or lack thereof. The feedback we received was, essentially, "We don't know how to market this."

Publishers typically acquire books that fall within clearly defined categories: such as literary fiction, women's fiction, romance, thriller, mystery. There is no "vegan fiction" category, nor one for the "environmental novel," and the lack of category, to large publishers, often implies a lack of a built-in audience. That's not to say that novels with vegan themes haven't been published over the past few years. *Elizabeth Costello* by J. M. Coetzee was published by a major press in 2003; however, this book was marketed as "literary fiction," and Coetzee had at that point already won the Booker Prize (twice) and was on the verge of winning the Nobel Prize.

My partner Midge Raymond and I both spent many years working in publishing, so we decided to publish *The Tourist Trail* ourselves. And by the end of the process we realized there might be other authors out there who have similarly struggled to find homes for their novels or short story collections. We founded Ashland Creek Press in 2011 with the goal of seeking out these manuscripts, and since then have published more than twenty novels and short story collections that have been variously labeled as "ecofiction" or "animal literature." And while labels such as these can be helpful, they can also be limiting, which is why we've pushed to expand the definition of *environmental literature* to include books with not only vegan characters but vegan worldviews.

REDEFINING ENVIRONMENTAL LITERATURE TO INCLUDE VEGAN LITERATURE

Pioneers of American environmental writing such as Henry David Thoreau, John Muir, and Aldo Leopold fished and hunted the land even while doing their very best to help protect it. And this belief system, wherein writers "get close" to nature by extracting from it or by doing battle with it, remains largely intact today. While a hundred years ago, hunting and fishing were generally undertaken as a matter of survival, today, there are too many alternatives to justify these acts. And yet this "survival" myth endures, even when justification for hunting and fishing has less to do with physical survival than emotional or creative survival. As contemporary environmental author Rick Bass wrote in the *Sierra*, the Sierra Club's Magazine, "I don't think I would be able to sustain myself as a dreamer in this strange landscape if I did not take off three months each year to wander the mountains in search of game; to hunt, stretching and exercising not just my imagination, but my spirit."

But there is a growing chorus of writers who believe that animals have suffered long enough at the hands of human civilization, and that all animals, including those labeled "game" and "livestock," deserve equal protection. And it is these writers who are helping to redefine environmental writing. For example, in the first volume of our short story anthology *Among Animals*, Charlotte Malerich's story "Meat" portrays a family that has brought home an animal to raise for food, with the belief this will lessen their guilt over eating meat from factory farms. The animal remains species-less, which adds to the power of the narrative. The little girl in the family asks her parents if the animal is part of their family. "'Of course she is,' Dad told me. 'We love her and take care of her, don't we?'" The mother remains silent and, later, after the animal is butchered, the girl finds her mother in the kill room holding the animal's lifeless body: "She was holding her against her chest, like the way sometimes she still held me even though I was too big for it" (Malerich 64).

Writers are also challenging the ethics of meat production and consumption in an age of climate change—not just in the US but globally. *The Green and the Red*, written by French author Armand Chauvel and translated by American Elisabeth Lyman, tells the story of a French meat company executive who is on a mission to shut down the local vegetarian restaurant in order to take it over for a pork museum. When Mathieu first enters the restaurant, he plays the role of vegan:

> To be on the safe side, Mathieu ordered pumpkin wonton soup as a starter, mushroom and polenta mousseline as his main dish, and flourless chocolate cake for dessert. He kept his menu to study while he waited. He noticed that certain dishes were labeled vegan—containing neither dairy nor eggs, according to the fine print at the bottom of the page—and figured that vegetarians must accept these two sources of animal protein in their diet. What a bunch of hypocrites! Where were animal rights in that equation? Vegans were at least consistent. Although if you looked closely enough, you would probably find larvae, termites, and other insects in a sack of grain. No, it was virtually fraudulent, just like these recycled-fiber napkins and those salt-and-pepper shakers made from old light bulbs. Ever since a girlfriend had dumped him because he had "the carbon footprint of a midsize airplane," he had hated anything and everything to do with the environment. (Chauvel 48)

What Mathieu doesn't bargain on is falling in love with the proprietor of this café and becoming a convert along the way, and throughout the novel, the dueling perspectives, along with light humor and a very real look into how meat gets to one's plate, offer up a romantic comedy that ultimately speaks to vegans and non-vegans alike.

At the far end of the animal rights spectrum are those insects that most of us would rather stay far away from. In the short story "Vivarium" by Claire Ibarra, in our collection *Among Animals 2*, a woman living alone in a Florida apartment captures a cockroach under a glass. Although initially terrified of it, finds herself bonding with this creature. She feeds it and introduces it to her friend as a companion animal:

> Eva tried to imagine how it would look to someone else, the tiny foil dish of water, the crust of bread, and the disgusting cockroach in her homemade insectarium. She began a rant: "There was this cockroach loose in my apartment, and I didn't know how to catch it, and the pillow didn't work, and the dustpan has a short handle—not a long, standing one like my mom's—and then it fell onto its back and couldn't roll back over, and it can survive one week without water, but I learned that cockroach fossils date back two hundred and eighty million years, and they have a heart and brain, and they make group-based decisions, which means they are social, like humans, but this one is alone, like me—," Eva paused for a breath.
>
> "Okay, hold on." Victoria knelt and peered more intently into the cage. "Relax for a minute. Look, it's eating the bread." Victoria pointed at the bug.
>
> Eva knelt next to Victoria, and both watched intently as the cockroach sat on the piece of crust, moving its head from side to side. (Ibarra 152)

THE BIRTH OF A PLANT-BASED VAMPIRE

One of the early novels we published was *Out of Breath*, the first of a young adult trilogy by Blair Richmond. In this series, readers witness not only the evolution of what constitutes environmental writing, but the evolution of the vegan vampire character.

The vampire has come a long way since the publication of Bram Stoker's *Dracula* in 1897. For many years, vampires preyed exclusively on humans, sometimes in installments so as to draw out the life of their victims. But over the past two decades writers have reimagined the vampire in striking ways. Anne Rice gave us a vampire with movie-star looks and little difficulty in assimilating into human society. The Sookie Stackhouse series by Charlaine Harris depicts vampires who exist on synthetic blood, albeit not without the occasional tragic lapse.

The *Twilight* series by Stephenie Meyer introduced the concept of "vegetarian" vampires—though this term referred to vampires who feed on nonhuman animals. As Laura Wright notes in *The Vegan Studies Project*, "in Meyer's creation of so-called vegetarian vampires that are actually carnivores, the natures of both vampirism and vegetarianism become muddled and contradictory to the point that neither signifier actually means what it means. Not being a cannibal does not make one a 'vegetarian,' just as simply being pale and cold should not make one a 'vampire'" (55–56).

Collectively, these books introduced vampires who were in constant state of evolving. In *Out of Breath*, Kat, a young woman on the run from a violent home, finds herself in a small Pacific Northwest town with an entirely new species of vampire, living right alongside the remaining traditional, bloodthirsty vampires, including the handsome and mysterious Roman. One day Kat discovers her friend Alex's secret—not that he's a vampire, but how he survives as one:

"As I told you, we're adaptable," Alex says.
"You eat only from plants?"
"Exactly." He smiles. "So you see why I could never hurt you."
"A vegan vampire," I say, amazed to hear these words coming from my own mouth. Amazed that such a thing exists. Mostly, I'm relieved. My instincts have been right, maybe not about Roman, but about Alex. I am safe with him.
"Yes, a vegan vampire," Alex says.
"I've heard about vegetarian vampires," I say, "the ones that eat animals, not humans."
"Anyone who eats an animal, human or vampire, is not a vegetarian," Alex says. "To be vegetarian is to spare all mammals, all birds, all fish. But then, you know that already."
"Are you the only one?"
"There are others, but only a few. We have to keep a low profile, which is why I've waited so long to tell you. Many—vampires like Roman— believe it's okay, even admirable, to kill a vegan vampire. We are lesser creatures in their eyes. And we threaten their existence." (86)

Out of Breath, as well as the subsequent two books, known as The Lithia Trilogy, took vampire evolution to its supernatural conclusion. On a higher level, these books posed the crucial question: *If vampires can change their diets for the greater good, why can't humans?*

"ACCIDENTALLY" VEGAN LITERATURE: FROM *CHARLOTTE'S WEB* TO *MOBY-DICK*

Just as we have "accidentally" vegan foods—foods, like Oreo cookies, that weren't created with veganism in mind but happen to qualify as vegan—we also have literature that appeals to vegans. Such books might begin when an author had an affinity for a particular animal species and then crafted an amazing novel about this species. For example, the novel *Love and Ordinary Creatures* by Gwyn Hyman Rubio tells the story of a captured cockatoo who has fallen in love with its owner (a common behavior pattern among the species). Readers spend the entire novel inside the head of this bird and, by the end of the book, they understand the tragedy that is the life of a caged bird and, by extension, all wild animals that must endure lives imprisoned.

As a man who raised and slaughtered pigs, E. B. White likely didn't set out to urge his readers to give up pork when he wrote *Charlotte's Web*—and yet this book has subtly and powerfully inspired countless readers to rethink their relationships with animals. Similar statements have been made about animal testing by fans of *Mrs. Frisby and the Rats of NIMH* by Robert C. O'Brien, or *We Are Completely Beside Ourselves* by Karen Joy Fowler. Sometimes a singular work of fiction can, intentionally or not, result in positive change.

I believe that *Moby-Dick* is in itself an animal rights novel, though not in the way we might define this type of novel today. I can't say with any degree of certainty that Herman Melville felt remorse for the whales he played a role in killing during his days on a whaling ship. But several times during the reading of the novel I got the feeling he was struggling with this issue through the narrator Ishmael. On occasion, Ishmael imagined the oceans from the whale's perspective, and was often amazed by the great intelligence, empathy, and bravery the species displayed through their actions:

The more I consider this mighty tail, the more do I deplore my inability to express it. At times there are gestures in it, which, though they would well grace the hand of man, remain wholly inexplicable. In an extensive herd, so remarkable, occasionally, are these mystic gestures, that I have heard hunters who have declared them akin to Free-Mason signs and symbols; that the whale, indeed, by these methods intelligently conversed with the world. Nor are there wanting other motions of the whale in his general body, full of strangeness, and unaccountable to his most experienced assailant. Dissect him how I may, then, I but go skin deep. I know him not, and never will. But if I know not even the tail of this whale, how understand his head? much more, how comprehend his face, when face he has none? Thou shalt see my back parts, my tail, he seems to say, but my face shall not be seen. But I cannot completely make out his back parts; and hint what he will about his face, I say again he has no face. (Melville 351)

In one passage in particular Ishmael calls out not only whale hunters specifically but carnivores in general:

It is not, perhaps, entirely because the whale is so excessively unc- tuous that landsmen seem to regard the eating of him with abhor- rence; that appears to result, in some way, from the consideration before mentioned: i.e. that a man should eat a newly murdered thing of the sea, and eat it too by its own light. But no doubt the first man that ever murdered an ox was regarded as a murderer; perhaps he was hung; and if he had been put on his trial by oxen, he certainly would have been; and he certainly deserved it if any murderer does. Go to the meat-market of a Saturday night and see the crowds of live bipeds staring up at the long rows of dead quadrupeds. Does not that sight take a tooth out of the cannibal's jaw? Cannibals? who is not a cannibal? I tell you it will be more tolerable for the Fejee that salted down a lean missionary in his cellar against a coming famine; it will be more tolerable for that provident Fejee, I say, in the day of judgment, than for thee, civi- lized and enlightened gourmand, who nailest geese to the ground and feastest on their bloated livers in thy pate-de-foie-gras.

But Stubb, he eats the whale by its own light, does he? and that is adding insult to injury, is it? Look at your knife-handle, there, my civilized and enlightened gourmand, dining off that roast beef, what is that handle made of?—what but the bones of the brother of the very ox you are eating? And what do you pick your teeth with, after devouring that fat goose? With a feather of the same fowl. And with what quill did the Secretary of the Society for the Suppression of Cruelty of Ganders formally indite his circulars? It is only within the last month or two that the society passed a resolution to patronize nothing but steel pens. (Melville 282).

I suspect, based on Melville's earlier writings, that he initially set out to write another epic adventure—the type of book that always sells—but at some point found himself writing something quite different, far more ambiguous, far more ambitious. While one could argue that the book glorifies whaling, I get the sense that Melville was playing more the role of the documentary filmmaker, displaying the gruesomeness of it all to show its cruelty. I'm not sure he was trying to turn people against whaling—the industry was already seeing its days numbered at this point in history—but I think he was deeply conflicted about the industry and America's role in leading it.

PUBLISHING INTENTIONALLY VEGAN LITERATURE

For the past three years we've sponsored the Siskiyou Prize for New Environmental Literature. The prize specifies "*new* environmental literature" to draw attention to the fact that we don't wish to publish books that glorify hunting and fishing as a means to humans' connection to nature, and this stance has raised awareness of the goals of our press. Today, we receive significantly more manuscripts from vegan authors than we did when we started, a sign that this chorus is growing not just in pitch but in numbers.

When looking at the vegan-centric books we have published over the years, we can loosely categorize them along a spectrum. On one side of the spectrum are books that raise awareness for one particular species, such as *The Dragon Keeper* by Mindy Mejia, which focuses on the Komodo dragon. On the other side are books that speak to *all* species, even species that may get very little love from any human; this would include our two *Among Animals* anthologies.

TODAY'S NICHE IS TOMORROW'S MAINSTREAM

It's one thing to find vegan literature, accidental or intentional, to publish. It's quite another challenge to find readers. While it can be difficult to remain optimistic in the face of such massive animal slaughter and abuse, as well as progressive environmental degradation, every day it seems there are more people interested in vegan literature. And the fact that veganism is, with each passing day, becoming a more familiar word in popular culture, more and more publishers are open to seeing manuscripts with vegan characters. For example, Midge recently published her novel *My Last Continent* through a major publisher (Scribner), and this novel had not one but two vegan protagonists as well as a strong environmental theme. As much as we love our press and the work we do, our greatest hope is that more books like this make it into the mainstream with the full force of the Big Five publishers behind them.

I believe this new era of writing will be best defined by the questions it poses, questions that were not commonly asked a generation or even a few years ago—like the question Alan Weisman asks in *The World Without Us*: "wipe us out and see what's left. How would the rest of nature respond if it were suddenly relieved of the relentless pressures we heap on it and our fellow organisms?" (5). So even though "vegan literature" sections may not yet exist in most bookstores (or online), we'll continue to contribute to them and, by patience and persistence, eventually see them into being.

WORKS CITED

Bass, Rick. "Why I Hunt." *Sierra Magazine*, July/August 2001. SierraClub.org, https://vault.sierraclub.org/sierra/200107/bass.asp.

Chauvel, Armand. *The Green and the Red*. Translated by Elisabeth Lyman. Ashland, OR: Ashland Creek Press, 2014.

Ibarra, Claire. "Vivarium." *Among Animals 2: The Lives of Animals and Humans in Contemporary Short Fiction*. Edited by John Yunker, 105–15. Ashland, OR: Ashland Creek Press, 2016.

Lowbridge, Caroline. "Veganism: How a Maligned Movement Went Mainstream." December 30, 2017. https://www.bbc.com/news/uk-england-leicestershire -40722965.

Malerich, Charlotte. "Meat." *Among Animals: The Lives of Animals and Humans in Contemporary Short Fiction*. Edited by John Yunker. 55–68. Ashland, OR: Ashland Creek Press, 2014.

Melville, Herman. *Moby-Dick; or, The Whale*. London: Constable & Co., 1922.

Richmond, Blair. *Out of Breath*. Ashland, OR Ashland Creek Press, 2011.

The Vegetarian Resource Group. "How Many Adults in the US Are Vegetarian and Vegan?" VRG.org, 2016. https://www.vrg.org/nutshell/Polls/2016_adults_veg.htm.

Weisman, Alan. *The World Without Us*. New York, NY: Thomas Dunne Books, 2007.

Wright, Laura. *The Vegan Studies Project: Food, Animals, and Gender in the Age of Terror*. Athens: University of Georgia Press, 2015.

CHAPTER 3

How We Feel about (Not) Eating Animals: Vegan Studies and Cognitive Ecocriticism

Alexa Weik von Mossner

Images can make powerful impressions, especially if they catch us unprepared. This may not be a new insight, but I recently was reminded of its validity on a deeply visceral level. A few months ago, I opened my own Twitter account and promptly started following a large number of accounts promoting veganism, plant-based eating, and animal rights and welfare. The result of this was that I quickly became afraid of my own Twitter feed. Scrolling down the tweets, I started to brace myself for whatever photograph or, worse, video might jump at me at any instant, confronting me with often secretly obtained footage of animal abuse. There were the close-ups of faces distorted by fear, pain, and anguish, faces with eyes bulging in terror and mouths foaming, faces of cows and calves, pigs and piglets, sheep and lambs, chicken and chicks. There was the footage of animals jumping off transport trucks in order to escape. There were the images of workers in slaughterhouses kicking animals with their feet, beating them with iron bars. There was a video that showed killings gone wrong, sentient beings being broken, crushed, scalded, and torn apart while still conscious, chicks shredded alive by the millions. More than once, I thought about unfollowing in order to protect myself, to stop the onslaught of empathic fear and pain I was feeling along with deep compassion and the raging fury and shame that goes along with a desperate desire to help and the recognition that one is in no position to do so. My only consolation, as I was tearing up, was that the particular animal I was looking at was no longer suffering because it was already dead. Not that that reality made me feel any better.

In this essay, I want to take my Twitter experience as a starting point for a discussion of the range of emotions that are cued by the strategic communication used by vegan activists. Much of my research in the past few years has been dedicated to the exploration of the emotionalizing strategies employed by the authors of environmental narratives from a cognitive ecocritical perspective. Ecocritical approaches that draw on the insights of cognitive science are a very recent development in the multifaceted field of research that is ecocriticism; so recent in fact that they go by very different names and build on a variety of theoretical and empirical discourses.[1] I have for now settled on the term "cognitive ecocriticism" to denote a mode of inquiry that draws on research in neuroscience and cognitive cultural studies in order to explore how our minds and bodies respond to environmental narratives.[2] The aim of this essay is to draw connections between this mode of ecocritical inquiry and vegan studies. Vegan studies scholars have often commented on the affective dimensions of both veganism and its scholarly exploration.[3] I believe that a cognitive ecocritical approach can complement the cultural studies side of vegan studies by turning our attention to the ways in which texts and films invite us to *feel* about animals, food, and the relationship between the two. The first part of the essay will demonstrate that cultural texts promoting veganism often use what the cognitive literary scholar Suzanne Keen has called "authorial strategic empathizing" (83). Relying on involuntary processes of embodied simulation, such texts—which include the ones in my Twitter feed mentioned above—cue parallel emotions of empathetic fear and pain as well as the complementary emotions of compassion, anger, guilt, and shame. Located on the other end of the emotional spectrum are the cookbooks, food blogs, and practical guides that aim to make a vegan lifestyle attractive and desirable. The second part of my essay is dedicated to the exploration of the *positive emotions* that are cued by such texts, and to the question of whether one of these affective narrative strategies is more effective than the other.

FEELING BAD: HOW CULTURAL REPRESENTATIONS OF ANIMAL SUFFERING MAKE US SUFFER

Why is it that many of us are so strongly affected by the representation of animal suffering on a website, a poster, a documentary film, or even in a novel? Documentaries such as Shaun Monson's *Earthlings*

(2005) and nonfiction books such as Jonathan Safran Foer's *Eating Animals* (2009) are frequently cited as triggers for people's decision to go vegan. Often, there is a preexisting uneasiness around the consumption of animal products, especially around the consumption of meat, but it seems that an exposure to representations of animal suffering can add something to those preexisting concerns, especially when they are so vivid and *visceral* that they make it difficult for recipients to remain in denial. "If you are like most people," writes psychologist Melanie Joy, "when you sit down to eat beef you don't envision the animal from which the meat was derived" (15). Most carnivores, Joy suggests, simply see "food," when they see a piece of meat, and thus "focus on its flavor, aroma, and texture," thereby skipping "the part of the perceptual process that makes the mental connection between meat and the living animal" (15). According to Joy, avoiding the mental connection between meat and the animal that was slaughtered for it is a case of *empathy inhibition* and thus the cognitive suppression of an affective empathetic response due to egoistical motives, cultural beliefs, habitualization, or outright denial. Joy also reminds us of the fact that such empathy inhibition tends to be limited to certain species of animals. Cultural belief systems, and the schemas they create in people's minds, dictate "which animals are edible, and it enables us to consume them by protecting us from feeling any emotional or psychological discomfort when doing so" (18). What is lacking in such situations are feelings of *empathetic distress*, according to psychologist Martin Hoffman a strong prosocial motive that tends to induce helping behavior (105). The lack of distress is the result of psychic numbing—"a psychological process by which we disconnect, mentally and emotionally, from our experience" (Joy 18).[4] Instead of feeling empathy, people are left with apathy.

Much vegan activism aims to cut through people's psychic numbing and push them into empathic distress by reminding them of the fact that the meat they eat used to belong to the body of a thinking, feeling, and suffering being not unlike themselves and nearly identical to their beloved pet. The photos, gifs, and videos in my Twitter feed are typical examples, as are books such as *Eating Animals* and films such as *Earthlings*, which all foreground that (1) eating meat means eating animals, (2) the production of other animal products such as eggs and dairy involves the ruthless exploitation and killing of animals, and (3) animals think, feel, and suffer just like humans. If they are successful in the sense of triggering empathic distress in their audiences, such cultural texts may be able to motivate personal lifestyle changes and even advocacy. In a 2005 interview with Katie Couric, the talk show host Ellen DeGeneres recalls that she went vegan after first reading Rory Freedman and Kim Barnouin's *Skinny Bitch* and then "forcing herself" to watch *Earthlings*, a film that is packed with secretly filmed footage of animal abuse. "I do it because I love animals," DeGeneres explains in the interview. "I saw the reality and I just couldn't ignore it anymore" (2005). Of course, DeGeneres did not actually *see* the reality in any straightforward sense when she watched Monson's documentary. What she saw was moving images flickering across a screen. But it is understandable that she felt that way because she was watching a film indexed as nonfiction and therefore assumed (correctly) that it was documenting reality.

The cognitive film scholar Dirk Eitzen has suggested that the most important difference between a fiction film and a documentary is how we *feel* about the events we see on the screen. Citing his own empathetic response to the display of a suffering dog in Robert Gardner's documentary *Forest of Bliss* (1985), Eitzen argues that nonfiction films involve our emotions in peculiar ways because we know that what we see on the screen is *consequential* in the actual world (183). Empirical evidence suggests that our empathic response to the display of animal suffering and human suffering is in fact very similar. A team of psychologists around Robert Franklin used functional magnetic resonance imaging (fMRI) to examine neural responses in (human) participants while they were presented with pictures of suffering humans and pictures of suffering dogs. They found "that viewing human and animal suffering led to large overlapping regions of activation previously implicated in empathic responding to suffering" (217). The results of the study indicate "that there are many overlapping [brain] regions in humans' empathic responses to viewing animal and human suffering, particularly in areas classically associated with empathic response" (225).[5] And while the researchers do not explicitly mention the fact, it should be noted that in this experiment, too, subjects were not confronted with the actual suffering animals but with their visual representations. Neuroscientific research on embodied simulation shows that it is quite normal for mirror neurons to respond in similar ways to the actual thing and its representation, and it also suggests that it makes little difference for our empathic response whether the representation is fictitious or not.[6] In all cases we are cued to feel along with the animal through involuntary processes of affective mimicry and emotional contagion, regardless of the fact that in the case of the fiction film the animal is—hopefully—not truly suffering.[7] What Eitzen suggests, however, is that in the case of the documentary our cognitive knowledge that the display of the animal's suffering is *authentic* will amplify our emotional response because we realize that the suffering is *real*.

In this context, it is telling that DeGeneres says she had to "force herself" to watch *Earthlings*. She does not go into any detail in the interview, but there are at least two likely reasons why she may have felt an inner resistance to watching the film. *Earthlings* is notorious for its graphic display of animal suffering, and so she may have been afraid of what the film would do to her, personally, on the emotional level. Film scholar Julian Hanich has suggested that when we are afraid at the movies it is often because we "fear a negative affective outcome, namely our own fearful experience of shock and/or horror" (12). The witnessing of animal abuse is frightening and painful for many people because, when the display is vivid, they will be cued to feel along with the animals through trans-species empathy. Since affective empathy involves involuntary processes of embodied simulation, it will be difficult for most people to disengage from such a vivid display (unless they stop exposure altogether), but research suggests that personal lifestyle habits—and related patterns of psychic numbing—can make a difference in the intensity of the emotional response.[8] DeGeneres calls herself an animal lover, which suggests that she is emotionally vulnerable to the display of their suffering. Just as painful as the empathetic suffering may be the accompanying negative feelings of anger and rage at the people who inflict the suffering, as well as the guilt and shame related to the recognition of one's own implication in the situation or the despair about one's inability to change it. None of this is pleasant, and so it is normal that one would try to avoid it. As philosopher Lori Gruen has argued persuasively, the very act of ontologizing animals as food precludes us from perceiving them as personalities with individual thoughts, emotions, needs, and desires (101). Monson's film works against such preclusion by using empathy strategically to communicate its entreaty most effectively.

In Keen's definition, authorial strategic empathizing occurs "when an author employs empathy . . . in the service of 'a scrupulously visible political interest'" (83).[9] Keen's analytical focus is on postcolonial fiction, but I have argued elsewhere that strategic empathizing is just as central to politically oriented nonfiction texts, be they literature or film, and texts that promote veganism are a case in point.[10] Although there is no visual documentation of animal suffering in a book like Foer's *Eating Animals*, its descriptions are vivid enough to allow readers to simulate those situations in their minds and then react emotionally to them. This, too, can be explained in terms of embodied simulation. As Gallese explains, "it appears that the MNS [mirror neuron system] is involved not only in understanding visually presented actions, but also in mapping acoustically or visually presented action-related linguistic expressions," ("Mirror Neurons" 443). The same is true for linguistic expressions that describe sensations and emotions, and so a vividly described moment of animal suffering is likely to trigger high levels of empathetic distress in those who are willing to expose themselves to the reading experience. We tend be less guarded when reading a literary text (Keen 82), and so involuntary processes of embodied simulation can more easily surprise us and override our normal inhibitions. "The literature doesn't simply cite statistics," complains former meat lover Ioan Marc Jones half-mockingly in an article on his vegan conversion. "In sanguineous detail, every book preaching the merits of veganism inexorably describes the caging of poultry, the failed stunning and throat-slashing of pigs and the yearly mass killing of turkeys. The authors recite these stories in explicit detail. They are supposed to disgust the innocent reader. They are successful" (I. M. Jones). While there is a good amount of ironic distancing in this assessment of the narrative strategies of vegan literature, it makes clear that vivid descriptions of animal suffering can also get to those who have long cultivated their empathy inhibitions. Jones leaves open whether he experienced physical or moral disgust in response to the "explicit detail" of animal suffering, but he freely admits that next to environmental and health-related concerns it was the narrative confrontation "with the slaughter of really cute animals" that led to his change of mind (I. M. Jones).

To be politically effective, then, the graphic display of animal suffering must be complemented by a larger argument and context, and this is what we typically see in literary texts and films that try to get viewers to change their eating habits.[11] The second possible explanation for DeGeneres's hesitation to watch *Earthlings* may be related to this larger argument and context and thus to the possible *consequences* of the viewing experience. Hanich argues that "we appraise scenes of dread as potentially harmful to our current (and even future) psychological well-being" (12). Aside from the immediate empathetic pain and the potential bad dreams and horrifying visual memories, we must therefore consider the potential long-term effects of what Eitzen calls a documentary's "special entreaty to viewers" (196). Because it is conse-quential in that it depicts a situation in the actual world, a documentary film (or a nonfiction text) about animal abuse in industrial livestock farming points beyond itself by calling upon us to *do* something about that situation. It may do so explicitly through a direct call to action, but even if that isn't the case we may feel the moral pressure to stop eating animals and their products, which might involve major changes in our personal habits and social circles. After all, not everyone reacts kindly to others' lifestyle choices, especially if such a choice is perceived as radical or aberrant. Vegan websites and self-help books are filled with anecdotes about people's arguments against veganism that reach from the concerned ("but where do you get protein?") to the stupid ("cows need to be milked, so we are doing them a favor") and the absurd ("if we didn't breed animals for food, they would go extinct"), and so there is no doubt that negative peer pressure is one of the main reasons why going vegan can be an emotionally trying experience.[12]

In combination, the fear of empathetic suffering with tortured animals and the anticipated personal suffering that may result from a sudden lifestyle change can seem daunting to people who expose themselves (or even just consider exposing themselves) to a film like *Earthlings* or a book like *Eating Animals*. Filmmakers and authors who use what we may call the "shock and awe approach" to promoting veganism must be aware of that risk and of how easy it is for poten-tial audiences to simply avoid their messages. And there is another, related, downside to the strategic cueing of negative emotions for political purposes. The fact that DeGeneres had to force herself to watch *Earthlings* is an indication of this, as is my own urge to unfol-low Twitter accounts that bombard me with images of helpless, suf-fering creatures that cannot be saved. Social psychologist Anthony Leiserowitz notes that it makes political sense to cue negative emo-tions such as fear, shame, and anger in people, since such emotions come with strong action tendencies; however, problems arise when there is no direct action that can be taken to alleviate the situation.[13] Negative emotions are quite painful and thus difficult to endure over a long period of time without falling into either apathy or despair. In the case of vegan activism, the lingering danger is that people—including people who are vegan—might become unwilling to expose themselves to depictions of suffering animals without being able to help them. Of course, it can be argued that going vegan is in itself a way of helping but, as Robert C. Jones points out, "an individual consumer's choice to refrain from the purchase or consumption of animal products *makes no difference at all* in decreasing the number of animals suffering and dying on factory farms" (19). This is known as the *causal impotence objection* to ethical veganism, and it is not only a potential obstacle to a person's individual decision to go vegan but also a motivational problem for vegan activists. While vegans have plenty of other reasons to continue their chosen lifestyle—among them the environmental and health-related reasons that Jones also cites—a felt impotence to reduce animal suffering can nevertheless be damaging to the cause.

That is why websites of vegan organizations frequently offer "tips for avoiding activist burnout" that include a limited exposure to cultural representations of animal suffering. "Ignore upsetting text and images," writes Mark Hawthorne on the World of Vegan website. "When you feel anger, guilt, grief, frustration, fear, or outrage come over you, that's probably not the best time to get out that DVD of *Earthlings* to watch with Uncle Fred . . . I agree we should be educated about the issues, but that doesn't mean we need to torture ourselves in order to feel empathy for those who are tortured" (Hawthorne). Both trans-species empathy and the related negative emotions that are cued by the film are here framed as double-edged swords that can be debilitating if overused. As important as cultural texts are in visceralizing the dry facts and numbers of livestock farming, it is important to pay close attention to the *kind* of emotions they cue. This may in part be the reason why vegan organizations often also rely on another empathetic strategy, one that foregrounds representations of *happy* animals: piglets, cows, and chickens that have been rescued and that now are enjoying their lives in one of the many sanctuaries around the world. Sometimes the representations are funny, but in all cases they are heartwarming and uplifting, cueing positive emotions that can be a great relief to someone who feels overwhelmed and desperate, in spite of the cognitive knowledge that the happy animal is vastly outnumbered by those who suffer and die unseen. This brings me to the second part of my essay and to the strategic use of *positive* emotions to convince people to adopt a plant-based diet.

FEELING GOOD: HOPE, FUN, AND DESIRE IN VEGAN CAMPAIGNING AND FOOD BLOGGING

An interesting example of the strategic use of trans-species empathy to cue positive emotions in recipients is the recent Veganuary campaign, which inspired Ioan Marc Jones and many other people in the UK and elsewhere in the world to go vegan. At the heart of the crowdfunded campaign is a thirty-one-day challenge that has been widely popularized in both the traditional media and various social media outlets, among them Twitter, Facebook, Instagram, and Pinterest. Since its inception in 2014, Veganuary asks people every year to "try vegan" for the month of January, a challenge that was taken up by 59,500 people worldwide in 2017 (and by over 160,000 people in 2018), a steep increase from the less than 5,000 people who took part in the campaign's first challenge three years earlier. One reason for this substantial increase is probably a general trend toward the consumption of plant-based foods, but I wonder whether the light-hearted and positive affective tone of the campaign isn't another important factor in its success.[14] As Tobias Leenaert has pointed out, the campaign organizer's decision to ask people to "try vegan" for a limited time rather than "go vegan" indefinitely already avoids unpleasant emotions by offering "people a way to opt out without losing face or being embarrassed" (Leenaert). Just as significant is the fact that the campaign for the most part avoids moral imperatives related to animal rights and welfare. Co-founder Matthew Glover explains on the Veganuary website that, "after being vegetarian for 10 years, [he] watched 'the video the meat industry doesn't want you to see' and was shocked to see the cruel realities behind the dairy and egg industries. He then went vegan." This is a by now familiar story involving a catalytic experience in the face of the representation of animal suffering, and so it is not surprising that the "Animals" page of the Veganuary website offers detailed information about farm animals and their abuse with accompanying images and videos.[15] However, this information is not foregrounded. Animal welfare in fact *does* play a central role in the Veganuary campaign, but it is mostly communicated through narratives and imagery that cue positive emotions such as affection, hope, desire, and pride.

The Veganuary website is a colorful hodgepodge of people and products that are "proudly vegan." Next to a "vegan starter kit," it offers recipes and personal success stories, product directories, and a restaurant guide that is supposed to make it easy for newcomers to find plant-based meals in both "ethnic and chain restaurants." The related social media campaign and the more than 2,500 posters that went up in the London Underground in December 2016 mostly stay away from showing suffering and mutilated animals in living conditions that evoke pity, disgust, guilt, shame, and other painful emotions. Instead, most of the visuals feature young, healthy-looking, and frequently *named* animals—among them the piglet Ernie, the calf Rocky, and the chick Eric—who are shown before brightly colored backgrounds with captions such as: "Save little Eric—Try Vegan this January." Other ads show the relaxed face of a calf that is being embraced by a child, a woman kissing the cheek of a sheep, and the image of a dirty-nosed, free-ranging piglet, captioned "Sprinkles would like you to try vegan this January." The campaign thus establishes imaginary connections between the consumption of plant-based food and the happiness of animals, but it does so through positive connotations rather than negative ones. It also positions itself in direct opposition to the causal impotence objection by raising the hope that going vegan for a month *directly* saves animal lives.

Once the challenge was underway, this emphasis on positive emotions continued and it was not limited to animal welfare. Participants almost immediately began sharing images and recipes of the vegan dishes they were preparing and consuming, together with stories of their adventures and successes, making the vegan challenge a communal phenomenon that is not only easy but also fun. This community-building phenomenon seems to be a particularly important aspect of Veganuary and other successful campaigns. Not only are individuals often participating in the challenge together with their partners, friends, or family members, but they also meet new people online and in person (for example, in one of the many participating restaurants). The positive emotions cued by the idea of saving actual animal lives are thus accompanied and amplified by the creation of new networks of like-minded individuals who share a challenging and exciting experience. This positively connoted community-building process works against social isolation and may thus be a significant factor in terms of whether people make it to the end of the challenge and whether they remain vegan afterward. It is a process that was strongly encouraged by the Veganuary organizers, who continued sending out uplifting messages all through January 2017, concluding in a tweet on January 31 that "Over five million animal-free meals were eaten during Veganuary" and offering statistical information about challenge participants (who were overwhelmingly female and below the age of forty). Another tweet shows Rocky, Ernie, and little Eric all in one picture with the caption "We need you" framed as a *direct appeal* from the animals to challenge participants to remind them that their future choices will continue to have a substantial effect on these animals' lives and on those of other animals like them. The organizers have also collected more than 600 vegan recipes from around the world—many of them shared during the challenge—in an interactive database on their website that makes it easy for Veganuary participants to continue their plant-based diet beyond the thirty-day challenge.

It would be easy to criticize the Veganuary campaign for its emphasis on positive emotions and its strategic use of images with happy-looking, baby-faced animals while at the same time downplaying (though not completely omitting) the horrific truth about the lives and deaths of the actual animals that are nevertheless slaughtered every day for human consumption. Another potential point of criticism is the campaign's strict emphasis on food rather than on other aspects of the vegan lifestyle and worldview. Other thirty-day-challenge programs, such as the one developed by the Turkish-German "self-taught cook" Attila Hildmann, go even further down this road by focusing entirely on anthropocentric health-improvement and weight loss. If animals are mentioned at all in Hildmann's books— books that bear titles such as *Vegan for Fit*, *Vegan for Fun,* and *Vegan for Youth*—it is to let us know that "[i]n addition to health and renewed vitality, you can also have a completely clear conscience about animals and the environment" (Hildmann website). Though not even remotely true, this bold assertion adds to the program's overall emphasis on feeling well and looking great, an emphasis that has greatly helped in promoting "nonideological" veganism in Germany in recent years. Much like the *Forks over Knives* campaign and Freedman and Barnouin's *Skinny Bitch* books, Hildmann predominantly speaks to people who are concerned about their health and/or good looks without necessarily embracing "radical" animal rights positions or other ideological dimensions of ethical veganism. When these books do cue negative emotions, they are usually related to readers' own health and body image which, they suggest, can be vastly improved by eating a clean, plant-based diet.[16] This message is corroborated in these campaigns' visuals which, on the one hand, foreground the transformation of unhealthy and unattractive carnivorous human bodies into healthy, strong, attractive vegan ones and, on the other hand, feature a wide variety of vegan dishes pictured in a most alluring way.[17]

This brings me to the last point I want to briefly touch upon before closing: the increasingly widespread phenomenon of *vegan food porn*, a phenomenon that owes its popularity not least to the intensely positive emotions it evokes.[18] Owing to the growing popularity of plant-based food, and at the same time also fueling that popularity, we have seen the publication of hundreds of cookbooks and the emergence of what must by now be thousands of food blogs that feature every vegan dish under the sun. Both are relatively recent phenomena that have exploded in just the last three or four years to a degree that led PETA (People for the Ethical Treatment of Animals) to declare 2016 "The Year of the Vegan." What is remarkable about this explosion is not only that it includes a wide variety of traditionally plant-based recipes from ethnic cuisines around the world and vegan alternatives to long-standing omnivore favorites, but also that—almost pervasively—these recipes are combined with extremely attractive food photography by both amateurs and professionals. In her study on the popularization of veganism through food blogs in France, Ophélie Véron states that early vegan food bloggers intended to provide like-minded people with information that at the time was difficult to get, and that over the past decade "this vegan blogosphere has helped build and develop the identity of the French vegan community" (290). In addition to helping create the sense of identity and community among like-minded people that we have also seen in the Veganuary campaign, Véron credits food blogging with expanding the acceptance of veganism in French society more generally through "highlighting the culinary delights offered by the vegan cuisine, and presenting it as a healthy and delicious alternative to meat-based food" (290). Almost without exception, such culinary delights are accompanied by what some consider "pornographic" food photography.

In a 2015 article, entitled "What 'Food Porn' Does to the Brain," the journalist Cari Romm relates the popularity of attractively depicted food items to psychologist Deirdre Barrett's research on supernormal stimuli and her insight that "exaggerated imitation can cause a stronger pull than the real thing" (Barrett 3). Food porn, argues Romm, "is defined in part by the senses [in] that it is a visual experience of something that other people can smell and taste" (Romm). Just like our negatively connoted imaginary experience of the suffering of animals depicted in photographs, films, or even literary texts, the appreciation and desiring of alluring representations of food is dependent on processes of embodied simulation. Vision, explains Gallese, "is far more complex than the mere activation of the visual part of the brain. Vision is multimodal: it encompasses the activation of somatosensory, emotion-related and motor brain networks; these play out in endocrine systems" ("Bodily Framing" 4). Not only can images "make you sweat" (4), but the multimodality of vision also allows for the activation of a wide range of other physical responses, allowing us to simulate on the imaginary level a range of sensual impressions that we do not perceive directly, among them smell, taste, and texture. "Sight is critical in eating," writes Barb Stuckey in her book-length study *Taste* (2012), and this is the case even when the food is physically present. In the case of food porn, however, the supernormal stimulus of a carefully arranged and lit dish (which may or may not be edible) can be even more powerful and emotionally engaging than the actual stimulus on your dinner table. You may never be able to produce a vegan French toast that will look quite as delicious as the one displayed on your favorite food blog, but if you like French toast, there is a good chance you will feel like making some whenever you visit that blog.[19]

Quite possibly you will not follow through on that feeling. Research has shown that people who love cooking shows do not actually cook more because of them, and Romm cites a study that suggests that food porn may in some cases even function as a substitute for food itself (Larson et al.). Véron nevertheless insists that vegan food blogs that emphasize "culinary enjoyments" (301) have an important function in popularizing veganism. While acknowledging that "their direct role in raising the general public's awareness of animal ethics seems limited," Véron suggests that food blogs can contribute to the recognition that vegan food is not only healthy and ethically correct, but also desirable and attractive. The same is true for vegan cookbooks and for the previously mentioned campaigns that foreground personal health, well-being, and beauty. There is no question that much is lost when vegan campaigning downplays or nearly omits the complex and often gut-wrenching issues surrounding animal rights and welfare. However, as Laura Wright reminds us, there is a wide variety of reasons why people embrace (nutritional) veganism (8), and it seems that an emphasis on positive emotions, humor, and self-centered motivations such as personal health and attractiveness can be just as effective as an ethically motivated animal-rights approach, perhaps reaching a different segment of the population. Gabrielle Starr has suggested that our sense of beauty has emotional and moral dimensions (2013), and so the aesthetic display of vegan food and the suggestion that "vegan bodies" are healthy and attractive are important strategies in the promotion of veganism that should not be looked down upon or ignored.

∽

In this essay, I have considered the emotional dimensions of vegan advocacy in a range of cultural texts. We need much more research before we can even begin to give a more sophisticated assessment, but it seems to be the case that cultural texts that emphasize positive, more pleasurable emotions can be just as effective in promoting veganism as those that predominantly cue negative, painful emotions. In fact, an argument can be made that an overemphasis on negative emotions such as empathetic fear and anger, pity, guilt, and shame can be problematic both for non-vegan and vegan audiences. Turning our attention to the enormous animal abuse and the unimaginable nonhuman (and human) suffering involved in livestock farming may be the ethically right and necessary thing to do, but it cues emotions that are so negative and painful that they are very difficult to endure. A recent study conducted with a range of viral videos produced by Mercy for Animals—among them those that made me afraid of my Twitter feed—showed that videos "focusing entirely on cruelty footage with scenes of farmed animal suffering, confinement, and abuse" were less effective than "videos comparing suffering farmed animals to happy farmed animals or non-farmed animals, such as dogs" when it comes to promoting a vegetarian or vegan diet (Caldwell). Such "comparison" videos were also more effective than merely "cute" animal videos and "videos describing vegan food and how to eat vegan." While the authors are careful not to overestimate the significance of their findings, they suggest that people's mostly positive emotions toward companion animals can be used strategically in vegan advocacy. Put bluntly, people love their pets and erasing the culturally established difference between a puppy and a piglet (in the Western context) may be a particularly effective way of changing their attitudes toward livestock farming and animal consumption more generally.

This gives us another good reason to look more closely into the role of emotions in the formation and maintaining of those attitudes. Books such as Joy's *Why We Love Dogs, Eat Pigs, and Wear Cows* (2010), Hal Herzog's *Some We Love, Some We Hate, Some We Eat* (2011), and Barbara King's *Personalities on the Plate* (2017) have already started that important work, but we need to continue and expand it with a particular focus on veganism. Establishing veganism as an academic practice, suggests Emilia Quinn in her insightful observations on the 2016 Towards a Vegan Theory conference at the University of Oxford, "appears to directly question how we might reconcile the seeming antagonism between emotions and rigorous scholarship" (Quinn). Perhaps this "seeming antagonism" is indeed a false dichotomy. More than twenty years ago, Antonio Damasio's *Descartes' Error* (1994) exposed from a neuroscientific perspective the problematic fallacies involved in the categorical separation of body and mind, emotion and reason, animals and humans. Cartesianism continues to dominate much of Western thought, but it is now increasingly questioned from a variety of disciplinary positions, among them ecocriticism and the environmental humanities more generally. Vegan studies scholars, too, have rejected the Cartesian dichotomy between sentient humans and animal automata, and so I see no reason why they should have to reconcile any seeming antagonisms between emotions and rigorous scholarship. Emotions are inevitably part of our scholarly investigations and, if we believe Damasio, constitutional for rational thinking. Cognitive ecocriticism, and the larger field of embodied cognition, may offer us ways to explore our emotions about (not) eating animals in ways that are both empathetic and rigorous.

WORKS CITED

Adams, Carol J. *The Sexual Politics of Meat: A Feminist-Vegetarian Critical Theory.* 20th anniversary edition. London: Bloomsbury Academic, 2010.

Barrett, Deirdre. *Supernormal Stimuli: How Primal Urges Overran Their Evolutionary Purpose.* New York: Norton, 2010.

Caldwell, Kristin. "Which Kinds of Pro-Vegetarian Videos Are Best at Inspiring Changes in Diets and Attitudes?" Mercy for Animals. March 14, 2017. http://www.mercyforanimals.org/kinds-of-viral-videos-are-best-at-inspiring?utm_content=buffere2727&utm_medium=Social&utm_source=Twitter&utm_campaign=AnimalCharityEv.

Damasio, Antonio. *Descartes' Error: Emotion, Reason, and the Human Brain.* London: Vintage, 1994.

Easterlin, Nancy. "Cognitive Ecocriticism: Human Wayfinding, Sociality, and Literary Interpretation." In *Introduction to Cognitive Cultural Studies.* Edited by Lisa Zunshine, 257–75 Baltimore: Johns Hopkins University Press, 2010.

Eitzen, Dirk. "Documentary's Peculiar Appeals." In *Moving Image Theory: Ecological Considerations.* Edited by Joseph D. Anderson and Barbara Fisher Anderson, 183–99. Carbondale: Southern Illinois University Press, 2005.

Filippi, Massimo, Gianna Riccitelli, Andrea Falini, Francesco Di Salle, Patrik Vuilleumier, Giancarlo Comi, and Maria A. Rocca. "The Brain Functional Networks Associated to Human and Animal Suffering Differ among Omnivores, Vegetarians and Vegans." *Plos One,* May 26, 2010. http://journals.plos.org/plosone/article?id=10.1371/journal.pone.0010847.

Foer, Jonathan Safran. *Eating Animals.* New York: Little, Brown & Company, 2009.

Franklin, Robert G., Anthony J. Nelson, Michelle Baker, Joseph E. Beeney, Theresa K. Vescio, Aurora Lenz-Watson, and Reginald B. Adams. "Neural Responses to Perceiving Suffering in Humans and Animals." *Social Neuroscience* 8, no. 3 (2013): 217–27.

Gallese, Vittorio. "Mirror Neurons and Art." In *Art and the Senses.* Edited by Francesca Bacci and David Melcher, 441–49 New York: Oxford University Press, 2011.

———. "Bodily Selves in Relation: Embodied Simulation as Second-person Perspective on Intersubjectivity." *Philosophical Transactions of the Royal Society B* 369 (2014): 1–10. doi.org/10.1098/rstb.2013.0177.

———. "Bodily Framing." In *Experience: Culture, Cognition, and the Common Sense.* Edited by Caroline Jones, David Mather, and Rebecca Uchill, 1–15. Cambridge, MA: MIT Press, 2016.

Gruen, Lori. *Entangled Empathy: An Alternative Ethic for Our Relationships with Animals.* Brooklyn: Lantern Books, 2015.

Hanich, Julian. "Judge Dread: What We Are Afraid of When We Are Scared at the Movies." *Projections: The Journal for Movies and Mind* (2014): 26–40.

Hawthorne, Mark. "Tips for Avoiding Activist Burnout." World of Vegan, http://www.worldofvegan.com/activist-burnout/. Accessed February 1, 2017.

Herzog, Hal. *Some We Love, Some We Hate, Some We Eat: Why It's So Hard to Think Straight About Animals.* New York: Harper Perennial, 2011.

Hildmann, Attila.attilahildmann.com, n.d. http://www.attilahildmann.com/.

James, Erin. *The Storyworld Accord: Econarratology and Postcolonial Narratives.* Lincoln: University of Nebraska Press, 2015.

Jones, Ioan Marc. "Veganuary: I Was Dreading Giving Up Meat—Now I Can't Find a Reason to Eat It." *Independent*, January 27, 2017. http://www.independent.co.uk/life-style/food-and-drink/features/veganuary-i-was-dreading-giving-up-meat-now-i-can-t-find-a-reason-to-eat-it-a6837716.html.

Jones, Robert C. "Veganisms." *Critical Perspectives on Veganism.* Edited by Jodey Catricano and Rasmus R. Simonsen, 15–40. Basingstoke, UK: Palgrave Macmillan, 2016.

Joy, Melanie. *Why We Love Dogs, Eat Pigs, and Wear Cows: An Introduction to Carnism.* San Francisco: Conari Press, 2010.

Keen, Suzanne. "Narrative Empathy." *Toward a Cognitive Theory of Narrative Acts.* Edited by Frederick Louis Aldama, 61–94. Austin: University of Texas Press, 2010.

King, Barbara J. *Personalities on the Plate: The Lives and Minds of the Animals We Eat.* Chicago: University of Chicago Press, 2017.

Larson, Jeffrey, Joseph P. Redden, and Ryan Elder. "Satiation from Sensory Simulation: Evaluating Foods Decreases Enjoyment of Similar Foods." September 12, 2013. http://dx.doi.org/10.2139/ssrn.2325157.

Leenaert, Tobias. "Why Veganuary Is a Great Campaign." *The Vegan Strategist,* December 23, 2016. https://veganstrategist.org/2016/12/23/why-veganuary-is-a-great-campaign/.

McDonald, Barbara. "'Once You Know Something, You Can't Not Know It': An Empirical Look at Becoming Vegan." *Society & Animals* 8, no. 1 (2000): 1–23.

Monson, Shaun, dir. *Earthlings.* Burbank: Nation Earth, 2005. DVD.

Panksepp, Jaak, and Jules B. Panksepp. "Toward a Cross-species Understanding of Empathy." *Trends in Neuroscience* 36, no.8 (2013): 489–96.

Peat, Jack. "Vegan Food Sales Up By 1,500% in Past Year." *The London Economic,* November 1, 2016. http://www.thelondoneconomic.com/food-drink/vegan-food-sales-up-by-1500-in-past-year/01/11/.

Priestley, Alexis, Sarah K. Lingo, and Peter Royal. "'The Worst Offense Here Is the Misrepresentation': *Thug Kitchen* and Contemporary Vegan Discourse." In *Critical Perspectives on Veganism.* Edited by Jodey Catricano and Rasmus R. Simonsen, 349–371. Baskingstoke, UK: Palgrave Macmillan. 2016.

Quinn, Emilia. "The Monstrous Vegan." *The History of Emotions*, 2016. https://emotionsblog.history.qmul.ac.uk/2016/06/the-monstrous-vegan/.

Romm, Cari. "What 'Food Porn' Does to the Brain: What's the Psychological Appeal of Looking at Food that Can't be Tasted?" *The Atlantic*, April 20, 2015. http://www.theatlantic.com/health/archive/2015/04/what-food-porn-does-to-the-brain/390849/?utm_source=SFTwitter.

Salih, Sara. "Vegans on the Verge of a Nervous Breakdown." In *The Rise of Critical Animal Studies: From the Margins to the Center*. Edited by Nik Taylor and Richard Twine, 52–67. New York and London: Routledge, 2014.

Sawer, Patrick. "Thousands Giving Up all Animal Products for a Month as Part of Veganuary." *The Telegraph*, January 2, 2017. http://www.telegraph.co.uk/foodanddrink/foodanddrinknews/12078341/Thousands-giving-up-all-animal-products-for-a-month-as-part-of-Veganuary.html.

Schüssler P., Kluge M., Yassouridis A., Dresler M., Uhr M., Steiger A. Ghrelin Levels Increase after Pictures Showing Food." *Obesity* 20, no. 6: 1212–17.

Starr, Gabrielle G. *Feeling Beauty: The Neuroscience of Aesthetic Experience*. Cambridge, MA: MIT Press, 2013.

Stuckey, Barb. *Taste: Surprising Stories and Science about Why Food Tastes Good*. New York, NY: Atria Books, 2012.

Véron, Ophélie. "From Seitan Bourguignon to Tofu Blanquette: Popularizing Veganism in France with Food Blogs." In *Critical Perspectives on Veganism*. Edited by Jodey Catricano and Rasmus R. Simonsen, 287–306. Baskingstoke, UK: Palgrave Macmillan, 2016.

Vukovic, Diane. "9 Awesome Answers to Stupid Vegan Questions like 'How do you get your protein?'" PlenteousVeg.com, January 4, 2016. https://plenteousveg.com/answers-to-stupid-vegan-questions/.

Weik von Mossner, Alexa. "Emotions of Consequence? Viewing Eco-Documentaries from a Cognitive Perspective." In *Moving Environments: Affect, Emotion, Ecology, and Film*. Edited by Alexa Weik von Mossner, 41–60. Waterloo, ON: Wilfrid Laurier University Press, 2014.

———. *Affective Ecologies: Empathy, Emotion, and Environmental Narrative*. Columbus: Ohio State University Press, 2017.

Wright, Laura. *The Vegan Studies Project: Food, Animals, and Gender in the Age of Terror*. Athens: University of Georgia Press, 2015.

END NOTES

1. The first scholar to introduce the term "cognitive ecocriticism" was Nancy Easterlin in her 2010 contribution to Lisa Zunshine's *Introduction to Cognitive Cultural Studies*. In her more recent work, Easterlin uses the term *biocul-*

turalism for her approach, which incorporates insights from cognitive narratology, cognitive science, and evolutionary psychology. The *econarratological* approach that Erin James develops in *The Storyworld Accord* (2015) combines cognitive narratology with contextual narratology in order to examine the formal features of environmentally minded literature.

2. I develop this approach more fully in *Affective Ecologies: Empathy, Emotion, and Environmental Narrative* (2017).

3. The affective dimensions of veganism are mentioned and/or discussed in Adams (1980/2010), Quinn (2016), Salih (2014), and Wright (2015), among others.

4. Joy is following the terminology of the psychologist Robert Jay Lifton.

5. While the study was limited to the display of dogs, a companion animal that lives in particularly close relationship to humans, it is likely that its results also have bearings on our empathic responses to other animals, especially when they are mammals. On trans-species empathy, see also Panksepp and Panksepp (2013).

6. A "non-conscious, pre-reflective functional mechanism of the brain–body system" (Gallese "Bodily Selves," 3–4), embodied simulation is a function of the mirror neurons in our brains that helps us understand not only the movements of other agents, but also their sensations and emotional states, both in real life and in our engagement with cultural representations.

7. The base assumption that suffering animals in fiction films are not truly suffering (often supported by the American Humane Association [AHA] disclaimer that "No animals were harmed in the making of this movie") found recently expression in the widespread outrage and boycotting of the film *A Dog's Purpose* after leaked evidence of animal abuse during the production of the film. For more information, see http://www.hollywoodreporter.com/news/peta-calls-boycott-a-dog-s-purpose-video-surfaces-965667.

8. A 2010 fMRI study conducted by Massimo Filippi and colleagues suggests that there are significant differences in brain activity among omnivores, vegetarians, and vegans who are exposed to images of human and animal suffering. The authors conclude that "empathy toward non conspecifics has different neural representation among individuals with different feeding habits, perhaps reflecting different motivational factors and beliefs" (2010).

9. Keen takes her cue from Gayattri Spivak's concept of strategic essentialism, which is a political tactic employed by minority groups that involves emphasizing a shared identity for political reasons even though strong differences may exist between members of these groups.

10. For my earlier arguments regarding strategic empathy in environmental nonfiction literature and film, see Weik von Mossner (2014) and chapters 4 and 5 of my book *Affective Ecologies* (2017).

11. See, for example, Robert Kenner's *Food, Inc.* (2006), Mark Devries's *Specisim* (2013), and Louie Psihoyos's *The Cove* (2009).

12. These examples are taken from the *PlenteousVeg.com* website (Vukovic 2016), but there are countless other sources that cite similar comments and questions along with reasonable ways of responding to them.

13. Leiserowitz comments on the motivating potential of negative emotions in a TV interview with Bill Moyers dedicated to "Ending the Silence on Climate Change." The interview is available at http://billmoyers.com/episode/ending-the-silence-on-climate-change/

14. According to a recent article in *The London Economic*, "[v]egan food sales are up by a whopping 1,500 per cent" in 2016 (Peat).

15. For a study on veganism as an activist animal rights position promoted by catalytic experiences, see McDonald (2000). Plant-based food sales also show significant growth rates elsewhere in Europe and in North America.

16. Laura Wright helpfully summarizes the criticism levelled at Freedman and Barnouin's *Skinny Bitch* books because of their promotion of thin female bodies (104–05). Hildmann's books address themselves to both genders, but they tend to feature Hildmann's own attractive male body as a constant reminder of the link between plant-based eating and physical attractiveness and desirability.

17. For a critical look at the use of ethnic identity in the popular food blog *Thug Kitchen*, see Priestley, Lingo, and Royal (2016).

18. The alluring depiction of food in ads, cooking shows, cookbooks, and food blogs is sometimes referred to as "food porn" because of what some consider a structural similarity to the psychological mechanisms of sexual pornography. Romm traces the term "food porn" back to feminist writer Rosalind Cowards's 1984 book *Female Desire*.

19. A 2012 study by Schüssler et al. found that just looking at pictures of food may be enough to cause an uptick in ghrelin, a hormone that causes hunger.

PART II

VEGAN STUDIES IN THE UNITED STATES

CHAPTER 4

The Sexual Politics of Meat in the Trump Era

Carol J. Adams

On January 20, 2017, the Trump presidency began.[1] But the Trump era precedes by more than a decade the cultural moment when Donald Trump, a TV game show host, often-failed businessman, thrice-married loudmouth, liar, and promoter of racist, anti-immigrant, anti-Muslim, and misogynistic positions, was inaugurated as the forty-fifth president of the US. Two events vie for the first-moment of the Trump era.

The initial event that might be claimed to have marked the beginning of the Trump era was the airing of the first episode of *The Apprentice* on January 8, 2004. *The Apprentice* is a game show that involves a variety of individuals vying to succeed at business-related tasks, and Donald Trump was its host for the first fourteen years. Some might argue that the era was initiated by the 1987 publication of Trump's ghostwritten *The Art of the Deal,* which created the idea of Trump as a wise businessman.[2] But even a best-selling book lacks the cathoid-ray, plasma-display, and LCD-power of the television, which sat in 118.4 million American homes in 2016 (Nielsen).

Comedian, actor, and writer Chelsea Handler suggested it was the reality show *Keeping Up with the Kardashians* (first aired in 2007) that initiated this era: "I blame the Kardashians, personally; the beginning of the end was the Kardashians. The way these people have blown up and don't go away—it's surreal. Everyone is for sale" (Delbyck, 2017). Handler argues that the mainstream media outlets maintained this reality television view of Trump: "They were treating [Trump] as an entertainer first" and permitted Trump, like the Kardashians, "to traffic in scandal instead of substance" (Delbyck). Emily Bell, director of the Tow Center for Digital Journalism at Columbia Journalism School, in arguing that Donald Trump should be seen himself as a media organization, refers to *The Apprentice* as "the vehicle that made his presidency possible" (Bell).

The other event that competes for the first-moment of the Trump era was the passing of "Ag-Gag" laws and a federal law that seeks to impede and criminalize animal rights activism. Alicia Prygoski separates Ag-Gag laws into two parts: the early laws, which began to appear in the early 1990s that

> were designed to deter animal rights activists from trespassing and causing physical property damage. They criminalized entering the premises of industrialized farming operations without permission and destroying or damaging property. Though this was the primary intent of these ecoterrorism laws, all three also contained language criminalizing recording at industrialized farming operations that is very similar to some of the modern-day ag-gag legislation. (Prygoski)

The current laws, passed subsequent to 2011, "shifted away from preventing property damage to focusing primarily on banning recording in an effort to curb resulting economic damage" (Prygoski). Like the changing focus of the Ag-Gag laws (in 2007, there were Ag-Gag laws in five states), the federal law (The Animal Enterprise Protection Act of 1992) was amended in a way that "chills First Amendment activity" (New York City Bar 2009). The amended law, passed in 2006, is known as the "Animal and Ecological Terrorism Act" (AETA). It greatly expanded the definition of "terrorism" and focused on animal rights and environmental activism. Drafted by the conservative (and corporate-influenced[3]) American Legislative Exchange Council, it expanded "the definition of terrorism to include not only property destruction, but any action intended to 'deter' animal enterprises," including nonviolence, civil disobedience, and witnessing and documenting corporate misconduct (Potter 128). Vegan Congressman Dennis Kucinich spoke against the bill, saying in essence that existing federal laws were adequate and that "trespassing is trespassing, theft is theft, harassment is harassment" (Potter 169). Kucinich said, "My concern about this bill is that it does nothing to address the real issue of animal protection but instead targets those advocating animal rights. This legislation will have a real and chilling effect on people's Constitutionally protected First Amendment rights" (Potter 2006). Kucinich urged Congress "to pay more attention to the issues raised by the millions of Americans concerned about the humane treatment of animals, and to consider legislation in response to those concerns" (Center for Constitutional Rights). With the passage of AETA, documenting animal abuse on factory farms by going undercover was illegal, but the animal abuse itself occupied a more fungible state. Traditional acts of civil disobedience, among other activities, were now labeled "terrorist."

The labeling of some animal activism as terrorism, the tight-knit relationship between big businesses and legislation, and the attempt to control embarrassing and revelatory information from being released, all "chilling" free speech, characterize not just these laws and legislation, but presage the Trump candidacy and transition period. During the 2016 presidential campaign, Trump demonized his opponent and the mainstream press in unprecedented ways, not only referring to Democratic candidate Clinton as "nasty" but also asserting "lock her up," while impeding release of information about his payment (or lack of payment) of his taxes and his sexually predatory behavior (see below). He also filled advisory posts during the presidential transition period with advisors such as Iowa Republican governor Terry Branstad, who was "the first governor to sign into law an 'ag-gag' measure that punishes whistleblowers, giving factory farmers free rein over animal welfare and worker safety" (Parker). Former Iowa state Republican representative Annette Sweeney, the bill's sponsor, was also a Trump adviser.

The question of who is a terrorist and what is terrorism has gained new relevance as activists hit the streets to challenge inhumane policies enacted during the Trump administration. Will Potter, author of *Green Is the New Red,* warned in an interview with me in December 2017 that, "the strategies and tactics used against animal activists aren't going to stop there. They are expanding to Black Lives Matter, to people protesting the Trump Inauguration, the Dakota Pipeline protestors. They are expanding this framing of who is subversive and who is dangerous, and as well, there is an attempt to narrow that discussion in terms of people in power. So that by definition whatever you are doing as a person in power is not part of the debate."

After Trump's inauguration, attacks on the mainstream press, the claim of "alternate facts," the rewriting of history, the efforts to roll back Obama-administration-led environmental protections, and the support of other sexual abusers like Fox News superstar Bill O'Reilly, confirmed what I had sensed during the painful campaign: President Trump is the avatar of the sexual politics of meat, as I will show in this essay. As Jill Filipovic persuasively argued in March 2017, the decision to show Trump among a large number of white men when announcing decisions (especially those having to do with women, like reinstating the global "gag rule" prohibiting organizations that receive US funding from mentioning abortion) isn't a gaffe, but a deliberate act:

> President Trump ran a campaign of aggrieved masculinity.... Mr. Trump oozes male entitlement, from his brash insistence that he's the best at everything despite knowing very little about anything to his history of crass sexism. . . . Mr. Trump promised he would make America great again, a slogan that included the implicit pledge to return white men to their place of historic supremacy. And that is precisely what these photos show. (Filopovic)

THE SEXUAL POLITICS OF MEAT

I have previously argued that a link exists between meat eating and notions of masculinity and virility in the Western world (Adams 2015). A belief exists that male-identified strength comes from eating meat, and that eating vegetables is equated with femininity. As Bruce Fleming's 2006 study *Why Liberals and Conservatives Clash* confirmed, conservatives find their political attitudes expressed in the association of maleness and meat eating. Countless cookbook titles, meat advertisements, and cultural moments remind us that, if one wants to "eat like a man" one needs to be eating meat, and all reinforce a conservative political perspective. Anxiety about meat eating and masculinity shows how they are both normative and unstable—so more steaks and more red meat are needed to secure what has been destabilized: masculinity. Meat eating becomes a marker—*this* is what real men do; they eat meat. They aren't "sissies," they aren't "effeminate." Fleming explains why conservatives scorn those who eat a veggie burger: "such a person is a 'wimp.' This word is surely a portmanteau word combining 'woman' with 'limp' to suggest impotence: Being strong or firm, as we say, is all about maleness which . . . is structurally congruent to the conservative worldview" (Fleming 34–35).

After primary contests and at other times during 2016 (press conferences!), candidate Trump offered steaks to those in attendance. The steaks made a statement about wealth, brand, conservative politics, and masculinity. As *The New York Times* describes it, "Branding, Mr. Trump's specialty, is the capitalist version of transubstantiation. The businessman-celebrity bestows his blessing on a humble slab of meat and lo, it becomes a Trump Steak" (Poniewozik). The steaks available to his followers in 2016 were not Trump Steaks. These had been marketed during a brief time in the summer of 2007 through the Sharper Image catalogue, on QVC, and sold online. The usual bluster appears in his promotion of a product: "When it comes to great steaks, I've just raised the stakes! . . . Trump Steaks are the world's greatest steaks . . . Treat yourself to the very, very best life has to offer. . . . One bite and you'll know exactly what I'm talking about. And believe me: I understand steaks. They're my favorite food" (*Business Insider*).[4] Trump Steaks were not a successful business venture. Jerry Levin of Sharper Image reported, "We literally sold almost no steaks," adding, "If we sold $50,000 of steaks grand total, I'd be surprised" (Opelka).

OBJECTIFICATION/FRAGMENTATION/CONSUMPTION

In *The Sexual Politics of Meat*, I identified how violence against women and animals used for meat is interconnected and occurs through the processes of objectification, fragmentation, and consumption:

> Objectification permits an oppressor to view another being as an object. The oppressor then violates this being by object-like treatment: e.g., the rape of women that denies women freedom to say no, or the butchering of animals that converts animals from living breathing bodies into dead objects. This process allows fragmentation, or brutal dismemberment, and finally consumption. . . . Consumption is the fulfillment of oppression, the annihilation of will, of separate identity. (27)

The patriarchal climate that normalizes this objectifying, fragmenting, and consuming behavior had seemed to exist just below the surface, erupting through advertisements and other ephemera, but not considered something one should admit to himself doing. But Trump's rhetoric during the 2016 presidential campaign empowered his followers to be blatant and obvious, rather than suggestive. Watching a three-minute video culled from *The New York Times*' reporters' coverage of Donald Trump's rallies revealed that formerly egregious behavior had become normalized. The video begins with a warning: "This video includes vulgarities and racial and ethnic slurs." Amidst anti-Muslim invective, xenophobic references to "build that wall," racist slurs against President Obama, and violent incidents, we learn that "perhaps nothing draws more ire than mentions of Hillary Clinton." We hear shouts of "Bitch," "Tramp," "Fuck you Hillary," and "Hang the bitch." At minute 2:31, a political pin appears with the wording "KFC Hillary Special: 2 Fat Thighs, 2 small breasts . . . left wing."

I first saw this reference to Hillary Clinton around 1993 when she was beginning her life as First Lady by working for health care reform. When I used the term "politics" in the title of my 1990 book *The Sexual Politics of Meat*, I meant, like Kate Millet, the power-structured relationships of a patriarchal world. Not surprisingly, politics—electing and governing—and *sexual* politics, the world constituted by everyday actions of misogyny, intersect.

In 2013 a characterization similar to the one used about Clinton appeared against Australian Prime Minister Julia Gillard. The opposition party held a dinner that included on its menu "Julia Gillard Kentucky Fried Quail: small breasts, huge thighs and a big red box." These were two of the most powerful women in the world, yet their opponents reduced them to sexualized body parts, participating in the viewpoint that women exist to please someone else, not to act in their own self-interest—it's not about their programs, their platforms, or their merits or demerits. Such characterizations disempower them; body parts don't have a voice or a will.

Using language that reduces women to their body parts is nothing new. It is part of the process of objectification. We know that batterers and rapists often avoid language that acknowledges the individuality of the victim (like someone's first name), and choose instead language that objectifies them (like bitch, cunt, cow, or slut). They aren't alone—violence against another person often begins with such distancing devices, making some*one* into some*thing* to enable their treatment as an object. An individual is unique, whereas body parts are interchangeable.

The language found at that dinner in Australia or on the pins at a Trump rally are only the most noticeable examples of the everyday degradations of this type that many women experience. For example, one Fox News host referred to the first female pilot in the United Arab Emirates Air Force who landed her plane as "boobs on the ground" instead of by her name, Major Mariam Al Mansouri. Or consider the Chicago restaurant where you can find a sandwich called "Double D

Cup Breast of Turkey," or the Carl's Jr. advertisement that announces that the "large breasts" it serves can't be shown on television. Kentucky Fried Chicken asks whether you are "a breast or a thigh man?" There's a steakhouse called "Adam's Rib," and it offers plenty of meat-related references to "racks," implying a woman's "rack," and not "a rack of ribs," is being consumed. All of these examples express misogyny.

From dead animals' sellable body parts—breast, thigh, wing, rib, and rack—come the slurs against successful women candidates, or the woman in the seat next to you in the restaurant, or any woman who encounters these ads, or ourselves. The double entendres create the question: *just who are we supposed to think is being consumed?* They are so deeply embedded in our culture that many people don't notice their assaultive and objectifying nature. They are just there—a joke. What's there to notice?

Meat advertisements often employ misogyny. Men will be called "ladies" as a put-down by someone who has just eaten a steak sandwich, or a man wearing a pink sweater may be asked, "Do they make that for men?" in an ad for Kentucky Fried Chicken. This misogyny extends to how dead animals themselves are depicted: as buxom females asking to be consumed. They *want* their left wing to be eaten, their thighs and breasts to be consumed. They live—or rather die—to please their consumers.

These sexual politics of meat attitudes are often expressed by Donald Trump, conveying a worldview that women are available as objects for his use, like the other animals. This behavior and accompanying attitudes became known in a video of Donald Trump leaked from the archives of *Access Hollywood* to the *Washington Post* on October 7, 2016. In the same way that animals are erased when they are rendered "meat," women are erased when they are rendered objects. I used the term *the structure of the absent referent* to represent this process of subjects being viewed and treated as objects. In the *Access Hollywood* video, the women being discussed are all "absent referents": their lives (and the integrity of their bodies) are not seen as mattering to them but only to how the patriarchal gaze experiences them (Adams, *The Sexual Politics of Meat* 21–23). In the video,

- Trump refers to women as objects ("Oh, it looks good").

- Trump tells the sycophantic Billy Bush: "I moved on her like a bitch but I couldn't get there." "I did try and fuck her. She was married." These comments illustrate her absent referent status, the absence of respect for her will.

- Trump fragments women into body parts ("Look at that face. Would anyone vote for that?"). The fragmentation continues as he discusses a woman's legs. She is a disaggregated collection of sexualized body parts, not a person.

- Consumption and consummation are referred to through Trump's mention of his previous incidents of sexual assault against women. Trump talks about his right to consume women. The *Washington Post*, the journalistic source that broke the news about the tape, provided a transcript:

> Bush and Trump can be heard commenting about actress Arianne Zucker. She was waiting to escort them onto the soap opera set.
>
> "Your girl's hot as s—, in the purple," says Bush.
>
> "Woah!" Trump says. "Woah!"
>
> "Yes! The Donald has scored," Bush says before commenting on Zucker's legs.
>
> As the men prepared to get off the bus, Trump made the comment that came to define the last month of the campaign and inspire rallying cries from women's rights organizations.
>
> "I just start kissing them," Trump says. "When you're a star, they let you do it."
>
> "Whatever you want," says another voice, apparently Bush's.
>
> "Grab them by the p—y," Trump says.
>
> They eventually exit the bus and greet Zucker, who is unaware of the conversation that had just taken place.
>
> "How about a little hug for the Donald?" Bush says. "He just got off the bus." (Hawkins and Mettler)

Women are the objects; Trump and Bush are the subjects. The women being discussed matter only to the degree that their bodies are seen as available to Trump and Bush. Male entitlement is circulated among men, who together create the object status of the women.[5]

In 2013, Trump tweeted about the rising number of reported sexual assaults in the military, saying, "What did these geniuses expect when they put men & women together?" From a dismissive "boys will be boys" to shrugging off the *Access Hollywood* video as "locker room talk," Trump normalizes sexual violence. He also normalized the objectification of women. At succeeding campaign appearances, men appeared holding signs such as "Rather grab a pussy than be a pussy," and "Jail the Cunt." In these responses, the misogyny seems to have moved to a pornographic fantasy of assault and bondage. From the pin reducing her to two fat thighs, etc., to references to Hillary as cunt, the demonization of Clinton—which was first observed more than twenty years earlier (Gates)—found its natural home: in the sexual politics of meat.

ANIMALIZATION OF WOMEN OF ALL COLORS

Trump participates in a worldview that objectifies others, that perpetuates hierarchies over those who are not white men, that spews hate speech against these nondominant others. Oppressive attitudes often reach beyond the species line to intensify themselves. For instance, when Trump called Alicia Machado—Miss Universe—"Miss Piggy" he combined fat-shaming with speciesism. He also racialized her by calling her "Miss Housekeeping," associating Latinas with the job of maid and housekeeper. As Claudia Rankine observes, "One benefit of white privilege is that whiteness has an arsenal of racialized insults at the ready" (Rankine 148).

During the GOP presidential candidates debate on August 6, 2015, Megyn Kelly—who was then one of Fox News' stars—said to Donald Trump, "You have called women you don't like 'fat pigs,' 'dogs,' 'slobs,' and 'disgusting animals.'" These examples of animalizing women are meant to demean them (in the view of the dominant culture) by seeing them as animal-like. As Leo Kuper notes, "The animal world has been a particularly fertile source of metaphors of dehumanization" (Kuper 88). Later to CNN, Donald Trump said of Kelly, "you could see there was blood coming out of her eyes. Blood coming out of her wherever" (Rucker). Trump's emphasis on bleeding women (this happened again in July 2017 when he said in a tweet about Mika Brzezinski of MSNBC's *Morning Joe* that "She was bleeding badly from a face-lift") is an effort at animalization of women, associating us with our bodies that bleed; the individual is both spotlighted for her abnormality while also being objectified as *less than*, and so loses her individuality. As Megan Garber pointed out in response to Trump's tweet about Mika, "the accusation [of bleeding] calls to mind the long cultural history of delegitimizing women as people because of their biological associations with blood. Blood, again, as weakness. Blood as dirtiness. 'Bloody' as an insult, largely because it suggests unruly femininity." (Garber)

These dualistic associations that "dehumanize" are hierarchical and interconnected: not just male *over* female, human *over* animal, animate *over* inanimate, but humanized male *over* animalized female, "legal [human]" over "illegal [animals]" (undocumented immigrants). As an example, language about undocumented immigrants often animalizes them, so that Mexican women in the US are said to "drop their babies" whereas US citizens "give birth"—yet another example of racism employing speciesism (Santa Ana 86).

THE POLITICAL CLIMATE: NOSTALGIA, RACISM, AND ANTI-FEMINISM

A survey in January 2017 by PerryUndem—described by *The New York Times* as "a nonpartisan research and polling firm"—found that Republican men underestimated the sexism women experience in their lives (Miller). Most survey respondents agreed that it was a better time to be a man than a woman; 75 percent of Republican men did not believe a lack of women in political office affected women's rights. About two-thirds of Republican men did not view unequal responsibilities in caring for families as affecting women's rights. All men, including those who said women were still treated unequally, underestimated women's experience of sexism, specifically women's experience of sexist language and inappropriate touching.

An earlier survey conducted shortly before the November 2016 presidential vote found that many voters for the Republican candidate, Donald Trump, wanted to return to the time of the 1950s: "Roughly two-thirds (66 percent) of Democrats say American culture has generally changed for the better since the 1950s, while roughly two-thirds of Republicans (68 percent) and a majority of independents (55 percent) say American society and way of life has only gotten worse" (Cooper et al). This nostalgia for the 1950s ignored that decade's history that saw the killing of civil rights activists, the rigidity of Jim

Crow laws, the numerous deaths of women from illegal abortions, and the simmering threat of nuclear weapons during the Cold War. Daniel Marcus in his 2004 study of the fifties and the sixties in cultural politics observes, "As students of memory have found, recollections of the past take shape out of current needs and pressures. Nostalgia thrives when the stability of personal identity is challenged by rapid social change, discontinuity, and dislocation" (Marcus 67).

In fact, scholars like Stephanie Coontz in *The Way We Never Were: American Families and the Nostalgia Trap* have shown that the 1950s were actually a departure from earlier decades, not a culmination. Drawing on Coontz's work, Marcus observes,

> The Baby Boom era's emphasis on the primacy of private, domestic family life, with tens of millions of Americans ensconced in single-family suburban homes, working in offices or large factories and going to church regularly, was not a continuation of traditional American practices, but a newly dominant norm that still described only a minority of Americans' lives. Rather than being an aberration from a previously unchanging norm, the Sixties' challenge to Fifties social forms and ensuing reversal of 1950s demographics in regard to marriage, divorce, and childbearing actually reconstituted trends from earlier in the century. (Marcus 68)

Control of female reproductivity is part of a return to the 1950s, when abortion was illegal and the birth control pill had not yet appeared on the market. Donald Trump campaigned on defunding Planned Parenthood. One in five women in the US have been to Planned Parenthood for health care (Richards).

The absence of respect for women's bodily integrity results in politics that restrict reproductive freedom. That female animals might also possess bodily integrity slips even further from ethical consideration when women's rights to reproductive care are restricted. In advertisements about female farm animals, I find attitudes that fuel the current rollbacks on reproductive freedom and access to abortion. To control fertility one must have absolute access to the female of the species. Cows, sows, hens, and female sheep are exploited in ways that merge their reproductive and productive labor. We can find a Bovi-Shield Gold advertisement about cows asking, "If she can't stay pregnant, what else would she do?" (National Cattlemen's Beef Association 2012). In their advertisements to animal agribusinesses, drug companies depict sexy, buxom animals who want to be pregnant, who want to give the farmers one more sow per year. A hen who holds her sexualized, hairless leg out, she wants those drugs too, wants to be the subservient reproducer as though she is saying, "Keep me pregnant down on the farm." Misogyny is hiding behind the depiction of sexualized farmed animals. As others, including Laura Wright, have noted, Republicans in power wish to keep *white* women pregnant and producing white children (Wright, note to author, July 2017).

When it comes to meat consumption, nostalgia for the fifties and the average consumer's unproblematized relationship to meat eating is perhaps more on point. Both Burger King and McDonald's began franchising fast-food burger-centered restaurants (with milkshakes) in the 1950s. Insta-Burger King opened on March 1, 1953. That same year Ray Kroc gained the right to be the exclusive distributor of franchises for the McDonald brothers. (The headline of the *Guardian* review of the 2017 movie on Kroc, *The Founder*, suggests the Trump era began then: "Michael Keaton [as Kroc] supersizes McDonald's and births Trump's US" [Bradshaw].)

In the 1950s, with more cars on the road and the stimulus of massive federal funding of highways, the "drive-in" with its meat- and dairy-centered meals, experienced its best decade. In 1956, the Institute of Home Economics of the Agricultural Research Service of the USDA introduced the Basic Four Food Groups, in which 50 percent of the food groups were from animals. The four food groups were milk, meat, vegetable-fruit, and bread-cereal. They replaced the Basic Seven that were introduced during World War II, which in itself had supplanted the "Twelve Food Groups" used in the 1930s:

1. Milk and milk products
2. Potatoes and sweet potatoes
3. Dry mature peas, beans, and nuts
4. Tomatoes and citrus fruits
5. Leafy green and yellow vegetables
6. Other vegetables and fruits
7. Eggs
8. Lean meat, poultry, and fish
9. Flour and cereals
10. Butter
11. Other fats
12. Sugars (Altman 12)

In 1960 beef consumption outpaced pork consumption for the first time (85.1 pounds to 64.9 pounds) (Ross).

Is it possible that twenty-first century Burger King and Carl's Jr. ads, featuring buxom women eating huge burgers, are part of Republican nostalgia, a longing for a time when sex roles were more determined and determinative, a time when oogling women was okay and women wanting to be oogled was the norm, and when burger eating was the casual prerogative of everyone?

CARL'S JR. GOES TO WASHINGTON

Legal scholar Cass Sunstein remarked that one job requirement for the people President-elect Trump nominated to cabinet positions was that they should "demonstrate a clear commitment to the fundamental mission of the department they seek to lead" (Sunstein). Many of Trump's nominees did not. Of particular concern was Trump's nomination of Andy Puzder to be Labor Secretary. Puzder was the CEO of CKE Restaurants, the parent company of the Carl's Jr. and Hardee's burger chains. He opposes unions, the minimum wage, paid sick leave, and the Affordable Care Act, among other programs: "Puzder is even critical of the federal relief programs, such as food stamps, that subsidize the poverty wages that he pays his employees" (Finnegan). William Finnegan hypothesized that Trump recognized in Puzder "a frat brother. Carl's Jr. is known for outrageous, salacious TV commercials starring young women in bikinis leeringly munching burgers." It was Puzder who created the Carl's Jr. brand "boobs and burgers." Puzder said, "I like our ads. I like beautiful women eating burgers in bikinis. I think it's very American" (Taylor).

In *Ways of Seeing*, John Berger proposed that "Men look at women. Women watch themselves being looked at" (Berger 47). As the chief executive of CKE Restaurants, Puzder oversaw—and justified—some of the most sexist and sexually provocative advertisements to air in the US, ads that teach men how to look at women and women how to look at men looking at women. Launched in 2005, these super-model-centric ads began at the beginning of the Trump era, crafted to appeal to their target market: eighteen- to thirty-four-year-old men. They offered a new platform for objectification, fragmentation, and consumption.

I wrote about Carl's Jr. and its brother company Hardee's in the afterword to the twenty-fifth anniversary edition of *The Sexual Politics of Meat*:

> Fast food burger chains like Carl's, Burger King, and Hardees' fall over each other in their attempt to find new ways of showing barely-clad women being objectified while eating or desiring hamburgers. Another aspect of the sexual politics of meat: the disempowerment of women is inscribed visually by depicting females in non-dominant positions, in which large burgers hang over their bodies, loom large beside their bodies, or are being stuffed into their mouths. The burgers dominate the visual space over or around a woman. They reveal (and enact) fantasies about women's big mouths and what we can swallow. Women are symbolically silenced by having their mouths stuffed with flesh— that innate and originating patriarchal symbol of power over and violence. (206)

The ads have other things in common: they sexualize a certain type of woman's body (in terms of size and figure), are often racist, reinforcing stereotypes about women of color, while also teaching men how to be voyeurs to women's sexuality. Carl's Jr. teaches that heterosexual men's sexuality is the referent point for dominance. One advertisement was shared on social media simply as "blow job woman." The ad exalted in a woman's humiliation as she tries (and succeeds) in stuffing a large burger in her mouth. Another simulates a man reaching orgasm through the spurting of his water hose at the apposite moment as he watches a large-breasted woman walk by taking bites out of a large burger.

Men who come to believe that entitlement allows them to look at women may also feel entitled to sexually harass women, especially, it turns out, female employees at fast-food restaurants operated by Puzder. (The #MeToo movement has taught us about the dimensions and phenomenon of sexual harassment.) New research suggests women at these restaurants "face far higher levels of workplace sexual harassment than the industry average. According to the research conducted by Restaurant Opportunities Center (ROC) United, around 66 percent of female workers reported sexual harassment at brands owned by CKE restaurants, run by Puzder, compared with the average of 40 percent across the fast food industry" (Bates, see also Laughland and Gambino).

On February 15, 2017, Puzder withdrew his nomination. Though Democrats, unions, and liberal groups had mounted a strong campaign against his nomination, it was thought that his withdrawal occurred after he lost the support of many conservative publications and congressman because of his previous pro-immigration stance and his own employment of an undocumented immigrant as a housekeeper. Resurfaced video of his ex-wife alleging domestic violence in 1988 did not help his case (Rappeport). In March, Puzder resigned as president of CKE Restaurants. A week later, CKE announced it was abandoning its use of bikini-wearing women in its advertisements.[6]

RESISTING TELEOLOGICAL TALES

What then do we do in response to the sexual politics of meat in the Trump era, as well as all that has accompanied it: the vitiation of environmental protections, the attack on health care, the attacks on the judiciary, and the growing evidence that the president has no comprehension of American history, compliments dictators, and is impulsive and ignorant? I've come to think of veganism as the ultimate anti-Trump diet (see Adams and Messina), and this act of resistance matters to vegan studies and to activism. The nature of veganism in itself resists some of the harms of the Trump era. By placing us lower on the food chain, veganism is much less environmentally demanding than meat and dairy consumption, thus reducing the harms associated with climate change. The daily action of veganism withdraws support for products that arise from deeply patriarchal attitudes. In addition, a healthy vegan diet offers protection against stress during times of political turmoil.

In *The Sexual Politics of Meat*, I argued that veganism disturbs the presumptions of meals by removing "the meat" thought central to them and by disrupting "the story of meat" that justified animals' oppression. I suggested this destabilizing process was akin to feminism's challenge to the dominant story narratives featuring active men and passive women (like those in which princesses need rescue). I wrote:

> We accept meat eating as consumers because this role is continuous with our role of consumers of completed stories. . . .With the lens of feminist interpretation we can see that the animal's position in the story of meat is that of the woman's in traditional patriarchal narrative; she is the object to be possessed. The story ends when the Prince finds his Princess. Our story ends when the male-defined consumer eats the female-defined body. The animals' role in meat eating is parallel to the women's role in narrative: we would have neither meat nor story without them. They are objects to others who act as subjects. (78)

Destabilizing traditional narratives is inherent to feminist-veganism, and that skill is called for now. Timothy Snyder has pointed out that the liberal assumption that progress occurs and things will work out is a fallacy and antihistorical, referring to this assumption as the "politics of inevitability." In a talk at Yale in December 2016, "Snyder pushed back against the idea that history trends towards justice by declaring, 'There's no arc of history. . . Sorry!'" (Ding). Snyder implies that the teleological assumption that holds that the federal government can withstand the assault it is experiencing under Trump may prevent us from responding accurately and fully. The functioning of teleological fictions that disarm activism and posit optimistic interpretations of the status quo is familiar to vegan activists and scholars. Teleological fictions inform some of the most deeply held justifications of eating meat and dairy: that humans are at the top of the food chain, that we are the evolutionary victors and allowed the spoils (of animals' bodies and products), and the belief that we are predators not prey. If vegan studies can unravel these fictions, can they contribute to the destabilization of the function of teleological naiveté and help equip people to see that we also can't assume the state will necessarily survive someone like Trump?

Vegans have something to offer to those resisting the regressive, anti-environmental, misognynistic, and anti-free-speech Trump administration. The social experiences of vegans—feeling alienated from current events, experiencing deep despair, dealing with challenges to free speech, and feeling powerless in the face of great power—provide vegans with skills for coping and responding. Vegans know about compassion fatigue and activism overload and have experience in seeking remedies for both. We have learned to interrogate the propaganda that encourages meat, dairy, and egg consumption. It comes from corporate advertising and with the full backing of the federal government. And we recognize the fallacies of an ahistorical teleology. A vegan diet can strike at the patriarchal roots of animal oppression. All of these skills and practices are needed now.

⁓

- I wish to thank Meera Atkinson, Pat Davis, Ian Elwood, Priscilla Feral, Melinda Fox, Leslie Robinson Goldberg, Danielle Kichler, Lisa Hussein Knaggs, Nora Kramer, Nancy Lancy, Eveline Lang, Evander Lomke, Mychael McNeely, L. C. Robertson, David Gavin

Steib, Julia Tanenbaum, Lee Ann Thill, and Jordan Toland for their suggestions for this article and Laura Wright for her astute edits.

- For this essay, I have included paragraphs from my op-ed that appeared in *Transformation* on August 22, 2016, www.opendemocracy.net/transformation/carol-j-adams/ sexual-politics-of-meat.

WORKS CITED

Adams, Carol J. *The Sexual Politics of Meat: A Feminist-Vegetarian Critical Theory.* New York: Bloomsbury, [1990], 2015.

———. *Neither Man nor Beast: Feminism and the Defense of Animals.* New York: Continuum, 1994.

———. *The Pornography of Meat.* New York: Continuum/Lantern, 2003/2015.

———. "The Sexual Politics of Meat." *Transformation,* August 22, 2016. www.opendemocracy.net/transformation/carol-j-adams/sexual-politics-of-meat.

———, and Virginia Messina. *Protest Kitchen: Fight Injustice, Save the Planet, and Fuel Your Resistance One Meal at a Time.* Boston: Red Wheel, Conari, 2018

Altman, National. "Nutritional Watergate: The Story of the 'Four Food Group.'" *Vegetarian Times* September/October, 21, 1977. pp. 9–14.

Barbaro, Michael and Megan Twohey. Shamed and Angry: Alicia Machado, a Miss Universe Mocked by Donald Trump. The *New York Times.* Sept. 27, 2016. https://nyti.ms/2kfoYKk.

Bates, Laura. "'Ugly Women Don't Sell Burgers'–The Trickle-Down Effect of Team Trump." *Guardian,* January 18, 2017. www.theguardian.com/us-news/2017/jan/18/trickle-down-effect-team-trumps-labour-secretary-nominee-andrew-puzder.

Bell, Emily. "Donald Trump Is a Media Organization." *Columbia Journalism Review,* January 10, 2017. www.cjr.org/tow_center/donald_trump_media_organization.php?Newsletter.

Berger, John. *Ways of Seeing.* New York: Penguin Books, 1972.

Bradshaw, Peter. "The Founder review: Michael Keaton Supersizes McDonald's and Births Trump's US." *Guardian.* January 16, 2017. https://www.theguardian.com/film/2017/jan/16/the-founder-review-ray-kroc-micheal-keaton-dick-and-mac-mcdonald.

Center for Constitutional Freedom. "The Animal Enterprise Terrorism Act (AETA)." November 19, 2007. ccrjustice.org/home/get-involved/tools-resources/fact-sheets-and-faqs/animal-enterprise-terrorism-act-aeta.

Chait, Jonathan. "The Abnormalization of Hillary Clinton." *New York Magazine,* September 22, 2016. nymag.com/daily/intelligencer/2016/09/the-abnormalization-of-hillary-clinton.html.

Coontz, Stephanie. *The Way We Never Were: Amercian Families and the Nostalgia Trap.* New York: Basic Books, 1992/2016.

Cooper, Betsy, Daniel Cox, Rachel Lienesch, and Robert P. Jones, "The Divide Over America's Future: 1950 or 2050?" *www.prri.org/research/poll-1950s-2050-divided-nations-direction-post-election/.*

Delbyck, Cole. "Chelsea Handler Thinks the Kardashians Are to Blame for Trump's Presidency." *The Huffington Post,* January 17, 2017. www.huffingtonpost.com/

entry/chelsea-handler-thinks-the-kardashians-are-the-ones-to-blame-for-trumps-presidency_us_587e1d6be4b0897228653b70.

Ding, Julia. "What Can European History Teach Us about Trump's America?" Yale MacMillan Center, December 7, 2016. http://macmillan.yale.edu/news/what-can-european-history-teach-us-about-trumps-america.

Fahrenthold, David A. "Trump Recorded Having Extremely Lewd Conversation about Women in 2005." *Washington Post*, October 7, 2016. www.washington-post.com/politics/trump-recorded-having-extremely-lewd-conversation-about-women-in-2005/2016/10/07/3b9ce776–8cb4–11e6-bf8a-3d26847eeed4_story.html?utm_term=.54e36b83f47f.

Filopovic, Jill. "The All-Male Photo Op Isn't a Gaffe. It's a Strategy." *The New York Times,* March 27, 2017. https://www.nytimes.com/2017/03/27/opinion/the-all-male-photo-op-isnt-a-gaffe-its-a-strategy.html?_r=0.

Finnegan, William. "Trump Against the American Worker," *New Yorker*, December 13, 2016. www.newyorker.com/news/daily-comment/trump-against-the-american-worker.

Fleming, Bruce. *Why Liberals and Conservatives Clash*. New York and London: Routledge, 2006.

Garber, Megan. "Mika Brzezinski and Donald Trump's Penchant for Blood Feuds." *The Atlantic,* June 29, 2017. https://www.theatlantic.com/entertainment/archive/2017/06/mika-brzezinski-and-donald-trumps-penchant-for-blood-feuds/532185/.

Gates, Henry Louis. "Hating Hillary: Hillary Clinton Has Been Trashed Right and Left—But What's Really Fueling the Furies?" *New Yorker*, February 26, 2016. http://www.newyorker.com/magazine/1996/02/26/hating-hillary.

Hawkins, Derek, and Katie Mettler, "Billy Bush Speaks Out about Trump 'Access Hollywood' Tape: 'I Wish I had Changed the Topic.'" *Washington Post*, May 22, 2017. https://www.washingtonpost.com/news/morning-mix/wp/2017/05/21/billy-bush-speaks-out-about-trump-access-hollywood-tape-i-wish-i-had-changed-the-topic/?utm_term=.5cd54d5e6d49.

Holodny, Elena. "11 Donald Trump Businesses and Where They Are Today." *Business Insider*, October 9, 2014. www.businessinsider.com/trump-businesses-that-no-longer-exist-2014–10#trump-steaks-2.

Kuper, Leo. *Genocide: Its Political Use in the Twentieth Century*. New Haven, CT: Yale University Press, 1983.

Laughland, Oliver, and Lauren Gambino. "Restaurants Run by Labor Secretary Nominee Report 'Disturbing' Rates of Sexual Harassment." *Guardian,* January 10, 2017. www.theguardian.com/business/2017/jan/10/andrew-puzder-cke-sexual-harassment-labor-secretary?CMP=Share_iOSApp_Other#img-1.

Marcus, Daniel. *Happy Days and Wonder Years: The Fifties and the Sixties in Contemporary Cultural Politics*. New Brunswick, NJ: Rutgers University Press, 2004.

Mayer, Jane. "Donald Trump's Ghostwriter Tells All." *New Yorker*, July 25, 2016. www.newyorker.com/magazine/2016/07/25/donald-trumps-ghostwriter-tells-all.

Miller, Claire Cain. "Republican Men Say It's a Better Time to Be a Woman Than a Man." *The New York Times*, January 17, 2017. https://nyti.ms/2jA7BXv.

Millet, Kate. *Sexual Politics*. Garden City, NY: Doubleday, 1970.

New York City Bar. "Re: The Animal Enterprise Terrorism Act, 18 USC. § 43." July 23, 2009. http://lawprofessors.typepad.com/files/aeta_animalcivilrights_letter072109.pdf.

Nielsen Media. "Nielsen Estimates 118.4 Million TV Homes in the US for the 2016–17 TV Season." August 26, 2016. https://www.nielsen.com/us/en/insights/news/2016/nielsen-estimates-118-4-million-tv-homes-in-the-us--for-the-2016-17-season.html

National Cattlemen's Beef Association. 2012. *National Cattleman: The Official Publication of the NCBA. 2012 Directions*. http://www.beefusa.org/CMDocs/BeefUSA/Member/NC/Directions2012.pdf.

Opelka, Mike. "Fact Check: Can You Buy Trump Steaks, Trump Water, Trump Wine and Trump Magazine?" *The Blaze,* March 9, 2016. http://www.theblaze.com/stories/2016/03/09/fact-check-can-you-buy-trump-steaks-trump-water-trump-wine-and-trump-magazine/.

Paiella, Gabriella. 2017. "Carl's Jr. Is Trying Desperately to Escape Its Sexist Past." *New York Magazine,* March 30, 2017. http://nymag.com/thecut/2017/03/carls-jr-ad-trying-to-pivot-away-from-its-sexist-past.html.

Parker, Kathleen. "Another Group that Loses if Trump Wins? Animals." *Washington Post.* September 6, 2016. http://www.washingtonpost.com/opinions/another-group-that-loses-if-trump-wins-animals/2016/09/06/270eb888–7478-11e6-be4f-3f42f2e5a49e_story.html?utm_term=.60d305576a42.

Poniewozik, James. "With Trump Water, Wine and Steak, Is It Primary Night or an Infomercial?" *The New York Times*, March 9, 2016. nyti.ms/2jSBPoL.

Potter, Will. *Green Is the New Red: An Insider's Account of a Social Movement Under Siege*. San Francisco: City Lights Books, 2011.

——. 2006. "Statement from Kucinich on the Animal Enterprise Terrorism Act." *http://www.greenisthenewred.com/blog/kucinich-aeta-statement/174/*.

——. "Animal Enterprise Terrorism 101". GreenIsTheNewRed, November 17, 2007. http://www.greenisthenewred.com/blog/aeta-101/313/.

Prygoski, Alicia. 2015. "Detailed Discussion of Ag-gag Laws." *Michigan State University College of Law:* Animal Legal & Historical Center, 2015. www.animallaw.info/article/detailed-discussion-ag-gag-laws.

Rankine, Claudia, interviewed by David L. Ulin. "The Art of Poetry No. 102." *The Paris Review, no. 219* (Winter 2016): 138–166

Richards, Cecile. "Remarks at the Women's March on Washington." *Medium,* January 21, 2017. https://medium.com/@CecileRichards/remarks-at-the-womens-march-on -washington-a579db98ff7e.

Ross, Eric B. "Patterns of Diet and Forces of Production: An Economic and Ecological History of the Ascendancy of Beef in the United States Diet." In *Beyond the Myths of Culture: Essays in Cultural Materialism.* Edited by Eric B. Ross, 181–225. New York: Academic Press, 1980.

Rucker, Philip. "Trump Says Fox's Megyn Kelly Had 'Blood Coming Out of Her Wherever.'" *Washington Post,* August 8, 2015. https://www.washingtonpost.com/news/post-politics/wp/2015/08/07/trump-says-foxs-megyn-kelly-had-blood-coming-out-of-her-wherever/?utm_term=.539f6e6995bf.

Santa Ana, Otto. *Brown Tide Rising: Metaphors of Latinos in Contemporary American Public Discourse.* Austin: University of Texas Press, 2002.

Singer, Mark. 2017. "New York Strip." *The New Yorker.* Jan. 16, 2017, 22

Stoltenberg, John. *Refusing to Be a Man: Essays on Sex and Justice.* London: Breitenbush Books, 1989.

Sunstein, Cass. "There's One Main Job Requirement to Lead a Federal Agency." *Bloomberg View,* December 6, 2016. www.bloomberg.com/view/articles/2016–12-09/there-s-one-main-job-requirement-to-lead-a-federal-agency.

Taylor, Kate. "The CEO of Carl's Jr. Doesn't Care If You're Offended by the Chain's Sexy Ads." *Entrepreneur,* May 20, 2015. www.entrepreneur.com/article/246487.

END NOTES

1. Because of the time lapse between originally completing this essay (January 2017), and its publication, I cannot address with specificity all the threats to the democratic institutions of the US, the dismantling of agencies such as the Environmental Protection Agency, the frightening autocratic-like behavior of Trump, the nepotism of the administration, whether Trump has a personality disorder or is sociopathic, his total lack of historic understanding, his inability to negotiate with other countries, his failure to condemn white supremacy, his ongoing objectification of women, or his nuclear threats. I would argue, however, that such a megalomaniac privileged white man having this kind of power is entirely consistent with a world that countenances the sexual politics of meat.

2. In 2016, Trump's coauthor and ghostwriter Tony Schwartz regretted his role in helping to create this image (Mayer 2016).

3. Specifically, according to Will Potter, one of the most knowledgeable journalists on the act, the National Association for Biomedical Research, Fur Commission USA, GlaxoSmithKline, Pfizer, Wyeth, United Egg Producers, National Cattlemen's Beef Association, and many more.

4.   Willie Degel, proprietor of Uncle Jack's steakhouse on West Fifty-sixth Street in New York, confirmed in 2017 Trump's preference for steaks. When Trump eats at Uncle Jack's, he "loves the New York strip steak" (Singer 22).

5.   On the role of other men in creating "manhood" and maintaining misogyny, see Stoltenberg.

6.   Puzder claimed that he introduced the idea of abandoning the scantily-clad women approach in its ads in December 2015. "'I went to our ad agency and said 'Look, young hungry guys aren't as affected by the racy ads with swimsuit models because you can get a lot of that on the internet now,'" Puzder shared. "'Young guys today, the millennial young guys, are concerned with where do you source your beef, what kind of cooking system do you have? . . . You and I certainly may like the ads we've been running a long time but the younger guys can get that on the internet . . . you can get sex on the internet you don't need a Carl's Jr. or Hardee's ad'"(Paiella, 2017).

CHAPTER 5

A Vegan Rhetorical Approach to Upton Sinclair's *The Jungle*

Ryan Phillips

Upton Sinclair's novel *The Jungle* (originally published in 1906) constitutes a rhetorical artifact at least as much as it does a work of literary fiction, in that the author employs language as an effective means by which to change social realities, rather than simply produce art for any aesthetic or monetary purpose. Sinclair sought not only to represent his social justice values through his literature, but purposefully engaged in writing fiction as a way to actively advocate for social change. In fact, many scholars note that *The Jungle*'s social significance is historical rather than artistic and that it is more likely to be taught in an American history or sociology course than an English literature course (Pickavance 88). The novel chronicles the plight of Lithuanian immigrant Jurgis Rudkus as he works in the Chicago meatpacking industry. Based on Sinclair's undercover journalistic work, *The Jungle* exposed through a dramatized narrative the myriad problems of the US meatpacking industry during the early part of the twentieth century. Sinclair's main interest among these social issues was in exposing, and thereby drawing empathy to, the exploitation and oppression of the American working class. However, Sinclair's best-selling novel instead riled the American public over the sanitation and health-related issues of the meat industry—a popular outrage that subsequently led to food and agricultural policy reforms such as the Pure Food and Drug Act and the Meat Inspection Act.

Although much public and academic discourse has focused on the intended goals and materialized outcomes of *The Jungle*, there remains a dearth of analysis focusing on the vegan implications of Sinclair's novel. Though a socially progressive individual who wrote about and experimented with various diets (including vegetarianism and even variants of raw veganism) (Bloodworth 448–50), Sinclair never explicitly expressed any intentions to curb the meat-eating behavior of his readers and the general public. Despite being a longtime vegetarian, Sinclair was himself dismissive of the moral arguments for vegetarianism (at least during and around the time of *The Jungle*'s publication) (*Fasting Cure* 27–28). Sinclair was also quite vocal throughout most of his life in promoting the social and health benefits of meat-free diets (Bloodworth 446). Additionally (and unlike with the resulting health-based policy reforms), the public did not misinterpret *The Jungle* as a call toward vegetarianism or animal welfare policy reforms. This essay will therefore analyze the rhetoric of animal exploitation and oppression within Sinclair's *The Jungle* and discuss how and why this concern was neither advocated by the author nor interpreted by the public— despite the obvious violence present in both the setting and plot of the novel. This essay is concerned with investigating why this best-selling, highly detailed novel about slaughterhouse work did not propel readers toward vegetarianism, animal rights advocacy, or animal welfare reform. In order to address these concerns, I will apply a vegan theoretical framework to my rhetorical analysis in order to further expand upon the growing academic field of vegan studies.

THE JUNGLE

In 1906, Upton Sinclair published *The Jungle*—a novelized version of the muckraking journalist's investigations into the slaughterhouses of early twentieth-century Chicago, Illinois. The novel revolves around Jurgis Rudkus, a recently married Lithuanian man who emigrates to the US along with his family in search of work. Though initially thrilled with new work in the slaughterhouses (stockyards) and eager to pursue wealth and happiness through hard work, Jurgis soon discovers, and quickly becomes disenfranchised with, the realities of the meatpacking industry. Early into the narrative, Jurgis and his family become affected in different ways by the harsh working conditions of industrial animal agriculture, rampant alcoholism and crime, prostitution, and deteriorating health concerns—all of which are addressed as interconnected phenomena by characters throughout the novel. In the story's climax, an alienated Jurgis is absorbed into the socialist political circles that were becoming more active in response to the exploitative and oppressive nature of early-twentieth-century US capitalism.

Perhaps unavoidably, due to the subject matter, the novel also contains running themes of animals, food, and the problematic combination of the two. For example, after fleeing the city following the deaths of his family members later in the novel, Jurgis rests briefly in the countryside. Here, he is happy and enjoys the kinds of healthy vegetarian meals for which Sinclair himself had advocated—eating beans, asparagus, mashed potatoes, and strawberries, far removed from the industrialized animal agriculture of the cities (Bloodworth 446). Even early in the text, Sinclair explicitly addresses the relationship between violence against human and nonhuman animals when he notes that "men who have to crack the heads of animals all day seem to get into the habit, and to practice on their friends, and even on their families, between times" (*The Jungle* 19).

Yet despite these recurring instances of something that at least seems like a call toward vegetarianism, veganism, or at least animal welfare reform, *The Jungle* is not often considered in these respects by either the public or academics. Indeed, even contemporary interpretations and analyses of the novel tend to focus on either the author's intended socialist critique of US capitalism (Lee ii-iii; De Grave xx) or else the material outcomes of subsequent food policies (*Fast Food Nation* 204–05). It is therefore crucial to understand the social history of both Sinclair and *The Jungle* in order to better understand why the author's rhetoric resulted in the social transformations that it did, rather than becoming a canonical work of animal rights advocacy.

Sinclair had become interested in the 1904 Chicago Stockyards workers' strike, which he had read about in the socialist newspaper *Appeal to Reason*. After Sinclair published an article regarding the strike *Appeal*, the newspaper's editor Fred D. Warren convinced and commissioned the young writer to produce a serialized narrative addressing the issue, which was later picked up by publishers, revised, and printed into its now more recognizable novelized format (Gottesman xxiv; Lee iii). Following its release, *The Jungle* created controversy both within the US and internationally. For American socialists and other international readers (including Winston Churchill in the UK), the book revealed the extent of US greed and the unrelenting drive of free-market capitalism through its realistic narrative of worker exploitation. Domestically, however, the novel's controversy revolved around the exposé of mislabeled food products, which included such public health concerns as rodent feces in food products, two-year-old meat repackaged as new, cow hearts labeled and sold as chicken, accidentally killed workers being ground up and sold as lard, and widespread tuberculosis amongst workers (Foreword x). Follow-up federal investigations into these and other claims revealed that much, if not most or all, of what Sinclair had reportedly witnessed and documented was indeed a reality in the industrial US meat industry.

As a result of the public outcry and subsequent investigations, President Theodore Roosevelt quickly enacted both the Pure Food and Drug Act and the Meat Inspection Act in order to more thoroughly regulate the industry and protect consumers from misleading or fraudulent food packaging (Foreword x; Pickavance 88). These reforms for consumer rights were reluctantly welcomed by Sinclair, who later quipped in his autobiography that he had "aimed for the public's heart, and by accident . . . hit it in the stomach" (as cited in *Fast Food Nation* 153). With this miscommunication in mind, I will now outline and engage with some possible rhetorical explanations for why Sinclair's message affected the US meat industry as it did in the first decade of the twentieth century, rather than triggering any large-scale, moral turn toward vegetarianism. First, however, I will address both the larger history of vegetarianism in the US, as well as rhetoric itself as a discipline and its significance for vegan studies.

A BRIEF HISTORY OF VEGETARIANISM IN THE US

Most popular histories of vegetarianism in the US frame the movement as an aspect of twentieth-century modernism, when in fact the political and philosophical reasons for organized mobilization promoting the abstention from meat consumption date back to at least the early nineteenth century. Proto-vegetarianism in the US began with the arrival of the Bible Christians in Philadelphia during the early nineteenth century. The Bible Christians based their new religious and political ideals around the values of "temperance, pacifism, and meat-free diets" (Shprintzen 11). Bible Christians fundamentally believed that the truth of the Bible could only be understood through the progression of time via continuous study of scripture, and that themes of vegetarianism were apparent throughout the text—including the original idealized state of the Garden of Eden, as well as Jesus's own diet (Shprintzen 13). Many tenets of this early vegetarianism in the US emphasized the relationships between moral debasement and the physiological ramifications of meat consumption, rather than the ethical considerations of farmed animals themselves. Indeed, individuals like Sylvester Graham argued that the consumption of animal flesh made humans no better than the animals of wild nature—a sentiment that reflects the speciesist basis of many proto-vegetarians in the US (Shprintzen 27).

By the late 1830s, physicians such as William Alcott also began to promote meat abstention, though increasingly from a scientific rather than ideological or religious perspective. In the early 1840s, abolitionist Charles Lane purchased farmland in Massachusetts and, along with other reformers such as William Alcott, established Fruitlands: a utopian socialist community based on the ideals of gender equality, the elimination of class systems, and abstention from meat (Shprintzen 48–49). However, unlike previous proto-vegetarians, the community members of Fruitlands addressed the concerns of animal welfare as well as the perceived relationships between individual health and ethical living (49).

In 1850, the American Vegetarian Society (AVS) was founded in Philadelphia, based on the model of the Vegetarian Society in England, and became an umbrella organization for individuals and groups of social reformers hoping to draw attention to the issue of dietary reform (Shprintzen 60). The AVS was also crucial to the conceptualization and definition of vegetarianism as a social reform movement, and further associated meat abstention with the abolition of slavery, gender equality, and pacifism (Shprintzen 60). While the British Vegetarian Society promoted meat abstention as an issue of personal choice, the AVS instead promoted the notion that not eating meat was actually the natural state of human diets, based on both contemporary anatomical sciences and Biblical teachings (Shprintzen 64).

While there had been significant vegetarian reformist activities happening in Philadelphia for decades, many vegetarians and social reformers in Chicago during the second half of the nineteenth century became increasingly concerned with the city's meatpacking industry and its resulting social problems (Shprintzen 150–51). In response to the issues of poverty, ill health, and urban decay resulting from the meatpacking industry, Chicago vegetarians became more organized and continued to grow in number throughout the 1880s and 1890s—largely due to the activism of figures such as Carrica la Favre, who started the Chicago Vegetarian Society (Shprintzen 151). In June of 1893, vegetarians from around the world visited Chicago for the World's Vegetarian Congress—widely publicized as the world's "largest gathering of like-minded food reformers in history" (Shprintzen

156). These organized and mobilized reformers in Chicago resulted in vegetarianism being increasingly discussed among the populace by the 1890s, whether or not individuals practiced vegetarianism themselves (Shprintzen 164). Indeed, by 1899 the AVS national magazine *Vegetarian Magazine* moved its headquarters from Philadelphia to Chicago (Shprintzen 170–71). Still, the US vegetarian movement during this time continued to focus on the health benefits of meat-abstention—rather than on the ethical concerns for nonhuman animals—and the Chicago vegetarian scene was no different. Figureheads of the late-nineteenth-century vegetarian movement, most notably the physician J. H. Kellogg, would have significant ideological impacts on Sinclair, and so the latter's eventual health-based advocacy of vegetarianism rather than ethical concerns for animal welfare make sense given the historical progression of meat-abstention in the US.

RHETORIC AND VEGAN STUDIES

The term *rhetoric* is often perceived negatively, as essentially equatable with discourse that is lacking in substance (Richards 3; Derkatch 13; Booth 139). As such, ostentatious or empty speech is now often denounced as rhetoric—that is, not truly espousing the views or opinions with which the speakers actually align themselves in order to achieve some hidden, self-serving purpose (Richards 3–4). However, rhetoric (or, effective or persuasive language) as both a theoretical and practical concern has a history that begins at least as early as ancient Greece, and its contemporary negative connotation in popular discourse is actually a relatively recent phenomenon (Richards 3–4).

The study of rhetoric (as an academic discipline) is concerned with the analysis of everyday language, and how that language affects and is affected by social realities in different ways (see Richards; McGee; Perelman and Olbrechts-Tyteca). Understanding rhetoric is therefore crucial for vegan studies, in that our relationships with other animals are in many ways mediated by our use of language. Laura Wright has outlined vegan studies as an academic subdiscipline concerned with studying and deconstructing representations of veganism—as both a practice and an identity—in the mainstream media, literature, television, film, and advertising (1). While the practice of veganism involves abstaining from the consumption of products wholly or partly made up of animals and animal by-products, the identifying element of veganism can reflect a number of different things (Wright 1–2). Specifically, the vegan identity can signify an ethical, health, religious, or environmental commitment, or even any combination of these identifying markers (especially with regards to dietary choices). Regarding the crucial relationship between vegan studies and language, Carol J. Adams notes that "animals are made absent through language" (*Why?* 304). Any time we see a billboard for cheeseburgers, we are being subjected to language that effectively works to commodify, depersonalize, and ultimately make absent the lives of individual, sentient beings. Similarly, the terms beef, pork, and venison all serve as euphemisms for dead cows, pigs, and deer, respectively. It is therefore important that we have a sound understanding of the rhetorical processes involved in shaping our everyday social relations with other animals.

TERMINISTIC SCREENS, CONTINUITY, AND DISCONTINUITY

One of the most prominent and influential rhetoricians of the twentieth-century was Kenneth Burke (1897–1993), who developed the concept of terministic screens. Terministic screens refer to the differing ways in which individuals, whether explicitly or implicitly, represent ideas through language (*Symbolic Action* 44–45). For example, Burke uses the analogy of a single photograph being subjected to different filters—though it remains the same image, our interpretations or responses to the photograph might be different if its brightness is augmented or decreased, if it is set in sepia tone or black and white, or if any red eyes are removed. In terms of language, then, our choices of words and phrases serve to select aspects of social reality that we wish to emphasize (or *reflect*), while simultaneously deemphasizing (or *deflecting*) other aspects (*Symbolic Action* 45). This is why, for example, the ongoing debate regarding abortion is often cast as being between pro-choice and pro-life advocates, rather than pro- or anti-abortion advocates. By presenting their position as pro-life, individuals opposed to abortion rights reflect an understanding of unborn fetuses as living organisms, while simultaneously deflecting their opposition to (at least some) individual reproductive rights for women.

Burke also outlined the significance of what he referred to as the *continuity* and *discontinuity* within terministic screens. Continuity refers to *differences of degree* (or treating different things as parts of a continuum), whereas discontinuity refers to *differences of kind* (or treating different things as wholly distinct from one another) (*Symbolic Action* 50). To illustrate these representations of difference, Burke differentiates between Darwin's and the Catholic Church's understandings of humans. While in the 1800s Darwin saw humans as one of many animals in the world, Catholic doctrine maintained that humans were fundamentally distinct from animals. In this sense, Darwin understood humans and other animals as continuous with one another, whereas the Church understood humans and animals as discontinuous with one another.

Burke's concepts of continuity and discontinuity, and the example of human and nonhuman animals, are particularly relevant to the analysis of Sinclair's novel. Throughout *The Jungle*, Sinclair differentiates between humans and animals through narration as well as character dialogue. However, Sinclair's rhetoric also works in an intricate and nuanced way that is sometimes disruptive of a simple human and animal binary of discontinuity or continuity.

Burke's main criticism of Darwin's continuity between humans and other animals was that Darwin's rhetoric did not also engage with the numerous discontinuities between humans and other animals. For example, only humans have investment bankers, corrupt politicians, and yellow journalism (*Symbolic Action* 50). Because this is the case, Burke argues that even from a secular position, Darwin can be understood as having overstated the continuity between humans and other animals. From this perspective, then, it is still important to acknowledge differences in kind even when a screen is primarily employing a rhetoric of continuity. This is also true of discontinuous rhetoric being more fully developed when it also acknowledges at least some differences of degree.

Sinclair manages to acknowledge subtle differences of degree even though his rhetoric is primarily based on the conception of humans and animals as discontinuous with one another. Upon first visiting the stockyards, for example, Jurgis watches the squealing hogs being lead to slaughter, noting that they "were so innocent, they came so very trustingly; and they were so very human in their protests—and so perfectly within their rights!" (*The Jungle* 38). However, this rhetoric of continuity is used by Sinclair mostly as metaphor in order to further highlight issues of human oppression, rather than to also raise empathy for the suffering of nonhuman animals. As Steven Rosendale has argued, "the sympathy [toward stockyard animals] is ultimately an anthropomorphism meant to symbolize and accentuate the emphasis on human misery" in Sinclair's novel (62). For example, immediately prior to this momentary address of the humanity of hogs, and upon first witnessing the hogs being taken to the killing floor, Sinclair notes that Jurgis and his friends "were not poetical, and the sight suggested to them no metaphors of human destiny" (*The Jungle* 36). This scene eventually climaxes with something of an ironic punchline from Jurgis, who simply states that he's "glad I'm not a hog!" (*The Jungle* 39), despite Sinclair's descriptions of workers as being equally doomed. Although the use of metaphor is common in rhetoric (Lakoff & Johnston 4–6; McCloskey 3; Charteris-Black 65–66), Sinclair's use of metaphor effectively works to further mask the moral issue of animal oppression. Taken as a whole, then, Sinclair's sparse instances of continuity between humans and other animals in this scene (as well as in various other instances throughout the novel) are employed in order to elicit sympathy for the fact that slaughterhouse workers are being treated as poorly as the cows and pigs that they are killing. However, Sinclair's more prevalent rhetoric of discontinuity between humans and other animals has the overall effect of deflecting any ethical consideration for nonhuman animals in their own rights.

The terministic screens employed in *The Jungle*'s narrative thus effectively serve to reflect the realities of slaughterhouses (both animal suffering and worker exploitation) during the early 1900s. However, the use of metaphor also deflects attention away from the issues of animal welfare or animal rights, as the suffering and oppression of pigs and cows are used as symbolic representations of human exploitation. In order to better understand these screens in Sinclair's work, it will be helpful to further examine the author's use of rhetorical identification.

IDENTIFICATION

Burke argued that for persuasive language to be effective, it is helpful if the audience is able to identify with the speaker or message (*Motives* 20). In fact, Burke even proposed that identification could be considered, as an alternative to persuasion, as the goal of effective social language (*Motives* 19–21). This *identification* does not necessarily need to be substantive; it is sufficient that the audience believe in, or be persuaded to believe in, some perceived identifying properties. It is important to note here that this sort of identification can involve either the individuals identifying themselves with another individual or group, and/or an individual identifying others as sufficiently similar to each other

(*Motives* 20). As a Canadian for example, I can identify myself with other individuals living in Canada based on a perceived understanding of geopolitical proximity, but I can also identify two Australian individuals as both sharing the similarity of living in Australia. As social beings, we are therefore able to identify ourselves with externalities (persons, places, sentiments, etc.) as well as identify various externalities as similar to one another. The rhetorical significance of this phenomenon, then, is that evoking sentiments of identification allows for a more persuasive message.

Interestingly, some of the more explicit passages that might help the reader identify the experiences of nonhuman animals with those of humans appear to have been excluded from the original publication of *The Jungle*. For example, when Jurgis first begins attending union meetings in the unedited version of *The Jungle* (not published until 2003), he notes that "what the unions were really trying to do was to put a stop to murder. For it was murder that went on upon the killing-floor, systematic, deliberate and hideous murder—and there was no other word for it, and nothing else to be said about it. They were slaughtering men there, just as certainly as they were slaughtering cattle; they were grinding the bodies and souls of them, and turning them into dollars and cents" (*Uncensored Original* 82). This passage thus works to help the reader identify "men" and "cattle" as sufficiently similar in their shared property of abuse (*Uncensored Original* 82). Though this passage, again, represents an instance in which the killing of nonhuman animals is meant to elicit sympathy for the exploitation and abuse of human workers, there is also a rhetorical effect of identifying humans with other animals. Indeed, the last line of the passage is fairly ambiguous, in that it is not immediately clear (in terms of the language used) whether the speaker is conveying moral outrage at the practice of turning either men or cattle (or both) into profits.

When considering individual bodies and food, Western cultures tend to identify more with the consumer and producer than with the consumed and produced. When the moral argument for vegetarianism arises, the meat-eating defense is that it is up to the individual agent (i.e., consumer) to decide what they choose to consume. While this position is often framed within the Enlightenment values of individual liberties and freedoms, there exists a contradiction in that the individual liberties and freedoms of the killed animal are ignored. Carol J. Adams conceptualizes this phenomenon as the *absent referent*, referring to how the individual subjectivities of animals are made absent through the language used to rhetorically transform them into consumable (and therefore morally ignorable) products (*Neither* 16–17). As a result, the relational violence that is required for the apparent transformation of an animal subject into a food object is rhetorically removed from the process of meat production and consumption (Twine 626). This is why, for example, it is common in Western societies to speak casually about cooking and eating pork rather than pig, or chicken rather than a chicken, while maintaining the appearance of discussing an amoral issue.

The absent referent has significant implications regarding the process of identification. Each individual animal has a unique personality, sentience, and completeness of self, yet there exists a contradiction in that they cannot possibly be identified as such if they are to become food for humans (*Neither* 17). This results in a process wherein animals become rhetorically constituted as things rather than beings, and any violence that goes into transforming them from subjects into products becomes masked by language. For example, the above passage from the uncensored version of *The Jungle* identifies the relationships between the violence toward both working-class humans and nonhuman animals in slaughterhouses, yet its removal from the original publication further serves to make absent the referent of individual animal "bodies and souls" (*Uncensored Original* 82). This edit is especially interesting given the use of the term *murder*, an act that is typically reserved for the killing of humans. By removing references to the murder of nonhumans, the original publication also effectively removes a significant example of identifying humans and nonhuman animals as moral subjects. As a result, identification with the produced animal subjects is ignored, while identification with the producers (i.e., human workers) becomes reinforced.

The reinforcement of identification between the reader and the human workers in Sinclair's novel therefore reflects a *division* or *dissociation*, which Burke noted was the logical (though often implicit) counter effect of rhetorical identification. While Burke argued that the primary goal of rhetoric was identification, he also understood that identification with someone or something naturally results in a dissociation with other people or things (*Motives* 22). This understanding helps to further explain the rhetorical effects of identification in *The Jungle*, given that the original uncensored edition included more identification (and therefore, minimized the amount of dissociation) between human and nonhuman animals within the story. While this is not to suggest that these sorts of passages were removed from the original text (by either Sinclair or his editors) for any ideological reasons, it is interesting to note that a number of the words and phrases that were removed also contained an aspect of rhetorical identification between humans and animals. As such, the edits to the original text might have had the unintended consequence of also removing some significant passages in which the reader is better able to identify the suffering of animals with the suffering of workers in slaughterhouses.

Maurice Charland also engages with a rhetorical theory of identification, though from a somewhat different perspective than that of Burke. For Charland, identification in rhetoric is concerned with constituting the reader or audience as an ideological subject (134). This constitutive rhetoric borrows from Louis Althusser's concept of interpellation, or, the act of constituting someone as an ideological subject through the process of hailing their attention (Charland 138). For example, when a police officer on the street exclaims "Hey, you there!" and I stop to address them, I am effectively constituted as an ideological subject—I am now a potential criminal based on my acknowledgment of the constituted social power relations (Althusser 174). The identification that occurs through constitutive rhetoric is therefore crucial to effective persuasion in that it positions the audience as a subject to whom the message can effectively be conveyed. In fact, Charland argues that identification is a necessary component of persuasion—since rhetorical subjects do not exist as such outside of a given discourse, rhetorically constituting them as subjects in the first place is a necessary predicate in order for them to be persuaded (138). Charland further notes that this identification is not itself persuasive, but is rather a rhetorical act that can then be manipulated for the purpose of persuasion (138–39).

Since *The Jungle* is a novel, Sinclair's narrative does not employ any constitutive rhetoric directly. Instead, the reader is constituted as an ideological subject through character dialogue at various moments. The most obvious instance of this interpellation occurs toward the climax of the story, when Jurgis attends a socialist meeting. During this scene, Jurgis joins a socialist event in order to briefly shelter himself from the streets (he is, by this point, out of work and homeless), though he becomes sufficiently interested in the lecture of a socialist orator. The speaker addresses the audience (and reader, effectively) as "you . . . whoever you may be, provided that you care about the truth; but most of all I plead with working men. . . . To you, whose lot it is to sow that others may reap, to labor and obey, and ask no more than the wages of a beast of burden, the food and shelter to keep you alive from day to day" (*The Jungle* 339). As most people care about some notion of Truth, and given that the majority of people fall into this laboring class, it is apparent that Sinclair is attempting here to interpellate a great number of subjects. What is important to keep in mind with this address is that the speaker is not directly speaking with Jurgis as a character—Jurgis is just one of many unidentified audience members at the event. Rather, the speaker is interpellating the reader as an ideological subject so that the rest of Sinclair's rhetoric can then be used to try to persuade the reader to take social action. This rhetorical strategy is used in many works of fiction in order for the author to engage more directly with readers, such as John Galt's lengthy speech in Ayn Rand's *Atlas Shrugged*, or the titular character's lecture in J. M. Coetzee's novel *Elizabeth Costello*.

However, while the constitutive rhetoric in *The Jungle* attempts to identify the reader as an economic and political subject with regards to capitalist exploitation, there is no attempt to identify readers as moral agents with regards to their food choices. Throughout the novel, any attempts to identify humans and nonhuman animals as continuous subjects are done so metaphorically rather than morally. Similarly, any interpellation of the reader is carried out for political or economic reasons rather than to identify the reader as a moral agent, or to identify the oppression of nonhuman animals in slaughterhouses as a moral concern in its own right.

There are also instances of Burke's concept of identification in this climactic socialist speech; the speaker notes that "I have been in your place, I have lived your life, and there is no man before me here tonight who knows it better" (*The Jungle* 339). Yet, again, this identification is in reference to the socioeconomic position of the speaker and his audience, rather than any appeals to moral duty or ethical considerations toward other animals or food choices. It is therefore logically consistent for readers to have not interpreted the novel as a call toward moral vegetarianism or animal rights, given that the reader is not identified as a moral subject—at least, not in the context of food choices or consumption habits—in the first place.

The Jungle's lack of moral interpellation thus further reinforces the absent referent of individual animals as moral subjects, and sustains the contradiction that dead animals are kept rhetorically separated from understandings of (and interactions with) food products. The absent referent of moralized animal subjectivities both results from and reinforces a deeply ingrained cultural ideology that makes eating animal bodies seem natural, normal, and acceptable (*Neither* 101). Melanie Joy has called this ideology of normalized meat-eating in human cultures *carnism*, which she contrasts with both vegetarianism and veganism (which reject the violent ideology of normalized meat-eating in human cultures) and differentiates from carnivores (i.e., nonhuman animals such as sharks that are biologically reliant on eating other animals) (29–30).

As an ideology, carnism works to reinforce and perpetuate the normalization of human dominion over other species (Joy 29–30). Carnism is insidious because, like other ideologies, it is difficult for individuals to identify and critically reflect upon the foundations of their own worldview. Carnism is also an inherently violent ideology given that it relies on violence to function, and without this violence toward other animals the system would cease to exist (Joy 33). Though *The Jungle* is itself a critical novel with regards to the realities of capitalist exploitation, it is nonetheless a product of modern carnist culture and thus perpetuates many aspects of this ideology's normalized violence. As such, Sinclair's rhetoric does not interpellate the reader as a vegan (i.e., ideological opposite of carnist) subject. This is because Sinclair's constitutive rhetoric throughout the novel focuses on interpellating the reader as an exploited member of the working class. By not being initially interpellated as a vegan subject, the reader remains fixed in a carnist ideological framework and thus can only interpret the novel through this ideological perspective. Any rhetorical instances of moralizing animal subjectivities (even metaphorically) are therefore unable to persuade the reader that eating animals is an ethical issue, as the reader has not been identified as an ideologically vegan subject in the first place.

This analysis of rhetorical mechanisms used throughout *The Jungle* has demonstrated some reasons (though certainly not an exhaustive list of reasons) for how and why the novel—though it deals closely with examples of animal suffering and oppression—was ineffectual in arousing any popular demands for increased animal rights or animal welfare reforms. While Sinclair expressed no intent to promote vegetarianism or animal rights issues through his novel, it is still worth questioning why and how these concerns were not interpreted by the public, given their significant role in both the plot and setting of the narrative. This is especially curious given the popular uproar regarding the unsanitary methods of food production and distribution in the US—an issue that was addressed far less prominently throughout the novel than the issue of animal oppression.

One interesting example of rhetoric employed in *The Jungle* is the use of terministic screens, especially in terms of the continuity and discontinuity between humans and other animals. Though Sinclair predominantly represents humans and other animals as discontinuous, he does evoke some rare instances of continuity between the two subjectivities. However, these instances of continuity tend to be metaphorical, and used in order to further accentuate the oppression of human workers in the slaughterhouses. As a result, it is difficult for readers to identify (from a Burkean perspective) either human and nonhuman animals as equally deserving moral subjects, or with the plight of slaughterhouse animals themselves. Additionally, Sinclair's rhetoric in *The Jungle* does not interpellate the reader as a moral subject with the political power to influence social reality through their food choices. By not identifying (or, hailing) the reader in this way, it is difficult for the reader to approach and engage with the issue of animal oppression as a moral issue. From this perspective, it is understandable why and how the issues of animal oppression and suffering in slaughterhouses were not interpreted by the general public as moral concerns.

These are important points to keep in mind for animal rights activists and vegan studies scholars, as all moral issues are also necessarily rhetorical issues—that is, effectively persuasive language is necessary for discourses concerning both the political and philosophical nature of what is Good. As such, though Sinclair's novel reveals some of the many injustices being committed against nonhuman animals in industrial agriculture, *The Jungle*'s rhetoric does not sufficiently present these practices as cause for moral concern. As mentioned above, vegetarianism and animal rights were never the intended goals of Sinclair's work. However, the rhetorical issues that have been addressed throughout this essay should be taken into consideration for anyone hoping to promote vegetarianism (or veganism) as a viable means by which to resist the current hegemony of nonhuman animal oppression.

WORKS CITED

Adams, Carol. J. *Neither Man nor Beast: Feminism and the Defense of Animals*. New York: Continuum Publishing, 1994.

———. "Why Feminist-Vegan Now?" *Feminism & Psychology*, 20, no. 3(2010) 302–317.

Althusser, Louis. "Ideology and Ideological State Apparatuses." *Lenin and Philosophy and other Essays*, 127–86. New York: Monthly Review Press, 1971.

Bloodworth, William. "From *The Jungle* to *The Fasting Cure*: Upton Sinclair on American Food." *Journal of American Culture*, 2, no. 3(1979) 444–53.

Booth, Wayne. "The Rhetorical Stance." *College Composition and Communication*, 14, no. 3(1963) 139–45.

Burke, Kenneth. *Language as Symbolic Action*. Berkeley: University California Press, 1966.

———. *A Rhetoric of Motives*. University of California Press, 1969.

Charland, Maurice. "Constitutive Rhetoric: The Case of the *Peule Quebecois*." *The Quarterly Journal of Speech*, 73, no. 2(1987) 133–50.

Charteris-Black, Jonathan. *Corpus Approaches to Critical Metaphor Analysis*. Basingstoke, Hampshire: Palgrave Macmillan, 2004.

De Grave, Kathleen. Introduction to *The Jungle: The Uncensored Original Edition*, by Upton Sinclair, vi-xxiv. Tucson: Sharp Press, 2003.

Derkatch, Colleen. *Bounding Biomedicine: Evidence and Rhetoric in the New Science of Alternative Medicine*. Chicago: University of Chicago Press, 2016.

Empson, William. *7 Types of Ambiguity*. New York, NY: New Directions Paperbook, 1966.

Gottesman, Ronald. Introduction to *The Jungle*, by Upton Sinclair, xvii-xliii. New York, NY: Penguin Classics, 2006.

Joy, Melanie. *Why We Love Dogs, Eat Pigs, and Wear Cows: An Introduction to Carnism*. Newburyport, MA: Conari Press, 2009.

Lakoff, George, and Mark Johnston. *Metaphors We Live By*. Chicago: University of Chicago Press, 1980.

Lee, Earl. Foreword to *The Jungle: The Uncensored Original Edition*, by Upton Sinclair, 1-vi. Tucson: See Sharp Press, 2003.

McCloskey, Donald N. *The Rhetoric of Economics*. Madison: University of Wisconsin Press, 1985.

McGee, Michael Calvin. "A Materialist Conception of Rhetoric." *Explorations in Rhetoric: Studies in Honor of Douglas Ehninger*. Edited by Ray E. McKerrow, 23–48. Dallas, TX: Scott, Foresman and Company, 1982.

Perelman, Chaïm, and Lucie Olbrechts-Tyteca. *The New Rhetoric: A Treatise on Argumentation*. Notre Dame, IN: University of Notre Dame Press, 1969.

Pickavance, Jason. "Gastronomic Realism: Upton Sinclair's *The Jungle*, the Fight for Pure Food, and the Magic of Mastication." *Food and Foodways*, 11, no. 2–3, (2003) 87–112.

Richards, Jennifer. *Rhetoric : The New Critical Idiom*. London and New York : Routledge, 2008.

Rosendale, Steven. "In Search of Left Ecology's Usable Past: The Jungle, Social Change, and the Class Character of Environmental Impairment." In *The Greening of Literary Scholarship*. Edited by Steven Rosendale, 59–76. Iowa City: University of Iowa Press, 2002, 59–76.

Schlosser, Eric. *Fast Food Nation: The Dark Side of the All-American Meal*. New York, NY: Harper Perennial, 2005.

Schlosser, Eric. Foreword to *The Jungle*, by Upton Sinclair vii-xv. New York, NY: Penguin Classics, 2006.

Shprintzen, Adam. D. *The Vegetarian Crusade: The Rise of an American Reform Movement, 1817–1921*. Chapel Hill: University of North Carolina Press, 2014.

Sinclair, Upton. *The Fasting Cure*. New York and London: M. Kennerley, 1911.

——. *The Jungle: The Uncensored Original Edition. See* Sharp Press, 2003.

——. *The Jungle*. New York, NY: Penguin Classics, 2006.

Twine, Richard. "Vegan Killjoys at the Table: Contesting Happiness and Negotiating Relationships with Food Practices." *Societies*, 4, no. 4(2014) 623–39.

Wright, Laura. *The Vegan Studies Project: Food, Animals, and Gender in the Age of Terror*. Athens, GA: University of Georgia Press, 2015.

CHAPTER 6

Soylent Veganism: A Meditation on Cannibalism, Consumerism, and Veg Politics

Tom Hertweck

"The capitalist exists by exploitation, lives out of the labor, that is to say life, of the working man; consumes him, and his code of morals and standards of ethics justify it and this proves that capitalism is cannibalism."
   —*Eugene Victor Debs, Address at the Grand Central Palace, New York (1905)*

"Indeed, a day may come when the idea that human beings in the past raised and slaughtered living things for food and complacently displayed slabs of their flesh in shop windows will inspire the same revulsion as what travelers in the sixteenth and seventeenth centuries felt about the cannibal meals of American, Oceanian, or African indigenous peoples."
   —*Claude Lévi-Strauss, "A Lesson in Wisdom from Mad Cows" (1996)*

One of the many surprising and insightful contributions to the critical engagement with carnism to be found in Laura Wright's *Vegan Studies Project* is the concerted attention given to cannibalism. Long a backstop for studies of the apocalypse—the worst-case scenario of culture, and attendant to any range of disasters—cannibalism in its myriad forms as represented by the culture industry has been an effective means for exploring issues such as colonialism, environmentalism, sexism, and other social anxieties.[1] At the same time, it frequently wends its way into vernacular conversations about veganism, usually in the form of the question *Can vegans eat other humans?*[2] Leaving aside that question, which is nearly always asked in jest or to serve as some cynical rejoinder to veganism as such, under scrutiny the concept of cannibalism has the power to reveal something compelling about vegan politics. Specifically in popular culture, as Wright showcases with McCarthy's *The Road* and Atwood's MaddAddam Trilogy, particular depictions of cannibalism contain the figurative energy sufficient to bear closer examination and thereby sustain new forms of cultural critique. Richard Fleischer's 1973 film *Soylent Green* is precisely one such cultural text that encapsulates a world ready-made for critical analysis, but is often overlooked because of a campiness in the film that has not aged well.[3] Once just the throwaway punchline/plot-reveal from a popular but nevertheless mediocre film, *Soylent Green*'s secret—that humans are being "recycled" into the film's eponymous food-wafer—has resurfaced as the brand name for a recently developed meal-replacement shake, Rosa Foods' Soylent, that apart from causing a stir among foodies is also a vegan (not cannibal) product.

In a narrow sense, this essay seeks to explore a single question: What does it mean to give a real vegan commodity the name of a famous fictional cannibal food? The brief answer ultimately has much to do with the circulation of value under the conditions of postcapitalism. At the same time, the circumstances of that circulation contain more than the ironic semantic play of naming and selling. Uniting *Soylent Green* the film and Soylent the meal-replacer with Claude Lévi-Strauss's recently recovered work linking cannibalism and carnism has the power to help us refigure the conceptual apparatus of vegan politics. More than positing a simple and well-trod continuity between humans and animals as potential food objects, the suggestive schema I lay out here has the potential to express something essential about the structural contingency of eating in a world of limited resources. Mildly polemic (for how could an argument involving the eating of other living beings ever be otherwise?), the apparatus of Soylent Veganism as I describe it provocatively represents nothing less than the reordering of society around the notion of eating such that the continued fate of the world and the human species depend on it.

SOYLENT GREEN ISN'T PEOPLE—OR ANIMALS

Richard Fleischer's *Soylent Green* neatly figures Wright's discussion of veganism *contra* cannibalism by placing both issues in the same film artifact. Because of a series of events in the not-too-distant past, the time-present of the film is one of industrial decay, mass unemployment, and relative lawlessness all stemming from the central problems of overpopulation and environmental destruction. A truly Malthusian nightmare, the overwhelming majority of people subsist on handouts from a partnership between the government and the Soylent Corporation, which produces the nutrition wafers that appear to make up the bulk of people's diets. A portmanteau of their two ingredients, *soy* and *lent*ils, the wafers—which are seemingly vegan—come in red and yellow (presumably because of the predominant colors of their legume constituent) and are highly prized by citizens who queue to collect their share. Food riots break out when supplies run low because the only other edibles in the film viewers see are single items (manky vegetables, a small jar of jam, etc.) bought and sold in extremely limited quantities on the black market. Soylent is therefore truly a subsistence food, and not a choice in the marketplace except for those who are connected to the highest echelons of power and prestige, are criminals, or the film's antihero, Detective Frank Thorn (Charlton Heston), who moves among them all.

The potboiler plot has Thorn trying to solve the murder of a Soylent executive, and the usual *noir* twists and turns follow. All of this, however, is prolegomena to the real scandal that he uncovers by following the food back to its source: a human corpse-recycling factory. The film's B-grade thriller/horror is thus: the revelation of industrial cannibalism that appears to be totalizing. Too many people and too little food? Let one problem solve the other, an efficient solution if ever there were one. Thorn, fatally shot, cries out the final lines—"Soylent Green is people!"—to a witless crowd, not a one seeming to understand that it means precisely what it says. For the perceptive vegan viewer, the horror is mixed with disappointment, however, as one more vision of veganism (through Soylents Red and Yellow, at least) that might feed a world goes wrong, though not from a failure of veganism itself but rather a breakdown in the world's provisioning systems.

Soylent Green, even as the film opens, is no vegan utopia. However, it is worth teasing apart the mechanics of food's depiction to make sense of what is at stake beyond the moral repugnance of consuming other humans. In a touching scene, Thorn returns after a long day in the heat and filth of the city and presents his research partner, Sol (Edward G. Robinson), with loot grifted from the crime scene: a piece of celery ("Isn't that beautiful?"), some lettuce, a tomato (which Sol calls by the antiquated name "love apple"), and shockingly a not insubstantial piece of beef. Stunned, Sol breaks down on seeing the extraordinary flank steak, through tears lamenting, "Oh my God, how did we come to this?" As an assertion of value, on Thorn's return to the apartment later, Sol has taken the meager bits of food and made a dinner of salad (just lettuce), apple, and something like beef stew, setting the table and pulling out a single place-setting that he had kept in the apartment as a relic of older times. At the table, the two undertake a quaint pantomime of bourgeois dining, pure emulation on Thorn's part as he copies Sol's actions, aping his wiping off the apple on his shirt before eating all but the nub of stem and being shown how to clink glasses. When at the end of the meal Sol declares with satisfaction that he hasn't "eaten like this in years," Thorn responds, "I've *never* eaten like this" and the viewer takes it literally. Food as we know it is simply gone from their world because climate change has wiped out traditional agriculture in Sol's lifetime.

Because of its genre-inflected horror, the film's insistent focus on food consumption overshadows a more subtle criticism of all aspects of life under conditions of overpopulation, but one that is nonetheless inflected by the food that does appear. To be sure, Sol's easy nostalgia for "real food" reveals the general disappointment with living off the Soylent handouts. His tears reflect a sincere longing for the past that helps the viewer identify with him as a sympathetic, moral character, as well as the meal's serving as a visual foil for the cannibalism at the end. At the same time, the dinner scene is as much a moment that critiques the structure and content of life in New York of 2022. Even within the context of this special moment, Thorn is unimpressed and shrugs off the lettuce while Sol relishes it; likewise, Thorn's gleeful enjoyment of the beef stew—which must be, given what was available, largely tasteless having been cooked without salt or fats—seems to be a reflection of Sol's nostalgia rather than genuinely enjoying it himself, like a child mimicking adult behavior. Beef stew presents therefore an empty pleasure, not for meat-eating itself, but in a longing for life robustly lived that Thorn has never before experienced.

The film's malaise—figured visually as sweaty bodies slumped somewhere between sleeping and waking, and a crowded, pervasive gray griminess—has less to do with food than it does with employment levels. Exceedingly few people have jobs at all (the "lucky ones," we learn), most living off government death benefits paid in credits or Soylent. Not starving, the citizenry nonetheless apparently lives right at subsistence levels. All the same, it seems reasonably clear that the zombie-like stare we see on most faces is less a result of not having a real food culture (though this is surely a part), and more about having nothing to do. The secondary characters in the film bear this out. The lack of food culture and employment also explains, for example, why the murderer seems so giddy when committing the crime Thorn investigates: not a sociopath, he has temporarily become one of the "lucky ones" and will get paid for work. Shirl, a prostitute that "furnishes" the high-rise penthouse of the Soylent executive, offers herself to the people coming and going after the murder, not out of a sense of love or meaningful companionship, but seemingly for want of anything to do in her life of plush, sequestered boredom; she will get laid off if she cannot find a way to provide the services she was hired for. Likewise, Sol's shock and delight when Thorn presents him with pilfered pencils and a few sheets of paper suggests not only their limited supply, but also Sol's appreciation that he now has the means to create. Taken this way, *Soylent Green* shows us a world that has placed a limit on the entirety of human capacities for robust living. The food is only the most obvious part. The film articulates a more totalizing criticism when Sol, despairing over the state of the world after seeing the bounty that Thorn gives to him, says, "We're doing lousy, just like when I was a boy. Nobody cares. Nobody tries." A more distressing terror lurks beyond food and reflects back to the viewer, that the troubles of human capability in their world are our own and have been ever thus.

CLAUDE LÉVI-STRAUSS AND THE STRUCTURES OF CANNIBALISM AND CARNISM

As an anthropologist, Claude Lévi-Strauss was concerned with how social formation takes place. For Lévi-Strauss, the symbolic and material intermingled to the extent they were both constructions of the necessary invention of order. Or, as Priscilla Walton has described in a discussion of his work, "Although Lévi-Strauss was and still is a controversial figure in his own discipline (if not others), he notably shifted the ways in which anthropologists perceived the tales they were told, transferring a reliance on language and its meanings into another philosophical sphere" (29). Language use—especially in myth—reflects order, and attention paid to its organization reveals the ways in which lived societies produce roles, beliefs, and customs. Lévi-Strauss's achievement in his *Structural Anthropology* (1958, trans. 1963) then was the elucidation of the synthetic practice of how societies build culture out of available materials, a process he comes to call *bricolage* in a later work, *The Savage Mind* (1962, trans. 1966). That term was received by the French linguistic and literary front as a centerpiece of poststructuralism, the critical practice that opened up the problems of postmodernism, an aesthetic (rather than anthropological) project that seemingly unmoored signification from absolute referentiality. As a result, the work of Lévi-Strauss and the work of poststructuralism appear, at least in broad strokes, to be two sides of the same coin: the organization of meaning with attention paid to what remains said and unsaid, presented and covered over, in every utterance to the degree that visible and invisible organization also makes possible the arrangement and value systems placed on life itself.

In a pair of essays only recently collected in English, Lévi-Strauss trains this form of criticism on the notion of cannibalism, but also in service to a broader critique. In the provocatively titled "We Are All Cannibals" (1993), part of Lévi-Strauss's interest in cannibalism is corrective in terms of anthropological discourse. Namely, there had emerged in ethnologic circles during the late 1970s and 1980s the claim, stemming from works like W. Arens's *The Man-Eating Myth*, that depictions of cannibalism around the globe were an invention of Western cultures to demean the so-called savages they encountered during the era of colonial empire-building. That argument, well-intentioned as it may have been for the ways it attempted to combat racism, has been generally refuted, and the history of cannibalism (real or imagined) has become a source of strength for some indigenous groups.[4] Lévi-Strauss, however, uses the occasion to push the case for cannibalism as a generalized practice and thus asserts the claim of his title. He cites a number of cases: the equivalent of human brain disease in New Guineans, likely stemming from anthropophagy (kuru) and that also appeared after use of medical therapies involving the grafting of brain tissue and pituitary fluids; organ transplants; and the enforced cannibalism of cows as a result of industrial agriculture that led to the spread of bovine spongiform encephalopathy (mad cow disease) and the human variant of Creutzfeldt-Jakob disease.[5] With this new understanding,

So varied are the modalities of cannibalism, so diverse its real or supposed functions, that we may come to doubt whether the notion of cannibalism as it is currently employed can be defined in a relatively precise manner. It dissolves or dissipates as soon as one attempts to grasp it. . . . The notion of cannibalism, thus exorcised, will now appear rather commonplace. (88)

As the epigraph for this chapter points out, Lévi-Strauss's attitude toward cannibalism, despite being widespread, is still negative and connects with his thoughts on vegetarianism. Strikingly, though, for both cases the repugnance he appears to express is structural, and not, as so often happens, linked to arguments from *pathos* or cultural superiority. In this way, "A Lesson in Wisdom from Mad Cows" explores in provocative brevity both cannibalism's and carnism's passing out of favor as the result of structural changes in society. Here Lévi-Strauss grounds a discussion of vegetarians. The resultant "revulsion" he intuits comes not from any sense of moral obligation we ought to feel toward animals or out of nutrition discourse (though he in no way discounts these arguments), but out of a sense that human capacities are best served by eliminating meat-eating and producing greater efficiency serving human needs:

An expanding human population will soon need the current grain production as a whole to survive; nothing will remain for cattle and barnyard animals. All humans will therefore have to model their diet on that of India and China, where animal flesh fulfills only a very small portion of protein and calorie needs. We may even have to give up meat completely since, as the population has increased, the surface area of cultivable lands has decreased as a result of erosion and urbanization. In addition, oil and gas reserves are dropping, and water resources are drying up. Conversely, experts estimate that, if humanity were to become fully vegetarian, the areas now cultivated could feed twice the current population. (117–18)

He is realistic about the fact that meat eating may never fall entirely out of practice (just as elective cannibalism has never been eradicated, even in so-called civilized countries), and thinks it will instead become a minority practice in areas that are able to sustain meat as food, likely at great personal cost. His depiction above sounds a great deal like the montage that opens *Soylent Green*: archive photos of immigrant populations, bustling cities, and farmers of livestock and bumper crops give way to real and doctored photos of smog, urban crowding, and seeming garbage-filled decay. While similar to how these fictional versions converge in their apocalypticism, as a reality veganism will become the smart choice not only for the planet, but for individuals seeking to express their optimal selves, as meat production (he implies) will become a singular pursuit at the expense of all others and in the hinterlands of culture and power. Rather than the dreary future of enforced veganism foretold by the film, humanity along the lines that Lévi-Strauss describes it will build a future based on what will serve human capacities best, a process that will require lowering our resource use and refiguring what we think of as food. Whatever food will be, however, we know it will not be wafers, so long as wisdom is used to restructure society in ways that make veganism a meaningful choice and not a last resort.

The lesson of Lévi-Strauss's argument as contained in these essays is therefore double. First, we see in the present that social structure is nuanced by the relationship between what is known and stated and what is hidden and unspoken. Cannibalism is one such aspect of contemporary human life that deserves an account to the extent that it permeates our social relations and organizes material actions like eating. Second, in a future orientation, the mechanism by which this will take place could be through a renegotiation with our own attitudes about cannibalism, which are always already tied up in food-systemic efficiency and the contingent nature of carnism's hegemony. In other words, we have the power to disassemble and rebuild systems as we need them, and—unlike *Soylent Green*'s world—we can do so in a way that allows us to choose how we express our wills. Such expressions therefore come from a conscious decision to audit the kinds of choices we wish to make and extend beyond the catastrophe avoidance both forms of Soylent have implied, and they come rather from an interest in our own efficiency as animal machines and moral agents.

"FOOD MADE SIMPLE": SOYLENT AND CAPITALISM'S SPECTACLE OF EFFICIENCY

The idea of Soylent leapt back into the public's consciousness in 2013 when a small group of tech entrepreneurs were trying to lower costs while working on their software start-up, Rosa Labs. One of them, Rob Rhinehart, thought that if they could reduce their food expenses they could make their seed capital last longer. As it turned out, however, the product Rhinehart cobbled together out of bulk supplements after apprenticing himself to the science of subsistence nutrition became the innovation they were seeking, and thus their product. No longer a software start-up, the Rosa group started off calling it Soylent as a gag. The name stuck, and one more product in the recent history of "disruptors" was born. Consisting only of those nutrients, vitamins, and minerals necessary to sustain human life, the Soylent meal-replacement shake is a food of bare subsistence, devoid of any flavor or frills other than the sum of its constituent parts (runny pancake batter, according to the *New Yorker*'s Liz Widdicombe). Sold as a supplement and therefore unregulated by government, and tested on the company's founders themselves, the product hit the market in 2014 to praise, criticism, confusion, and various other think-pieces cranked out by legitimate media outlets and the internet's content mills.[6] Since then Soylent has expanded its line to add flavored options and to introduce a coffee-infused version, Coffiest,[7] and been followed into the market by a number of other international meal-replacers, including Huel (Great Britain), Ambronite (Finland), and Mana (Czech Republic).[8]

If the phenomenon of *Soylent Green* came about because of food horror and concerns about population and environment, its ironic resurgence forty years later happened because of a looming concern about capitalism. As Rhinehart describes, "I created Soylent because my existing options for food were limited. I wanted to have more freedom with my time and money" (Merchant). While it may sound strange to hear a venture capitalist complain about access to food, Rhinehart nonetheless clues in on a problem many people have and that he and his tech-sector friends shared: limited time and resources. In microcosm, the issue at Rosa Labs was not unlike the problem Lévi-Strauss addresses, but represented in a far more practical way as Widdicombe details in the Labs' origin story. Food was generally too expensive, or if cheap (fast-food dollar menus, Little Caesar's $5 pizzas), far too unhealthy to be a sustainable option; the start-up also had a miniscule kitchen to provide for the employees, so cooking was not a real option. In short, traditional notions of food had become a burden for people who wanted success and to use their time and money in its pursuit. Instead, Rhinehart and his colleagues elected to put themselves on a subsistence diet to optimize their productive efficiencies. The product thus appeals to consumers who feel harangued not just by logistical issues, but by food culture in general. Discourses surrounding nutrition, ethical sourcing (materials and labor involved), cultural sensitivity, localism/globalization, and food fads compete for consumers' attention to the point where choice fatigue sets in. Regularly, pieces about Soylent contain interviews of users who are relieved of this burden and happy to give up choice for bare sustenance.[9] Soylent's slogan, "Food Made Simple," reflects a simplification in the process of reducing food to its essential components and nothing more, but also a limiting of the consumer's set of choices to one, short-circuiting the choice mechanism to save time and mental energy for other pursuits. Like the film, Soylent is a one-stop food solution; unlike the film, its efficiency allows space for an increase in human capacities for self-fulfillment.

Soylent ironizes its source material. Soylent is at once a sign that refers to cannibalism in the eater's vague assumption that "Soylent Green is people," but also a material consumer product meant to increase the eater's efficiency under capitalism. It is unremarkable to merge cannibalism with capitalism, as it is one of the basic conditions of Marxist critique that commodities are themselves the residue of life force and social relations: we consume each other and ourselves through labor by our consumption of commodities.[10] And yet, Soylent is a product of mis-signification: it undercuts cannibalism/capitalism by also referring to the vegan Soylents Red and Yellow that are overshadowed by the plot in the film. Carnism seeks to redouble that cannibalism by linking the production of animals with human labor and technological exigencies, by inserting human energy into systems of industrial husbandry that is then consumed in the commodity forms of meat. As such, in a final compelling way does Soylent's vegan formulation avoid the terror of cannibalism, literally *and* conceptually, by avoiding animal products, but also by minimizing the forms of labor—physical and mental—that would otherwise be spent on the worry over and selection of traditional foods that are hegemonically directed toward animal products. When Rhinehart describes the choice to make the recipe vegan, he is in many ways describing the Soylent customer: "We try to get the optimal amounts of all these different nutrients. Then from there you're optimizing for bioavailability, cost, sustainability—which is why we, you know, went to vegan" (Merchant). In terms of its ability to maximize human potential, Soylent holds great appeal, not because of the ethical relationship between eater and eaten it provides (though it does this too), but because it positions itself to solve a problem under capitalism by reducing overhead and reclaiming otherwise lost time.

SOYLENT VEGANISM: CULTURAL STUDIES AS RESTRUCTURING

These three vignettes of Soylent are important because they work synergistically to examine how the future can take place. The restructuring of society along vegan lines requires a reorganization not only of the material conditions of life, but also in the ways that we conceive of our lives within the symbolic order. "Soylent" as a signifier is instructive in this regard. While it begins its life as a marker of the supreme anthropocentric horror of cannibalism, through its ironic revival in our time, Soylent now stands as a meaningful alternative to so-called foodie culture and the pressures of consumer capitalism, two things absent from the world of the film. Though professing to be obsessed with issues such as food ethics, sourcing, animal welfare, light environmental effects, and the like, foodie culture is nonetheless self-obsessed, bent on presenting narratives about the moral and social effects that choices produce or condone, to say nothing of the epicurean prestige to which it aspires.[11] It goes almost without saying that these same complaints are leveled regularly against vegans, whose critics claim that abstaining from animal agriculture shores up feelings of superiority over omnivorous eaters. More is needed.

The lessons in cannibalism that Lévi-Strauss describes provide a conceptual unity to the discussion that transcends the material and moral concern. Necessity will dictate the degree to which society must reorder around less resource-intensive modes of being. But, in order to energize that movement, the curious paradox contained in the play between *Soylent* to Soylent produces a literal future out of a fiction. Inasmuch as the film serves as a contemporary mythology—a future-oriented way of considering possible societies—something like a "Soylent Veganism" produces a counter-friction to meat consumption. If anything, then, the normalization of carnism across the globe and as an object of critique proves to be a drag both on the moral character of humans, to the extent that they disregard how violence toward other species is an act of self-violence and self-consumption, and a structure that is not static and can be retooled. This is Lévi-Strauss's argument in a nutshell, one that the film and food bear out. What is

more, however, is that, in the close examination of both Soylents' relationships to simplicity under capitalism, the ways that Soylent bears
an important message about how we use our finite time resources is
revealed. To think in terms of *Soylent*/Soylent means to think about
longevity, fulfillment, and our duties to ourselves and others without
having to engage the data-driven objectivity of nutrition discourse (so
often vexed to begin with) or *pathos*-soaked narratives about animal
welfare (that often cover over First World, racialized privilege) that
make up the bulk of activist veganism. It instead becomes a conceptual marker of a robust way of life. Rather than consuming other lives,
to practice Soylent Veganism means one is able to consume more of
one's own lived experiences and minimize the consumption of others'
capacities. Taken this way, Soylent is not just a product but a position, taken within food and social politics as well as within a symbolic
order that prioritizes veganism. To be sure, Soylent Veganism is not
a call to eat/drink Soylent as such. At the same time, I believe that
thinking through the political possibilities of something like a Soylent
Veganism has the potential to reorient the gaze with which we might
audit the world around us. Too often does veganism rely on a twinned
set of narratives about its healthfulness and its moral certitude. These
are valuable narratives that, when deployed in rational ways and with
a high level of sensitivity to a listener's own values, have the potential to—and indeed do frequently—change people's minds in lasting
ways. At the same time, there remains a limited utility to nutritional
and ethical discourses. For every argument about lowered cholesterol,
increased vitality, environmental impact, and animal intelligence,
emotions, and interests, there are dozens of arguments produced
each year in the forms of diets, spurious health advice, or miscon-
strued research in nutrition and animal cognition that cast doubt on
these two strands of thought. As such, carnists perennially outgun
veganism—but what else would one expect in a society that has
made the subjugation of animals for raw materials, food, entertainment, and profit a foundation of its very existence?

Soylent Veganism proposes instead to change our approaches. By
opening up veganism to a more chaotic, contingent, and fluid form
of symbology—of mythmaking—vegans have the potential to engage
popular opinions about what is and is not appropriate as a form of
existence, to refigure veganism as a way to live one's full potential.
The means lie within bricolage, to dwell in the semiotic ecology
of all versions of Soylent. Lévi-Strauss's two brief essays provide a

theoretical model for reconceiving of veg-politics to the degree that they upend and trouble (in a truly morally panicked way) received knowledge about cannibalism and require their readers to face the possibility that much of one's life is the product of a wide-ranging form of self-consumption. This is not a purely rational argument, but rather a presentation of certain facts about the world reordered to undermine conventional wisdom, a nonrational (rather than irrational) exploration that relies on the affective reality of what is entailed by choices made by all people. Likewise, the act of invoking cannibalism ironically in order to sell an eater a more efficient, productive life suggests the application of such a conceptual framework. Soylent is therefore purest bricolage. It picks up spare parts from the popular culture of a society obsessed with its own vanity (as producers or "winners" under capitalism, but also in the food chain) and builds with them an apparatus to overcome an entrenched, systemic reliance on carnism in service to self-fulfillment entirely of the eater's choosing.

This goes much further than producing new slogans for veganism by crafting new metaphors ("Meat is cannibalism!") as it reorients a whole point of view. C. Richard King has written well of his doubts about the ability of cannibalism to function as a suitable metaphor for doing the work of cultural critique when he explains, "Although [cannibalism] defamiliarizes practices of cultural production and consumption, it does not enhance understanding of the contexts in which individuals and institutions deploy them and does less to effectively challenge or undermine them" (108). This work of making strange does little else than upset or unnerve. For the case of food, however, tightly bound as it is to our identities, this may be sufficient to spur change. Perhaps more compelling than the possibilities posed by Soylent Veganism at a philosophical-conceptual level are those posed by the ways that popularizing links between carnism and cannibalism can affect everyday eaters. These are not metaphors, but rather the bodily signals that serve to awaken eaters and scholars to the complex interrelation of how we think of ourselves and our actions. In the space between Soylent and *Soylent Green* that cultural studies can narrate resides the reminder that the work to fuel our bodies, and also the struggle to be successful and efficient within a vexed web of ecological and social relations, are one in the same movement and coalesce within meals. To varying degrees a person can choose—at least for the time being, apocalyptic narratives warn us—to eat lower on the food chain and lessen both ethical and consumer impacts. In this way, the specters of cannibalism that haunt all acts of eating should serve as a reminder, to borrow a phrase from vegan comrade Jeffrey Moussaieff Masson, that the face on your plate is your own.

WORKS CITED

Adams, Carol J. *The Sexual Politics of Meat: A Feminist-Vegetarian Critical Theory.* New York: Continuum, 1990.

Avramescu, Cătălin. *An Intellectual History of Cannibalism.* Translated by Alistair Ian Blyth. Princeton, NJ: Princeton University Press. 2010.

Barker, Francis, Peter Hulme, and Margaret Iversen, eds. *Cannibalism and the Colonial World.* New York: Cambridge University Press, 1998.

DeAmicis, Carmel. "Vice Investigates Soylent, Finds Rats and Mold." Pando.com, November 12, 2013.

Estok, Simon C. "Cannibalism, Ecocriticism, and Portraying the Journey." *CLCWeb: Comparative Literature and Culture* 14, no. 5, n.p.

Fleischer, Richard, dir. *Soylent Green.* Performances by Charlton Heston, Edward G. Robinson, and Brock Peters. Santa Monica, CA: MGM, 1973.

Hutchinson, Lee. "Ars Does Soylent." ArsTechnica.com, September 5, 2013. https://arstechnica.com/gadgets/2013/09/ars-does-soylent-the-finale-soylent-dreams-for-people/

Johnston, Josée, and Shyon Baumann. *Foodies: Democracy and Distinction in the Gourmet Landscape.* 2nd ed. New York: Routledge, 2014.

King, C. Richard. "The (Mis)Uses of Cannibalism in Contemporary Cultural Critique." *Diacritics* 30, no. 1 (2000): 106–23.

Lévi-Strauss, Claude. *We Are All Cannibals and Other Essays.* Translated by Jane Marie Todd. New York: Columbia University Press, 2016.

Lipschutz, Ronnie D. "'Soylent Green . . . is . . . PEOPLE!': Labour, Bodies and Capital in the Global Political Economy." *Millennium: Journal of International Studies* 34 (2006): 573–76.

MacCannell, Dean. "Cannibalism Today." In *Empty Meeting Grounds: The Tourist Papers,* 17–73. New York: Routledge, 1992.

Manjoo, Farhad. "The Soylent Revolution Will Not Be Pleasurable." *The New York Times,* May 28, 2014. https://www.nytimes.com/2014/05/29/technology/personal-tech/the-soylent-revolution-will-not-be-pleasurable.html.

Merchant, Brian. "Soylent: How I Stopped Eating for 30 Days." Vice Media. November 30, 2013 https://motherboard.vice.com/en_us/article/539bpd/soylent-how-i-stopped-eating-for-30-days.

Morin, Roc. "The Man Who Would Make Food Obsolete." TheAtlantic.com, April 28, 2014. https://www.theatlantic.com/health/archive/2014/04/the-man-who-would-make-eating-obsolete/361058/.

Murray, Robin L, and Joseph K. Heumann. "Environmental Nostalgia and the Tragic Eco-Hero: The Case of *Soylent Green* and the Eco-Disaster Film." In *Ecology and Popular Film: Cinema on the Edge,* 91–108 Albany: SUNY Press, 2009.

Pohl, Frederik, and C. M. Kornbluth. *The Space Merchants.* New York: Ballantine, 1953.

Stewart, Martha. "A Collective Case Against Soylent." MarthaStewart.com, May 19, 2014. https://www.marthastewart.com/1072739/martha-stewarts-collective-case-against-soylent.

Travis-Henikoff, Carole A. *Dinner with a Cannibal: The Complete History of Mankind's Oldest Taboo.* Santa Monica: Santa Monica Press., 2008.

Walton, Priscilla L. *Our Cannibals, Ourselves.* Urbana and Chicago: University of Illinois Press, 2004.

Widdicombe, Liz. "The End of Food." *New Yorker*, May 12, 2014. https://www.newyorker.com/magazine/2014/05/12/the-end-of-food.

END NOTES

1. On the topic of colonialism, which roots the majority of critical inquiries making use of cannibalism, see, e.g., Avramescu and the excellent collection edited by Barker, Hulme, and Iversen; on environmentalism, see Estok. Adams's path-breaking account of gender and meat consumption deserves special recognition for its not infrequent invocation of cannibalism as one mode of meat-eating among others, though it is not the extended focus of any one chapter.

2. The answer I give my students when it comes up serves the pedagogical function of language precision: *Vegans (like all people) can eat whatever they want; they (like all people) abstain from eating certain things for certain reasons.*

3. Little serious work has been done with the film, though it gets frequent mention in passing. For a rare (but brief) treatment, see Lipschutz; see also Murray and Heumann for a full-length contextual exploration.

4. On native pride, see Travis-Henikoff. The Arens affair as an event in this history of anthropology appears to be largely settled, as contemporary reviews and subsequent research has undercut his totalizing thesis; however, it remains useful as a stepping-off point for the cultural studies work that followed, as his skepticism suited the needs of those working in critical theory and launched an industry of reading metaphors of cannibalism without having to take account of actually-existing cannibalism. Of this latter issue, see the opening of King.

5. Since his essay came out, a synchronicity of sources has addressed the same issues: see, e.g., King, MacCannell (who also includes communion's transubstantiation), and Walton.

6. For a range of examples, see Deamicis, Hutchinson, Manjoo, Merchant, and Morin. Even Martha Stewart and her team have chimed in "A Collective Case Against Soylent," which not coincidentally includes mostly meat.

7. Coffiest also hails from a dystopian science fiction property, Frederik Pohl and C. M. Kornbluth's 1953 novel *The Space Merchants*, in which the drink is sold to customers who are unaware that it is highly addictive—an excellent satire of caf-

feine's addictive properties, but far darker.

8. Liquid meal-replacers have been available over the counter and by prescription for targeted use (e.g., weight loss) for many years; however, Soylent is the first meant to replace food totally.

9. See, e.g., Casey Friedman in Merchant who laments coming home and not wanting to cook dinner as the reason he ordered Soylent. Out of curiosity, in every foodcentric course I teach, I ask the question of how many students don't like eating, having to make all sorts of decisions about eating, or would be happy to have all their eating choices made for them: never once has a class had fewer than 25 percent who raised their hands, making the feeling more common than we might like to admit.

10. Marx expresses as much in *Capital*, though in the language of vampirism; Avramescu helpfully tracks this moment through critics of early capitalism through to the writers that influenced Marx directly (253–54).

11. For a nuanced treatment of foodies, see Johnston and Baumann.

CHAPTER 7

Scarecrow Veganism:
The Straw Man of Buddhist Vegan Identity in Richard Powers's
The Echo Maker and Jonathan Franzen's *Purity*

Christopher Kocela

Early in Richard Powers's 2006 novel *The Echo Maker*, one of the main protagonists, Karin Schluter, rekindles her relationship with a former lover and environmental activist named Daniel Riegel. On seeing Daniel naked for the first time in years, Karin is surprised at his leanness and labels him a "scarecrow vegan" (58) for the animal-free diet and near-ascetic lifestyle he has adopted. Although this term is never repeated in the text, "scarecrow vegan" perfectly describes Daniel's subsequent role in Powers's novel: a fervent Buddhist, he meditates four times per day, refuses to let Karin eat meat, smoke, or even curse in his presence, and maintains such a high-minded view of environmental conservation that he alienates those around him, finally quitting the bird refuge at which has worked for years rather than compromise his principles. As I will discuss in this chapter, Daniel's character represents a straw man argument about the relationship between veganism and Buddhism that effectively neutralizes the political and ethical potential of vegan subjectivity. This argument has recently been seconded by Jonathan Franzen's 2015 novel *Purity*, which likewise contains a major character, Anabel Laird, who becomes a dangerously thin, "chronically depressed" (4) Buddhist vegan in protest of the treatment of women and animals in contemporary American culture. If a crucial task of vegan studies is the analysis and deconstruction of mainstream representations of vegan identity, these high-literary, post-9/11 American novels warrant consideration not only by virtue of the critical esteem in which Powers and Franzen are held (*The Echo Maker* won the National Book

Award, as did Franzen's 2001 novel, *The Corrections*), but also because both authors have been celebrated as contemporary "nature writers" whose work advocates for environmental awareness and conservation (Burn 82–87; Houser 383–86; González 22–25; Sielke 249–50). That Powers and Franzen have achieved this reputation despite their largely disparaging characterization of veganism, which has gone unremarked in scholarship to date, provides an opportunity for exploring how the political and ethical significance of vegan practice can be neutralized through too narrow an association with specific religious or spiritual traditions.

My examination of "scarecrow veganism" in Powers's and Franzen's works aims to assess how the equation of veganism with Buddhism in these texts limits a broader and more comprehensive understanding of vegan and Buddhist identity in contemporary American culture. Those with even a cursory understanding of veganism or Buddhism know that not all vegans are Buddhist and not all Buddhists are vegan. Perhaps especially in the US, individuals who choose a vegan lifestyle do so for a variety of ethical, religious, and health-related reasons. In a 2013 survey of over four hundred self-identified American vegans, less than half of those surveyed attributed their decision not to consume animal products to ethical or religious motivations (Johnson 40); among these ethical vegans, only five percent further identified as Buddhist (Johnson 45).[1] Meanwhile, although strict vegetarianism has been advocated in some Mahayana Buddhist traditions (particularly in China and Southeast Asia), Buddhism has never been a uniformly vegetarian religion. In fact, the Buddha explicitly forbade his community of mendicant monks from adopting rules that would prohibit meat-eating since, in his view, donation of food to monks comprised a source of spiritual merit for the laity that should be rejected only in exceptional circumstances.[2] Yet despite how rarely Buddhist and vegan identities overlap in the US, Powers and Franzen do not portray Buddhism as incidental to, nor even the impetus for, their characters' vegan practice. Instead, *The Echo Maker* and *Purity* portray Buddhism as the inevitable *outcome* of veganism. Daniel Riegel and Anabel Laird both become vegans in early adulthood after exhibiting a lifelong concern for animal welfare; both subsequently take up Buddhist practice, meditating regularly and embracing the ideals of "no-self" and emptiness; and both suffer profound social alienation as a result of this spiritual trajectory. As a result, these novels construct a model of vegan subjectivity filtered through the lens of what Timothy Morton calls

"Buddhaphobia," an "irrational fear of Buddhism" (187) that, in these texts, functions to deny the appeal and viability of vegan practice as a basis for individual identity and community.

By tracing the contours of Buddhist vegan identity in these novels, my goal is not to suggest that these representations necessarily reflect the attitudes or prejudices of their authors. Powers has spoken in interviews about the challenges he faced as an adolescent living for five years in Thailand (Dewey 6), one of the most homogenously Buddhist countries in the world; but he has not, to my knowledge, publically expressed any opinion about either Buddhism or veganism. Likewise, although some reviewers of *Purity* have interpreted the most outrageous aspects of Anabel's character as outgrowths of Franzen's controversial statements about feminism, Anabel's fanatical adherence to veganism and Buddhism does not reflect, so far as I know, any expressed hostility on Franzen's part toward these practices.[3] Rather than seek biographical explanations, I read these reductive characterizations of vegan identity as indicative of the need for flexibility and variation in defining vegan practice and identity in contemporary US culture. My chapter is divided into two parts. In the first I argue that *The Echo Maker* and *Purity* portray vegan subjectivity as an *orientation* in the sense defined by Laura Wright in *The Vegan Studies Project*—as "an *essential* or *fundamental* position" that, like sexual orientation, is "much more deeply rooted than a mere preference" (7). While this depiction enables Powers and Franzen to highlight the ethical seriousness and marginalized status of vegans, it also becomes the basis for a Buddhaphobic rendering of veganism as an antisocial and self-destructive drive. In the second part of the chapter I examine two scenes, one from each novel, in which the tenuousness of vegan identity is symbolized by the preparation of inedible or rejected "vegan food." As I will argue, failed vegan cooking becomes, in these texts, a means of reinforcing gender stereotypes and casting veganism as incapable of serving as the basis for collective identity or community, throwing into doubt the oppositional significance of vegan practice relative to mainstream consumer culture.

VEGANISM AS ORIENTATION

In *The Vegan Studies Project* Laura Wright interrogates the relationship between vegan identity and practice, comparing several accounts of why individuals might be motivated to become vegans. She takes seriously the possibility that, for some people, veganism is not merely a preference or choice but the expression of an innate orientation toward concern for animal welfare: "considering veganism as an orientation allows for an understanding of that minority position as a delicate mixture of something both primal and social, a category—like sexual orientation or left- or right-handedness— that constitutes for some people, just perhaps, something somewhat beyond one's choosing" (7). While Wright is careful to point out that this interpretation applies only to a small portion of real-world ethical vegans (8), this model is crucial to understanding the depiction of vegan identity in *The Echo Maker* and *Purity*. In contrast to most mainstream representations, Powers and Franzen portray veganism as an inborn drive toward animal advocacy that is explicitly linked to sexual identity. In these novels, however, veganism also becomes an *orientation* in the original etymological sense of "turning or facing eastward, esp. in an act of worship" (*Oxford English Dictionary*). For these vegan characters, an innate concern for animals propels them in the direction of Buddhist practice and faith that has unsettling implications in the eyes of those closest to them.

The Echo Maker has been widely interpreted as a "neuronarrative" or fictional examination of contemporary neuroscience that aims to heighten awareness of both the human need for storytelling as well as the threat to survival posed by climate change. In the former vein Harris describes the book as "the first fully realized novel of neurological realism" (243); Hawk portrays the novel as a "locus of the dialogue taking place between science and narrative" (21); and Roxburgh, Kirchhofer, and Auguscik argue that *The Echo Maker* "deploys established neuroscientific knowledge about the universality of stories and the human need for them" (78). Emphasizing the novel's environmental message, Houser argues that the novel offers a neurological account of wonder and mental illness so as to "increase readers' awareness of their surroundings as a way to promote ecological protection" (381); Sielke maintains that Powers's novel "honors a long tradition of conservational ethics and nature writing" (250); and Malewitz reads it as "bring[ing] together ecological modes of representing the natural environment with technological modes of understanding" (727). Powers's depiction of veganism emerges early in the novel when Karin Schlute, one of the main protagonists, returns to her hometown of Kearney, Indiana, following news that her younger brother has suffered a near-fatal automobile accident. Trying to speed her brother's recovery from a rare neurological disorder, she calls on a variety of Mark's friends, past and present, to help him reconstruct his memories. One such friend is Daniel Riegel, a fellow "nature boy" with whom Mark had an unexplained falling-out in high school:

> Until the age of thirteen, her brother and Daniel had been joined at the hip, twin nature boys turning up ornate box turtles, stumbling on bobwhite nests, camped outside burrows that they dreamed of inhabiting. Then, in high school, something happened. . . . Danny stayed with the animals and Mark abandoned them for people. (46)

In Karin's view, Daniel's decision to "stay with the animals" explains his veganism and his current work at the Buffalo County Crane Refuge, which is dedicated to preserving the local habitat of the sandhill crane. As Karin reestablishes a romantic relationship with Daniel, she learns that his veganism and concern for animals have led him to become a Buddhist: "[h]e simply wanted people to be as selfless as they should be, humbled by the million supporting links that kept them alive, as generous with others as nature was with them" (54). This description alludes to the well-known Mahayana Buddhist doctrine of emptiness (in Sanskrit, *sunyata*), which posits that no entity retains a permanent essence or self because each is part of an infinite network of interdependent relations with other things. According to this teaching, all beings are capable of realizing the truth of emptiness because they possess the "Buddhanature" or "Buddha womb" (*tathagatagharba*) that, as defined in the *Lankavatara Sutra*, is "imminent in everyone" (47). Initially, Karin is attracted to Daniel's spirituality: her first show of affection for him is to buy him a secondhand Buddha lamp, which she finds at a county auction. But as their relationship intensifies and she decides to move into his "dark monk's cell" (Powers 70), she is quickly alienated by his ascetic lifestyle and discipline. Beyond his vegan diet, Daniel uses no hot water and keeps his apartment at sixty degrees in the winter (70); he frequently punctuates his conversation with statistics on extinctions and environmental degradation (72); and he allows nothing to impinge on his meditation schedule, which consumes a considerable amount of the few hours he is not working for the Crane Refuge. For Karin, Daniel's commitment to meditation and veganism prove the most difficult aspects of his lifestyle to embrace. Angered by his obliviousness to her during meditation, she interrogates him about the practice:

> "What do you want from it?" she asked, trying to sound neutral.
> "Nothing! I want it to help me want nothing."
> She fisted her skirt hem. "What does it do for you?"
> "It makes me more . . . an object to myself. Disidentified." (73, ellipsis in original)

Rejecting meditation outright, Karin compensates by adopting Daniel's vegan diet, only to find herself physically and emotionally drained within weeks. While dining out with him at a Chinese restaurant she fantasizes about ordering meat: "The beef and broccoli sounded like a dream, a cure to her growing whole-foods anemia. Weeks of living with Daniel had left her wasted" (262). Although she resists the beef and orders tofu instead, her decision is followed shortly after by Daniel's reproof of her desire to have children, which he portrays as selfish and ecologically unsustainable (287, 408). By the time her brother finally reveals why he severed his friendship with Daniel a decade earlier, the reason for their falling out appears oddly commensurate with the troubles Karin faces in her current relationship. Mark confesses that, early in high school, Danny attempted to come on to him sexually—an event he describes as an effort to "queer me. Out of the blue" (376). Despite attempting to downplay the incident as mere juvenile homoerotism, it is evident to the reader that Karin also feels "queered" by Daniel, whose veganism and Buddhism threaten her health and reproductive future. Where Mark's revelation hints at a connection between Daniel's love for animals and sexual orientation, Karin's relationship with Daniel calls to mind the etymology of the word *orientation* mentioned above. From Karin's perspective, Daniel's veganism is only a waypoint in the achievement of Buddhist "no-self," which appears to her as an object-like state of asceticism and alienation befitting her early characterization of him as a "scarecrow vegan" (52).

Published nine years later, Franzen's *Purity* has yet to receive substantial scholarly attention, although two book-length studies of Franzen's fiction have already registered its formal and political differences from his previous novels. Weinstein portrays *Purity* as the "least comedic of Franzen's fictions" (222) and argues that its exploration of Oedipal themes leads Franzen to deploy "casually sexist language" more freely than ever before (209); similarly, Hidalga describes *Purity* as Franzen's

first "American Gothic novel" (220) in which, in contrast to his earlier
fictions, "display of ecofeminist concerns is obviously satirical" (233). [4]
In the present context the interest of Franzen's book resides in its construction, through the character of Anabel Laird, of an account of vegan
identity remarkably similar to that of Powers's novel. Like Daniel, Anabel
is introduced as a vegan Buddhist with a mysterious past. A reader of
Sanskrit who meditates every morning and refuses to drive a car or even
keep a photo ID, Anabel (who goes by the name Penelope) has raised
her only daughter, Pip, in a secluded cabin near Felton, California, so as
protect them both from an abusive husband and father whose identity
she refuses to disclose. Although Pip has long disbelieved her mother's
explanation for their underground lifestyle, she cannot persuade her
to reveal her real name or even her age; to personal inquiries Anabel/
Penelope responds with a "smile suitable to the posing of a koan" (6).
But when she refuses to help Pip find her father in order to help pay
back her $130,000 student loan, Pip accepts an internship with a hacker
and internet whistleblower whose efforts to conceal a past murder
lead Pip unwittingly into the employ of her lost father, Tom Aberrant.
Snooping through Tom's computer files, Pip discovers an unpublished
memoir that describes his relationship with Anabel and fills in the gaps
in her life story. Daughter of the owner of a large agribusiness conglom-
erate, Anabel rebels against her father in adolescence through rampant
drug use and sexual promiscuity. By the time she meets Tom in college,
she has embraced feminism and veganism and is working on a thesis
film entitled "A River of Meat," which juxtaposes the exploitation of
women and animals in American culture by intercutting images of Miss
America with slaughterhouse footage of cows being bolt-gunned (384).
To be sure, Tom's account of his "feminist marriage" (436) to Anabel
paints a heavily biased portrait of his ex-wife; but in the present context,
the interest of this narrative is that it mirrors the relationship between
Karin and Daniel at a number of key points. Early on, Tom becomes a
vegetarian in order to please Anabel and finds himself "constantly half
nauseated" (372); Anabel grows stick-figure thin as a result of her vegan
diet and exercise regimen, to the point that she carries "as much body fat
as a Shaker chair" (405); and although she, unlike Daniel Riegel, wants
children, her veganism makes this impossible for many years because
she is usually too malnourished to ovulate (403–04). Finally, Anabel's
Buddhism emerges as a seemingly unavoidable outcome of her lifelong
concern for animal welfare. Shortly after their divorce Tom visits her
at a secluded cabin in the New Jersey woods, where she has turned to

meditation and communion with nature as an "invisible" evolution of her experimental protest films (432). For Pip and the reader of Franzen's novel, this account of Anabel's meditation practice authenticates Tom's story and establishes its continuity with the life of Pip's mother, whose "spiritual Endeavor was itself a kind of art—an art of invisibility" (6).

Through the characters of Anabel and Daniel, *Purity* and *The Echo Maker* portray vegan identity as firmly grounded in an ethical orientation toward animal welfare and protection.[5] By linking this orientation to sexual identity and, particularly in Powers's novel, to queerness, these novels depict the marginalization of vegan, female, and queer identities as intersecting, reinforcing the arguments of queer ecofeminists such as Greta Gaard and pattrice jones that "sexism and speciesism, having grown up together across the centuries, are codependent siblings of dysfunctional patriarchal families" (jones 51). Gaard's original call for a queer ecofeminism advocates historical analysis of Western Christian and imperialist "erotophobia," or the "fear of the erotic so strong that only one form of sexuality is overtly allowed, only in one position, and only in the context of certain legal, religious, and social sanctions" (25). In *The Echo Maker* and *Purity*, however, ethical veganism does not advance a queer ecofeminist perspective but, instead, becomes the basis for a "Buddhaphobic" representation of vegan subjectivity as antisocial, self-destructive, and subsumed within a Buddhist spiritual teleology.[6] In his essay of the same name, Timothy Morton defines "Buddhaphobia" as an "allergic reaction" to the "always-already presence of Buddhism, and of what we shall call nothingness, within Western thinking" (189). Analyzing a range of Western discourses from philosophy to psychoanalysis to neuroscience, Morton finds that the construction of selfhood in these discourses frequently depends on a fundamentally Buddhist concept of emptiness that is disavowed as a foreign object or "object-like entity at the core of human being, an entity felt as an object precisely because it is inhuman, a-human" (228). Freud's initial characterization of the death drive as the "nirvana principle" perfectly exemplifies this Buddhaphobic reaction, as does Slavoj Žižek's demonizing of meditation as a practice that encourages passive acceptance of capitalist exploitation (Morton 215–16, 227–28). Similarly, the conflation of ethical veganism and Buddhism in *The Echo Maker* and *Purity* constitutes a Buddhaphobic reaction to the presence, in contemporary American culture, of a disturbingly "foreign" body that refuses to sustain or adorn itself with animal products. Daniel and Anabel are driven by an irrational Buddha-nature that shifts their allegiance from humans to animals and propels them toward a state of selflessness depicted in terms of isolation, stasis, and near-starvation. This negative representation of Buddhism differs markedly from that described by scholars such as John Whalen-Bridge and Gary Storhoff who, in examining the "indigenization" of Buddhism within contemporary American literature, tend to privilege authors and texts sympathetic to Buddhist ideals (3). In *The Echo Maker* and *Purity*, the effect of linking Buddhist and vegan practice is not only to Orientalize veganism through association with cultural otherness but, perhaps more radically, to deny the status of veganism as an ethical or political position in its own right.

Over the course of both novels, the idea that veganism is culturally or ideologically opposed to mainstream consumer values gives way to the impression that vegan practice is incapable of supporting any coherent ideology of its own. The political and ideological emptiness of veganism becomes manifest in a variety of ways. Most obviously, neither Daniel nor Anabel are able to articulate their concern for animals in a manner that is persuasive or even comprehensible to others; instead, both appear as hollow mouthpieces for what Lawrence Buell calls "toxic discourse," or discourse whose sole function is to generate "anxiety arising from perceived threat of environmental hazard" (31). As an art student in college, Anabel has difficulty making friends because "she kept alienating people with her moral absolutism" (350); by her own admission, her thesis film on slaughterhouses is "unwatchable" and reviled by all of her classmates except a fellow vegan (358). Even Tom, who is initially sympathetic to her views, repeatedly complains about her lapses in logic and compares talking with her to climbing a precarious "logic tree" (321, 326). That she gives up filmmaking once she starts meditating suggests that, at root, her ethical orientation is incommunicable to others. In *The Echo Maker*, Daniel is comparably challenged when it comes to arguing his moral and environmental convictions. His early attempts to explain his dedication to the Crane Refuge appear to Karin as a sustained reproach to her human need for self-affirmation: "One million species heading toward extinction. We can't be too choosy about our private paths" (72). When he is called on to speak at a public meeting on behalf of the Refuge, he "preache[s] with such messianic passion that she felt the room discount him as yet another finger-pointing Jeremiah" (346). Eventually Daniel, like Anabel, embraces the Buddha's "noble silence"

(338) and quits the Refuge for a job in Alaska where, free of human interference, he can appreciate the cranes on their breeding grounds (445). Given the seemingly inevitable progression from veganism to Buddhism in these novels, the fact that Anabel and Daniel give up their primary forms of political expression in favor of meditation and exile reinforces a Buddhaphobic thesis that runs throughout Western philosophy: "Buddhism is what must be rejected in order to have logic at all" (Morton 198). By the logic of these novels, Daniel and Anabel, as vegans, cannot avoid a Buddhist fate that reduces their practice to inconsequence and meaninglessness. As if to further discount the coherence of vegan and Buddhist subjectivity at a formal level, both novels, despite oscillating between multiple centers of consciousness, refuse to allow the reader access to the inner lives of these scarecrow-like characters.

In addition, the fact that the reader learns everything about Daniel and Anabel from the perspective of those who attempt, unsuccessfully, to adapt to their vegan lifestyles reinforces the impression that veganism is unsustainable for those unwilling to risk their health and even their lives in devotion to "Buddha-nature." The fatigue and nausea suffered by Karin and Tom while trying to stick to their diets obviously does not reflect the experiences of many real-world vegans and vegetarians who were previously omnivores. The scarecrow-like thinness of both Daniel and Anabel does, however, reflect a large body of writing in medical journals and the mainstream media that insists on linking veganism to forms of "disordered" eating, particularly among women. Commenting on this trend, Wright observes: "in a culture that is so fixated on a meat-based diet as standard, the language of deviance is the only language available with which to render non-normative dietary choices" (100). The fact that Anabel "simply stop[s] having her periods" (Franzen 404) for months at a stretch establishes a strong link between her veganism and anorexia, a key symptom of which, in the DSM-IV, is the "absence of at least three consecutive cycles" in a menstruating woman. Likewise, Daniel's lean physique—he is repeatedly described as "scrawny" and "skinny" (Powers 57, 89)—and his status as a "gentle seed-eater" (53) constitute a form of "hybrid masculinity" outside the mainstream of hegemonic American masculine norms (Greenebaum and Dexter 6); in this context, the plausibility of Daniel's queerness derives from his association with a thoroughly feminized sphere of animal advocacy (Luke 11–15) and from his lifelong refusal to perform the "carnivorous virility" (Adams 36) fundamental to heterosexual male identity in the West. Moreover, beyond reinforcing these gender stereotypes, the incompatibility between veganism and childrearing in both novels also recasts potentially progressive associations between vegan identity and non-normative sexuality as a threat to what Lee Edelman calls "reproductive futurism," the heteronormative ideology that, by portraying queerness as the enemy of the Child, attempts to deny "the possibility of a queer resistance to this organizing principle of communal relations" (2). In *Purity* and *The Echo Maker*, vegan identity is overdetermined as a figure for the death drive through its ties to Buddhist emptiness, anorexia, and queerness. This overdetermination is perhaps nowhere more evident, however, than when Daniel and Anabel are depicted as unable or unwilling to eat meals that are specially prepared for them by those most solicitous of their dietary restrictions. In both novels crucial turns in the narrative take place around acts of cooking and defining "vegan food." Daniel's and Anabel's refusal to eat this food not only reinforces the portrayal of veganism as a form of disordered eating differentiated in terms of gender stereotypes, it also buttresses the underlying argument of these novels that Buddhism, despite endorsing a "middle way" between austerity and indulgence, actually elevates asceticism above all other values.

RECIPES FOR EMPTINESS: INSTRUCTIONS FOR THE VEGAN COOK

In *Purity*, connections between vegan food, religious asceticism, and gender emerge early in the novel, following Pip's decision to bake a vegan birthday cake for her mother. Because Anabel refuses to celebrate her actual birthday, their annual tradition is to regard the summer solstice as her "not-birthday" (5)—a tradition about which both women are ambivalent. Pip regards it as another strategy by which her mother babies her, attempting to shield her from the truth about her past, while Anabel dislikes any attention to her age or appearance. As she teaches her daughter, "This is the terrible thing about bodies. They're so *visible*, so *visible*" (4, emphasis in original). Respecting her mother's veganism and rigorous avoidance of sugar, Pip eventually procures a recipe for dairy-free cake, which she devotes half a day to baking and frosting with "putty-like vegan icing" (66). Despite the unappetizing texture of her finished cake, however, it is not until she attempts to transport it to her mother's house in Felton that her plans are finally dashed. Boarding the Oakland bus carrying the cake in a roller-skate box, Pip needs to urinate but has to endure hours of bladder ache and fear of incontinence before she is able to use the ladies' room at the Santa Cruz bus station. There, in her rush to relieve herself, she upends the skate box, "dumping the cake facedown onto tiles smeared with condensed fog and cigarette ash and the droppings and boot residues of girl buskers and panhandlers" (67). Crying, Pip attempts to salvage what she can, but the cake's previously "putty-like" icing, spread across the bathroom floor, now looks to her like "smeary albino shit" (68). She arrives at her mother's house carrying only fragments of the salvaged cake and, "sobbing like an eight-year-old" (69), submits once again to Anabel's infantilizing care before departing to meet the internet whistleblower who will help her uncover her parents' identities.

The story of Pip's vegan cake provides a visceral example of the abjection of a food culture. Not only is her cake metaphorically linked, over the course of the narrative, to increasingly inedible and disgusting materials (from stevia to putty to shit), even her request for a vegan recipe renders her an object of mockery to her coworkers, whose comparison of "vegan cake" to "a party with no booze, desserts, or dancing" (37) makes Pip wonder if she is "starting down the road to being a friendless person like her mother" (37). As Lorna Piatti-Farnell observes, abjection of specific foods and cooking traditions is a recurring feature of contemporary ethnic American literatures and frequently serves, particularly in Asian American literature, to highlight boundaries between mainstream and immigrant cultures: "What is acceptable and what is not—what is edible and what is disgusting—can be interpreted as evidence of a group's distinction and organization; these elements are ultimately what construct the cultural boundaries of taste" (105). But while there is an Orientalizing element to Franzen's Buddhaphobic depiction of veganism, the central effect of abjection in *Purity* is not to define the otherness of vegan culture or community but, as I have argued above, to deny that such a community exists. Pip's early intuition that being vegan means "being a friendless person" is borne out, over the course of the narrative, by her inability to fashion the cake into an expression of respect or shared identity between her mother and herself. This failure is not hers alone but reflects the lack of communication that, largely as a result of her mother's Buddhism, has characterized her upbringing. Pip seems completely oblivious to the fact that Anabel's "not-birthday" tradition is in keeping with her Buddhist views. Well-known Vietnamese Zen (or Thiên) master Thich Nhat Hahn, for example, advises his students to honor "continuation days" rather than conventional birthdays in order to put into practice core teachings about suchness, emptiness, and impermanence (*No Death* 78–83).[7] Pip is unable to see this significance, however, because for her, as for Karin in *The Echo Maker*, Buddhism appears little more than a form of escapism through meditation. All her life Pip has had to contend with Anabel's retreat to silent breathing whenever their dialogue takes an uncomfortable turn, prompting her to tell her mother at one point, "I need you to stop being Buddhist and try to have an adult conversation with me" (550).

On one level, Franzen's depiction of Buddhism as an ineffective means of winning converts to veganism resonates with Corey Lee Wrenn's argument that religion and spirituality are largely inappropriate to the pursuit of animal rights causes (141). In Wrenn's view, this is not because all religions are fundamentally compromised by speciesism (she identifies Jainism as a vegan religion) but because spirituality tends to displace rights-based arguments at the heart of vegan practice, giving rise to a popular misconception in which "[a]ny person with an interest in sexual 'empowerment,' personal purification, detoxing, enlightenment, or 'following their heart' can be counted as a representative of veganism" (16).[8] As practiced by Anabel, Buddhism is clearly a path to personal purification by which she intensifies the rigor of her ascetic vegan practice. During the final months of her marriage to Tom, she eats only a single meal a day and works out three hours every evening—a regimen Tom describes as a quest to become "morally irreproachable" (441). Yet where Wrenn interrogates connections between veganism and religion so as to refocus attention on the ethical objectives of veganism (175–77), Franzen's depiction of Anabel's quest for purification through dietary restriction sheds no light on the validity of animal rights discourses but instead reflects ethnographic accounts of anorexia that attribute the disease to the subject's equation of asceticism with moral empowerment (O'Connor 51–52). By these readings, the unifying feature of anorexia is not trauma or a distorted body image but the seductiveness of asceticism in a world without clear moral choices: "In our sample, ascetic activity always initiated anorexia. Whether it begins with eating or exercise, self-denial focuses and finally consumes the person's life. Here the history of religious asceticism tells us devout austerities tempt death. Today's anorexia secularizes that scenario" (O'Connor 32). Although tradition teaches that the Buddha achieved enlightenment only after trying and *rejecting* ascetic practice, Anabel regards meditation as an ascetic "art of invisibility" (6) that, through retreat from worldly responsibility, solves the problem of embodiment, so terrible because "so *visible*" (4). To return to Pip's ruined cake: although it is impossible to criticize Anabel for not eating it, her response anticipates the many other refusals—of trust, honesty, adult engagement with the world—that come to define her vegan Buddhist practice over the course of Franzen's novel. While raising the possibility that shared vegan foods might form a basis for female solidarity and community, this narrative forecloses that possibility by failing to challenge pervasive cultural associations between female veganism, abjection, and disordered eating.

In contrast to *Purity*, the significance of vegan food in *The Echo Maker* is not explicitly addressed until late in the novel, when Karin decides to prepare a "vegan feast" (409) for Daniel. By this point in the novel she has been working alongside him for months at the Crane Refuge in an effort to repair their relationship and to distract herself from her brother's mental illness. To her surprise, she finds it "the most meaningful work she'd ever put her hand to" (338); but her communication with Daniel has not improved. Thwarted in his efforts to protect the cranes' habitat from development, he is increasingly silent and withdrawn and "meditates more now, sometimes an hour at a shot" (408). In compensation, Karin has begun meeting secretly with a local real estate developer and former lover willing to provide information useful to the Refuge. In an effort to jolt Daniel out of his apathy, Karin decides to cook a meal at which she will disclose all that she has learned from her secret romantic meetings:

> She spends the day preparing him a vegan feast: broccoli almond seitan, skordalia, and coriander chutney. Even tahini rice pudding, for the man who considers dessert a sin. She flies around the kitchen, mixing and assembling, feeling almost steady. Blessed distraction, and the most effort she has expended on him since moving in. (409)

Although she realizes that her confession will likely destroy their relationship, Karin believes Daniel will use her information to fight back against the real estate developers threatening the cranes' habitat.

When he arrives home, however, he proclaims the meal a "separation party" (409) because he has quit the Refuge earlier that day, no longer able to associate with an institution that regards "[c]ompromise as the better part of valor" (410). Even when Karin reveals her secret knowledge of the developers' plans, Daniel's anger does nothing to rejuvenate his faith in their environmental efforts; instead, he simply walks out, leaving Karin alone with the uneaten food.

Karin's "vegan feast" crystallizes the novel's gendered depiction of veganism as well as its equation of vegan and Buddhist practice. Throughout the novel Daniel exhibits features of what Jessica Greenebaum and Brandon Dexter call "hybrid masculinity"—a gender performance through which vegan men call into question traditional masculine traits while also reinforcing aspects of gender privilege (6). Although Daniel eschews the aggressive language and assertions of health and athletic prowess utilized by some vegan men to offset their association with traditionally feminine values of compassion and empathy, he clearly regards his independence and spiritual discipline as key to his status as a "good man"; in the process he "reinforces certain hegemonic ideals of masculinity by emphasizing individualism and non-conformity, toughness and heroism" (Greenebaum and Dexter 7). By preparing a meal designed to spark Daniel's outrage on behalf of the Refuge, Karin clearly aims to tap into his sense of moral uprightness in order to correct what she regards as his most unmanly character trait: his refusal to assert himself and to act out of anger. Throughout the novel she criticizes his passivity—in meditation (73), in arguments (206), even while driving (344)—and at one point she wonders how he could ever have "grown up in rural Nebraska without her brother's friends beating the life out of him" (89). In this context, although the meal she prepares consists of seitan, a meat substitute made from wheat gluten, its restorative symbolic function is in keeping with the sexual politics of meat in Western culture, which "imply that a man needs meat and that a woman should feed him meat" (Adams 34). The substitutive use of the seitan to reaffirm traditional gender values also reflects Christopher Ciochetti's view that vegan foods have the power to offset the loss of meaning associated with refusal to consume animal products (416). But Daniel's rejection of the meal, which turns out to be his last meeting with Karin prior to his departure for Alaska, signifies once and for all his inability to be reclaimed within mainstream models of masculinity.

Although Karin has been romantically attracted to another man for the last third of the novel, the symbolic weight of their failed relationship falls squarely on Daniel since it is his "queer" veganism that, from the outset, has presented the most formidable obstacle to their happiness together.

Furthermore, where Pip's vegan cake is rendered abject, in part, through its failure to reflect Anabel's Buddhist values, Karin's "vegan feast" is rich with Buddhist resonance. Seitan has long associations with Mahayana Buddhism owing to the fact that it was originally developed by Buddhist monks in sixth-century China (Stepaniak 28). That Karin experiences "[b]lessed distraction" (409) while making this vegan dish implies a self-consciously spiritual motivation for her efforts: through the meal, she hopes to restore not only Daniel's righteous anger but also his faith in the community of conservationists, which she has embraced with "all the fervor of a convert" (377). Her view of cooking here reflects the spiritual practice endorsed in Zen master Dogen's *Tenzo Kyokun,* or *Instructions for the Cook,* which famously portrays food preparation as a means of expressing and leading others to enlightenment:

> When you select and serve up crude greens, if you do so with a true mind, a sincere mind, and a pure mind, then they will be comparable to superb delicacies. Why is that so? Because when one enters into the pure and vast oceanic assembly of the buddha dharma, superb delicacies are never seen and the flavor of crude greens does not exist: there is only the one taste of the great sea, and that is all. (30)

For Dogen, writing in medieval Japan, the monastic cook had to make the best of his ingredients whatever their quality because the spiritual community of practitioners, or *sangha,* was dependent on him; likewise, a monk's grateful acceptance of even the most humble meal exemplified the proper response to all circumstances of life, from happiness to disappointment, success to failure.

Daniel's refusal to eat the vegan meal here thwarts Karin's intentions and showcases again the extent to which his own practice differs from the Buddhist ideal. His decision to leave the Refuge over a setback in public and environmental policy not only displays a lack of equanimity out of keeping with the tolerance and compassion he has promoted throughout the novel, it also amounts to turning his back on the *sangha* which, alongside the Buddha and the *dharma* (or teaching), is one of the three "jewels" of Buddhism. Given that *The Echo Maker* portrays Buddhism as the outcome of veganism, the fact that Daniel reveals his decision over an uneaten vegan meal lends further symbolic relevance to the breach of communal values involved. Karin's view that Daniel's withdrawal from work at the Refuge constitutes a form of "[d]eath by disengagement" (410) brings his story full circle from his adolescent decision to remain "with the animals" (46), reinforcing the idea that vegan practice, despite its seeming reverence for animal life, is the product of a fundamentally antisocial death drive. Although veganism continues to gain popularity and acceptance in the US, Daniel's refusal to eat this last meal, followed immediately by his decision to move to Alaska, reads as a denial of veganism's social relevance and sustainability as a political and ethical practice.

Viewed together, *The Echo Maker* and *Purity* offer similar representations of vegan subjectivity which, while highlighting the social marginalization of ethical vegans, also attribute that marginalization to the antisocial Buddhism of the vegan characters themselves. The fact that Powers and Franzen create these representations despite their reputation for in-depth character development and sensitivity to animal welfare suggests that vegan identity still remains underthought and under-examined in contemporary American culture. By trying to elucidate the troubling connections between veganism and Buddhism in these novels, I do not mean to suggest that a more sympathetic engagement with Buddhism could have no part to play in defining vegan identity in the US. Not only do some Americans take up vegan practice as an important aspect of their Buddhist faith, but Buddhism, as an established non-deistic religion, could play a valuable role in debates about the status of veganism as a religion under US law.[9] Even if such efforts are successful, however, it is crucial not to allow any secular or religious construction of veganism to predominate at the expense of others. Perhaps the most troubling aspect of veganism as depicted by Powers and Franzen is that it appears rooted in a fundamental drive or orientation that is rigidly deterministic of one's life choices and preferences. Ultimately, by constructing this straw man equivalence between veganism and Buddhism, these novels highlight the importance, to vegan studies, of preserving an understanding of vegan identity that does not overemphasize orientation at the expense of agency, and which enables fluid relationships between vegan practice and other spiritual and religious traditions.

WORKS CITED

Adams, Carol J., and Matthew Calarco. "Derrida and *The Sexual Politics of Meat.*" In *Meat Culture.* Edited by Annie Potts, 31–53. Boston: Brill, 2016.

Buell, Lawrence. *Writing for an Endangered World: Literature, Culture, and Environment in the US and Beyond.* Cambridge, MA: Belknap Press of Harvard UP, 2001.

Burn, Stephen J. *Jonathan Franzen at the End of Postmodernism.* New York and London: Continuum, 2008.

Ciochetti, Christopher. "Veganism and Living Well." *Journal of Agricultural and Environmental Ethics* 25 (2012): 405–17. JSTOR.

Colb, Sherry F. "Is Veganism a Religion Under Anti-Discrimination Law? An Ohio Federal District Court Says Perhaps." *Verdict: Legal Analysis and Commentary from Justia,* March 6, 2013. *https://verdict.justia.com/2013/03/06/is-veganism-a-religion-under-anti-discrimination-law.*

Dewey, Joseph. *Understanding Richard Powers.* Columbia, SC: University of South Carolina Press 2002.

Dogen, Eihei. *Instructions for the Cook.* Translated by Griffith Foulk. In *Nothing is Hidden: Essays on Zen Master Dogen's* Instructions for the Cook. Edited by Warner et al., 21–40. New York: Weatherhill, 2001.

Edelman, Lee. *No Future: Queer Theory and the Death Drive.* Durham and London: Duke University Press 2004.

Franzen, Jonathan. *Purity.* New York: Farrar, Strauss, and Giroux, 2015.

Gaard, Greta. "Toward a Queer Ecofeminism." In *New Perspectives on Environmental Justice: Gender, Sexuality, and Activism.* Edited by Rachel Stein, 21–44. Foreword by Winona LaDuke. New Brunswick: Rutgers University Press.

Gay, Roxane. "A Compelling Plot Gives Way to Farce in Franzen's Purity." NPR, September 1, 2015. *https://www.npr.org/2015/09/01/435543843/book-review-purity-jonathan-franzen.*

González, Jesús Ángel. "Eastern and Western Promises in Jonathan Franzen's *Freedom.*" *ATLANTIS: Journal of the Spanish Association of Anglo-American Studies* 37, no. 1 (2015): 11–29. JSTOR.

Green, Jeremy. *Late Postmodernism: American Fiction at the Millenium.* New York: Palgrave Macmillan, 2005.

Greenebaum, Jessica. "Veganism, Identity, and the Quest for Authenticity." *Food, Culture & Society* 15, no. 1 (2012): 129–44. EBSCOhost.

——, and Brandon Dexter. "Vegan Men and Hybrid Masculinity." *Journal of Gender Studies* (2017). *https://doi.org/10/1080/09589236.2017.1287064.*

Harman, Elizabeth. "Eating Meat as a Morally Permissible Moral Mistake." In *Philosophy Comes to Dinner: Arguments about the Ethics of Eating.* Edited by

Andre Chignell, Terence Cuneo, and Matthew C. Halteman, 215–31. New York and London: Routledge, 2016.

Harris, Charles B. "The Story of the Self: *The Echo Maker* and Neurological Realism." In *Intersections: Essays on Richard Powers*. Edited by Stephen J. Burn and Peter Dempsey 230–59. Champaign and London: Dalkey Archive Press, 2008.

Hawk, Julie. "The Observer's Tale: Dr. Weber's Narrative (and Metanarrative) Trajectory in Richard Powers's *The Echo Maker*." *Critique: Studies in Contemporary Fiction* 54 (2013): 18–27. EBSCOhost.

Hidalga, Jesús Blanco. *Jonathan Franzen and the Romance of Community: Narratives of Salvation*. New York: Bloomsbury, 2017.

Houser, Heather. "Wondrous Strange: Eco-Sickness, Emotion, and *The Echo Maker*." *American Literature* 84, no. 2 (2012): 381–408. JSTOR.

Johnson, Lisa. "The Religion of Ethical Veganism." *Journal of Animal Ethics* 5, no. 1 (2015): 31–68. JSTOR.

Jones, pattrice. "Fighting Cocks: Ecofeminism Versus Sexualized Violence." In *Sister Species: Women, Animals, and Social Justice*. Edited by Lisa Kemmerer, with a foreword by Carol J. Adams, 45–56. Urbana: University of Illinois Press, 2011.

The Lankavatara Sutra: An Epitomized Version. Translated by D. T. Suzuki, 1932. Edited by Dwight Goddard, with a foreword by John Daido Loori. Rhinbeck, NY: Monkfish, 2003.

Luke, Brian. *Brutal: Manhood and the Exploitation of Animals*. Urbana: University of Illinois Press, 2007.

Malewitz, Raymond. "Climate-Change Infrastructure and the Volatizing of American Regionalism." *Modern Fiction Studies* 61, no. 2 (2016): 715–40. Project MUSE.

Mallory, Chaone. "The Spiritual Is Political: Gender, Spirituality, and Essentialism in Forest Defense." *Journal for the Study of Religion, Nature, and Culture* 4, no. 1 (2010): 48–71. ATLAS.

Mizuno, Kōgen. "Eating Customs in the Early Sangha in India." In *Nothing is Hidden: Essays on Zen Master Dogen's Instructions for the Cook*. Edited by Jisho Cary Warner, et al, 105–15. New York: Weatherhill, 2001.

Morton, Timothy. "Buddhaphobia: Nothingness and the Fear of Things." In *Nothing: Three Inquiries in Buddhism*. Edited by Marcus Boon, Eric Cazdyn, and Timothy Morton, 185–266. Chicago and London: U of Chicago P, 2015.

Nhat Hahn, Thich. *No Death, No Fear: Comforting Wisdom for Life*. New York: Riverhead, 2002.

O'Connor, Richard A, and Penny Van Esterik. *From Virtue to Vice: Negotiating Anorexia*. New York and Oxford: Berghahn, 2015.

Piatti-Farnell, Lorna. *Food and Culture in Contemporary American Fiction*. New York and London: Routledge, 2011.

Powers, Richard. *The Echo Maker*. New York: Picador, 2006.

Price, Austin. "Jonathan Franzen Pulls a Convincing Authorial Disappearing Act in 'Purity.'" *PopMatters*, October 12, 2015. *www.popmatters.com/review/purity-by-jonathan-franzen/*. Accessed 11 Dec. 2016.

Rooney, Kathleen. *Reading with Oprah: The Book Club that Changed America*. Fayetteville: University of Arkansas Press, 2005.

Roxburgh, Natalie, Anton Kirchhofer, and Anna Auguscik. "Universal Narrativity and the Anxious Scientist of the Contemporary Neuronovel." *Mosaic: An Interdisciplinary Critical Journal* 49, no. 4 (2016): 71–87. Project MUSE.

Sielke, Sabine. "The Subject of Literature, or: (Re-)Cognition in Richard Powers' (Science) Fiction." In *Ideas of Order: Narrative Patterns in the Novels of Richard Powers*. Edited by Antje Kley and Jan D. Kucharzewski 239–61. Heidelberg: Universitätsverlag, 2012.

Sittenfeld, Curtis. "Purity by Jonathan Franzen Review—Dazzling, Hilarious and Problematic." *Guardian*, August 26, 2015. *https://www.theguardian.com/books/2015/aug/26/purity-by-jonathan-franzen-review*.

Stepaniak, Joanne. *Vegan Vittles: Recipes Inspired by the Critters of Farm Sanctuary*. Summertown, TN: Book Publishing Co., 1996.

Weinstein, Philip. *Jonathan Franzen: The Comedy of Rage*. New York: Bloomsbury, 2015.

Whalen-Bridge, John, and Gary Storhoff. Introduction to *Writing as Enlightenment: Buddhist American Literature into the Twenty-first Century*, 1–15. Edited by John Whalen-Bridge and Gary Storhoff, with a foreword by Jan Willis. Albany: SUNY Press 2011.

Wrenn, Corey Lee. *A Rational Approach to Animal Rights: Extensions in Abolitionist Theory*. New York: Palgrave Macmillan, 2016.

Wright, Laura. *The Vegan Studies Project: Food, Animals, and Gender in the Age of Terror*. Athens: University of Georgia Press, 2015.

END NOTES

1. The survey in question was designed in response to several recently litigated cases of employment discrimination against ethical vegans in the US (Johnson 32). Its purpose was to determine whether, based on the views of self-identified vegans regarding their own practice, ethical veganism should be "recognized as a religion and a protected characteristic under US law" (Johnson 31). Of the 439 vegans surveyed, 163 identified as ethical vegans and eight of those identified as Buddhist. Based on the discursive responses to the survey questions, Johnson concludes that, regardless of additional religious affiliations, "[e]thical veganism is itself a surface sign (a practice) of a religious belief (of ethical veganism)" (60).

2. One circumstance in which it was acceptable for monks to turn away meat was when they had reason to suspect that an animal had been slaughtered specifically to feed them (Mizuno 109).

3. Sittenfeld, noting that Franzen's name is "synonymous with sexism" in some circles, complains of the "tedious stereotypes embodied by the female characters" in *Purity*; Gay, focusing on Anabel's insistence that her husband sit down to pee, portrays Anabel's characterization as "so over the top as to feel like farce." Debates about Franzen's alleged sexism have persisted ever since his public feud with Oprah Winfrey over inclusion of his novel *The Corrections* in her Book Club in 2001. For scholarly analysis of the feud, see Green 79–116 and Rooney 33–66.

4. For a discussion of Franzen's serious engagement with ecofeminism in his second novel, *Strong Motion*, see Burn 74–75.

5. Some ethicists distinguish between ethical vegans who are concerned for animals and those who are concerned more broadly with the environment (Harmon 230; Greenebaum 130). Daniel is clearly concerned with both, while Anabel seems more narrowly focused on animal protection.

6. While existing scholarship has not commented on the depiction of veganism in either *The Echo Maker* or *Purity*, their negative representation of Buddhism has been recognized in passing. Houser notes that Daniel's spirituality constitutes an "improbable disorder that compromises personhood" (401); Price observes that "*Purity* wholly rejects the kind of Western Buddhism that would have made Schopenhauer proud."

7. Numerous Zen koans also challenge students to conceive of their lives outside the confines of birth and death. Perhaps the most famous is case 23 of the *Mumonkoan*, or *Gateless Gate*, in which Huineng challenges his pursuer, "Show me your original face before you were born."

8. For an alternative account of the relationship between spirituality and environmental activism, see Mallory, who portrays spirituality as a "dynamic site of dialogue and self-reflection . . . within the women's and transgender forest defense movement" (70).

9. To date these debates are largely academic in nature and represented in arguments like those of Johnson and Colb. In Ontario, Canada, veganism was recognized as a legally protected "creed" in January 2016.

PART III

VEGAN STUDIES BEYOND THE WEST

CHAPTER 8

South Africa

"My Culture in a Tupperware": Situational Ethics in Zoë Wicomb's *October*

Caitlin E. Stobie

With critical animal studies unsettling conceptions of humanity and personhood, there is a rising interest in the role—and nature—of the so-called global citizen in modern times. For example, in a 2011 article on the cosmopolitan aspects of South African–Scottish writer Zoë Wicomb's oeuvre, Dorothy Driver mentions that the theme of globalization allows readers to focus on contradictions "which we may apply not just to humans (as much cosmopolitanism tends simply to do) but also to animals and the environment" (94).[1] Wicomb's latest novel, *October* (2014), is perhaps her most globally minded text to date: set in the United Kingdom, South Africa, and East Asia, it alternates between a range of characters and diverse settings including Glasgow, Kliprand, Cape Town, and Macau. At surface level, the opposition of such contrasting spaces could suggest that the novel is mostly concerned with a simplistic rural-urban binary. Considering situational animal ethics in the text, however, it is evident that the "nature/culture" divide is more nuanced: it is a device that foregrounds the complexities of principled eating (and living) as a modern woman. In this chapter I consider postcolonial positioning to argue that images of animality and fertility link various privileges, demonstrating how ethical eating is troubled by classist complicity or miscommunication. Characters in *October* reconceptualize veganism to suit their material conditions and lived realities. Through repeated ruminations on trauma and transculturalism, Wicomb gestures toward culinary hospitality, but also warns that cosmopolitan creatures must be open to conflict, futility, and imperfection.

In 1826, the French physician Anthelme Brillat-Savarin wrote *"Dis-moi ce que tu manges, je te dirai ce que tu es"* (qtd. in Hamblin 4). Since then, the phrase "you are what you eat" has been used in popular discourse to justify various diets: low-carbohydrate "paleo" meals, catabolic foods for weight loss, and even a version of strict vegetarianism practiced by some in the Hare Krishna movement (Goswami 17). What the current environmental crisis necessitates, however, is for us to reflect on the complexities of communal identity which *we* face, rather than individualist concerns about "you" or "I". As industrialization causes not only deforestation but also the growth of factory farms, it is clear that the ethical treatment of nonhuman organisms is a worldwide concern wherein all humans are complicit. Yet it is crucial to remember that many individualist or neocolonial norms, which propagate both meat consumption and the fashionable rise of plant-based diets, originate from what is known as the "Global West." Indeed, one of the most prevalent (yet problematic) arguments against veganism is that it is an absolutist form of moralizing which can only be practised by classist elites. There is anthropocentrism in posing veganism as a beneficent act of "helping" and "speaking for" animals: these idioms imply that (some) humans are "saviors" who will rectify all environmental woes. Even people who espouse anarchic veganism—that is, the decision to abstain from both carnist consumer processes *and* capitalist hegemony (Dominick 4)—are forced to concede that they are in a relatively privileged position, because they are able to choose not to partake in dominant social systems. Finally, no matter what form of veganism one adopts, it is inevitable that one will be constantly derided for one's supposedly "personal" decision not to consume animal products. Adapting Sara Ahmed's queer theoretical conception of the feminist killjoy, sociologist Richard Twine observes that the most significant challenge which vegan and vegan-curious people face is not a lack of nutritional variety or access to resources, but rather contempt from friends and family members who view them as "difficult" (626).[2] The problem of coexisting in an omnivorously normative society is as old as the very practice of ethical eating (or, more accurately, the abstention from carnism). Roman philosopher Seneca records that he abandoned his vegetarianism after a year because "foreign rites were . . . being inaugurated, and abstinence from certain kinds of animal food was set down as a proof of interest in the strange cult. So at the request of my father . . . I returned to my previous habits" (25). The threat of interpersonal alienation is therefore one of the oldest and greatest challenges which ethical eaters may face.

Transcultural issues do not help with this perception of animal activists. Southern Africa is a culturally diverse area which has fallen under scrutiny for its protection policies regarding megafauna (such as the recent shooting of Cecil the Lion by American dentist Walter Palmer in Zimbabwe or rhino poaching in South Africa). Animal welfare scandals mean that the global community remains relatively ignorant about how citizens view the lives of animals in a more general sense; countries in the so-called "Global South" are often victims of generalizations. For example, the fact that "animals have historically been regarded . . . as sacred and/or sacrificial, as source of food and as a spiritually privileged link with the ancestors, [and] as part of originary myths" means that it is assumed that autochthonous South Africans cannot be interested in animal welfare or rights (Woodward and Lemmer 3). Yet as websites like Black Vegans Rock and A. Breeze Harper's recent work suggest, the issue is not that animal rights movements are inherently "white" but rather that media coverage is often biased or unrepresentative of cultural nuances (Harper, "Preface"). In a sociological overview of postcolonialism and animal studies, Philip Armstrong writes that "[t]he most promising collaborations between [the two fields] lie in the production of sharp, politicised, culturally sensitive, and up-to-the-minute *local* histories" (416; my italics). Following his observation about the importance of regional specificity, I wish to briefly clarify the state of animal rights in South Africa. The Vegetarian Society of South Africa states that it has no statistical studies of the number of vegetarians or vegans in the country ("Vegetarians Also Enjoy" 21)—but Aragorn Eloff, founder of the South African Vegan Society, asserts that the movement is "far more mainstream" than it was ten years ago (qtd. in Dodd 10). Certainly, the popularity of Fry's Vegetarian products (a South African family startup) and growth of websites like Vegan Review suggest that the movement extends beyond the country's wealthy white minority.

The term "food relationships" connotes two connections: a personal bond with one's diet and one's affiliation with the community at large. Whether one is faced with traditional expectations or the

homogenizing forces of modernity, inaction, or refusal to participate in normalized practices can prompt bafflement (at best) or
outright hostility (at worst). This is particularly true in the case
of veganism, a movement which is infamous for adopting puritan-
ical rhetoric and fostering "all-or-nothing" approaches to animal
rights. However, *October* is an example of "the animal text" that
illustrates a situational and communal sense of identity (Nyman
19); it is simultaneously critical of humanist cultural norms *and*
perfectionist categorical imperatives. South African literary critic
Wendy Woodward promotes "reading for animals by foreground-
ing literary or philosophical representations in relation, implicitly, to 'real' embodied animals" (354). Similarly, my argument is
informed by the idea that there is merit in "reading for" an inclusive
veganism by considering how fiction treats human *and* nonhuman
life. Through the technique of repetition, Wicomb's novel inherits
qualities of literary modernism (which is well known for its trans-
gression of aesthetic boundaries). The text simultaneously disrupts
hegemonic culture by thematizing intersectional issues,[3] from class
boundaries to gender roles and sexuality, while remaining firmly
situated in its socio-geographical setting. Exploring the formal
complexities of trauma and repression, the narrative opens itself to
the concept of imperfection—whether this is in the form of family
feuds or political futility.

A flexible and situational understanding of praxis would help to
immunize vegan studies against problems like classism and racism, as
well as academic colonization.[4] As Cathryn Bailey notes, "contextual
vegetarianism is not about privileged white theorists condescending
to 'permit' disadvantaged women and people of colour to eat meat,"
because "[i]magining that theory necessarily functions this way is
itself elitist and colonialist" (53). The challenge for vegan studies, then,
is to rethink not only human-animal relations but also the very nature
of philosophical praxis itself. Admittedly, there are few philosophers
outside the Western canon who have referred to critical animal theory
in these exact terms, or by solely reflecting upon the lives of nonhuman animals. This does not mean, however, that interspecies ethics
have not permeated postcolonial reading cultures. Through my textual analysis of the animal imagery, experimental forms, and narrative
nuances in Wicomb's novel, I show that fiction serves the same purpose as theory in overturning anthropocentric discourse to focus on
intersecting struggles.

October is primarily focalized through Mercia Murray, a self-identify-ing "coloured" academic in contemporary Glasgow who journeys to rural South Africa when her brother writes a cryptic letter asking for help with caring for his son.[5] When Mercia returns to her home country, she spends more time looking after her alcoholic brother than her nephew. Much of the narrative involves conversations with her brother's wife, Sylvie. Initially, the female characters appear to be foils: one is a childless and well-traveled "modern woman" whose partner has recently left her in order to start a family (*October* 56, 168), while the other is a rural wife and mother who works part-time at the local butchery (61, 99). As the narrative progresses, however, both its content and form reveal that Mercia and Sylvie have much in common. An absence of quotation marks in the third-person narration and multiple transitions between temporal and geographical set-tings lend a sense of modernist opacity to the text, causing segments of reported speech to seem uncharacteristic or some internal monologue to appear unattributed. By way of illustration, a paragraph that starts from Mercia's observation that "there is no stopping Sylvie when it comes to [talking about] sheep" is transformed into Sylvie's stream-of-consciousness narration as she tells her sister-in-law about "being just a little girl . . . given her first kid" (59), raising the lamb, and then praying to take the animal's place before it is slaughtered. Wordplay and associations are used to further explore repressed memories, such as Sylvie's recollections of "Handwork . . . The good, the holy, done by hand alone. Busy hands to keep you out of trouble. . . . [H]ands [that would] rather make sausages" (99). Mercia's own perspective is rendered complex by references to her autobiography, which she intends to write as a self-reflexive and "ironic depiction of home" (14). Initially, it may appear to the reader that her memoir and the novel are meant to be the same text. However, at the end of the narrative her auto-biography remains incomplete, and the reader is left without so much as an excerpt; we are only told that it is "more invention than memoir" (13). These experimental stylistic choices assist in illuminating the women's shared experiences, such as the fact that they were gifted, precocious chil-dren with aspirations of education and greatness. They are equally ambiv-alent about motherhood and—although they enjoy preparing it—are reluctant to eat meat. But the most important similarity is the plot's central revelation: both were abused by the same man.

Flashbacks set during apartheid initially portray Mercia's father Nicholas as a seemingly upstanding member of the community; the preacher boasts of his partially Scottish heritage and earns the nickname *Meester* ("Master"), a signifier of respect (3). Behind closed doors, however, he chastises his children with a whip which is referred to by the Afrikaans word *aapstert* (23), literally translated as "monkey's tail" (but made from the cured tail of a donkey). In the present, Mercia's truculent brother Jake remembers their deceased father as a "sanctimonious pig" who he "should have had the courage to kill" (178); yet, ironically, he inflicts similar harm upon his own family by threatening them with a butcher's knife (174). Viewed alongside this abusive cycle, wherein images of animals and slaughter recur as a justification or euphemism for masculinist violence, the public image of the supposedly dignified "Master" should be called into question. Yet exchanges between Mercia and her sister-in-law reveal that her father used both his social standing and nonhuman animals to create a violent legacy which extends far beyond his son's drunken threats; toward the end of the narrative, Jake reveals that he may not be the father of Sylvie's child by referring to his wife as his father's "leftovers" (184).

In Sylvie's childhood, Nicholas takes a shine to the young girl, whom he rewards with the gift of a live sheep after she starts to work on his farm. His internalized racism is revealed when she asks him about the spiritual fate of a herd of goats: he likens the "backward" Namaqua people to these "less advanced creatures" (188). To the impressionable Sylvie, the irony of the situation—namely, that both she and Nicholas are coloured—is lost. The socioeconomic element of their relationship intersects with their age and gender identities, creating a threefold power dynamic which he wields over her until he tells her "to unbutton her shirt and free her new breasts, small as green apples" (190). When a farmworker discovers the repeated molestation and reports it, Sylvie is devastated. In a disturbing passage, the young girl asks, "What kind of God was he who interfered so cruelly? The answer: a cruel God" (194). After losing her faith, the young girl regains inner fortitude by working in a butchery: it is only "[w]ith her arms plunged into the alchemy of sausage meat [that] she stopped crying" (194). Here, the reader is aligned with God as a potential judge of Nicholas and his sexual abuse—but a complication arises in the fact that Sylvie *enjoys* her relationship with the older man. A further difficulty is that after being degraded and compared to fruit, she regains her confidence by turning to meat production, the very practice that Carol J. Adams and other ecofeminists argue to be the ultimate signifier of female objectification. When reviewing the reasons why there are feminists who resist ethical vegetarianism or veganism, Bailey remarks that some

may adopt carnist practices in order to deny any emotional connect-
edness to animals and therefore appear "equal to men" (45), while others still might see steaks and other (typically expensive) meat-based
dishes as signifiers of class privilege which are typically denied to those
who are not regarded as fully human (45–46). From this perspective,
the rural girl's decision to work as a butcher could be seen to represent a desire to transcend her class and racial identity, and to enter
the cosmopolitan world which Nicholas claims to inhabit. Certainly,
she does initially use sausages as a very literal signifier of social status,
even going so far as to wrap herself in *boerewors* "like a rich silk scarf"
and take a series of risqué photographs (101–02).[6] She also repeatedly
asserts that she does not want to be mistaken for a mother and that
meat "may be damp as babies, but she knows which she prefers" (102,
99). To the young girl, then, it appears that a homely fellow-feeling
with all creatures is naïve and limiting, whereas the production of sausages is a lucrative business which can help her to gain autonomy.

This reading, however, does not account for the (seemingly contradictory) decisions that Sylvie and her sister-in-law make. The former's
paradoxical attitudes to conformity and carnism are displayed early
in the narrative, such as when she claims to always slaughter her own
sheep and is then guiltily relieved when Mercia asks her not to do so
(57, 61). It is also important to note that her relationship with meat
processing is not simple: she initially finds the cleaver to be terrify-
ing (99) and is disgusted when she realizes that the sausage wrapped
around her resembles a penis (103). Mercia's classist complicity in
omnivorous eating habits similarly highlights how issues of gender,
race, and social standing intersect. In Glasgow, she initially trades on
her cultural background as exoticized capital by hosting dinner parties
and cooking traditional Cape Malay dishes. However, one night she
reveals to her guests that this traditional food was created by necessity by "slaves from Goa, Malaysia, East Africa, sizzling their spices
in the shadow of Table Mountain," after which her partner Craig pretends that she "had had too much to drink" because "[n]o one said
that eating meat was not nice" (171). Her concern about racial equality is therefore silenced by the rationalist discourse of a white, British
man who admits elsewhere that he has only visited South Africa once
and therefore has little conception of her home country's complex history (51). As Sylvie prepares a batch of minced meat, Mercia imagines
that "an even, steady sausage of speech issues from the girl's mouth,"
and admits that she "is embarrassed, critical of her own snobbery, but

really there is no chance of correcting herself while the girl shouts as if she were in another room" (31). Here, meat codes conversely to how it did for the young Sylvie; that is, Mercia sees *boerewors* as a symbol for her sister-in-law's unerudite language, which is further associated with the poverty which her father encouraged her to escape by studying and earning scholarships. She is therefore partially complicit in the elitist, hegemonic narrative which dismisses her own experiences as a coloured woman.

As she matures, Sylvie seemingly overcomes her fears of fertility and becomes a hyperbolic example of a "natural mother" by marrying Nicholas and giving birth to a son, whom she breastfeeds until he is five (4). By choosing to continue with her job, she defies stereotypical, dualistic associations of motherhood with pastoralism and working womanhood with unemotional ruthlessness. Yet the butcher repeatedly ruminates on Dorpers or "Chosen Sheep" from her childhood, which are so named because they are "[c]hosen for this arid veld where they'd eat anything, chosen for their fecundity, and for being such good mothers" (188). The implication is that the rural wife who prepares and eats "anything" is like livestock that is conditioned to be docile and domesticated—and, furthermore, expected to produce offspring. These flashbacks to her younger years problematize her apparent enjoyment of her roles as a working wife and mother. The mirroring of procreative responsibilities between human and non-human cosmopolitan subjects thus highlights the ambivalence which many women may feel toward gender expectations and normalized eating practices, and the sacrifices involved with conforming to a masculinist and carnist society's ideals.

Although Sylvie is only a few years her junior, Mercia repeatedly refers to her as "the girl" (53)—an infantalizing term which is steeped in South Africa's colonial history of slavery and oppression. The irony is that while her sister-in-law has had a child (which, in repronormative traditions, is the ultimate rite of passage into womanhood), she has not. She struggles to even relate with children as an extended family member: when her nephew asks if humans eat tortoises, for instance, she is "horrified" (155). Mercia's own mother views the preparation of meat-based dinners reluctantly: she prepares beef stews and similar dishes for her family, but avoids eating flesh by serving herself smaller portions containing bones. No ethical reasons are ever vocalized for these actions. However, it is important to note that Nettie's words are only ever recalled through her daughter's narrative;

her *own* voice is never granted autonomy. Mercia recalls that her mother was also averse to raising children, but concluded that both cooking and childbearing were a "duty" which a "good wife" must fulfil (119, 114). Nettie's misgivings about meat and squeamishness when breastfeeding, however, have a negative impact upon her bond with her daughter. Her struggle to nurse Mercia—who, in turn, finds it difficult to form close emotional attachments with others—foregrounds the traditionalist concern that "one creates one's own identity *and those of one's children* through foodways" (Bailey 47; my italics). To deviate from foods favored by omnivorously normative culture, it is implied, is to risk alienation or isolation; as the protagonist ages, she finds that she neither has the tenacity to kill animals, nor the desire to abandon her freedom in favor of repronormativity. Similarly to how the toxic masculinity of the (symbolic and literal) father is transmitted to Jake, it is implied that Mercia's "growing fastidiousness about meat" and other normalized symbols of "cultural refinement" like idealized motherhood is a symptom not only of broader societal influences (168–69), but also of her troubled upbringing.

Given these achronological and varied meditations on relationships with both food and fellow creatures, one may wonder whether the text advocates *any* form of ethical certainty. At this point, it is vital to focus on the various instances of culinary hospitality which occur throughout the text. When Sylvie hesitates at the thought of slaughtering a sheep to welcome Mercia, she chooses instead to wake early and bake *roosterbrood* as a "substitution" (60).[7] Her choice to serve an ascetic dish which is free from all animal products may seem coincidental upon first reading, but I would argue that this decision deliberately foregrounds the possibility of situational veganism in transcultural scenarios. After Mercia expresses her pleasure in eating the bread, her sister-in-law responds, "take back some of my culture in a Tupperware, just add flour and warm water and leave in a warm place" (55). The pun indicates that Sylvie's willingness to share the yeast (a living organism) is not only an extension of hospitable warmth, but also an invitation for her to partake in those traditional practices which she is still comfortable performing. Furthermore, this "breaking of bread" evokes an earlier exchange of rare compassion between Mercia's parents: when a weak Nettie struggles to nurse, Nicholas picks lucerne from a pasture, packs it on buttered bread and convinces her to eat. By serving "cow's food" alongside a dairy product (116), he surprisingly deviates from the carnist stipulation that only meat can provide adequate nutrition for humans.[8] Another formulation of a flexible food exchange is exemplified by Mercia's vegetarian Scottish friends, who "allow [her] to bring along [her] own frying pan and pig chops" when they invite her on a weeklong camping trip (68). All of these small, simple acts show that while food is an important component of cultural identity, it does not follow that it should be a dividing force which causes groups to distinguish between "us" and "others."[9] Promoting veganism as "the" feminist way of eating is problematic, because women's bodies and choices are already policed enough by patriarchal culture. Instead, these interpersonal exchanges suggest that we should imagine dietary preferences as "a mean *relative to us*, falling on a continuum between the vice of doing injustice to ourselves, on the one hand, and the vice of doing injustice to others, on the other" (Van Dyke 40; original italics). In other words, the women's memories reveal how one's relationship with food overlaps with connections to both friends and family.

As Mercia returns to her cosmopolitan life, however, it remains dubious whether communal and situational veganism can be applicable when miscommunication often remains an issue. After learning about the sexual abuse, she leaves South Africa, imagining that Sylvie "must wish she were a fucking tortoise" so that she too could escape and begin a new life elsewhere (220). She then visits the University of Macau for a job interview. In the campus gardens she is "drawn to the strange movements of a small turtle," which provokes the following rumination:

> Perhaps, unlike its land cousin, the tortoise, who can walk away from its eggs, this lot left against nature in the same pond, thrown together in the same waters as their parents, will not be abandoned. Will keep on circling the elder in abject supplication. Will stutter through those quivering hands, Acknowledge me, it is I I I I . . . (234)

In this internal monologue, which is imbedded in the third-person narration, experimental form is evoked again by repetition of the first-person singular pronoun.[10] It is important to note the absence of subjects in the sentences beginning "will keep" and "will stutter," which implies a slippage between nonhuman babies and the human self. Mercia's fellow-feeling for Sylvie (and, by implication, the turtles) is therefore motivated not so much by an empathetic urge, but rather by memories of her *own* trauma and abandonment. Her self-involvement is confirmed when she returns to South Africa following the death of her brother. After Mercia offers to take her nephew back to Glasgow, the widow flies into a rage which resonates with the earlier meditations on meat and maternal roles: "I'm his mother. *Even a sheep screams when its lamb is taken*, so how could I have asked you to take him away? *What do you think I am*?" (238; my italics). Here, Sylvie's use of pronouns contrasts strongly with her sister-in-law's description of the personified tortoise. Referring to herself with the word *what* rather than "who," she implicitly accuses Mercia of dehumanizing her by questioning her agency and authority. Yet the final words of the novel, which are focalized through the butcher, are just as problematic as Mercia's misplaced sympathy. She assures her son that "one day he will visit Auntie Mercy in England" (239), but this statement is factually inaccurate for three reasons. Perhaps the most obvious is the name that has been anglicized to mimic one of the humanist virtues from the faith which Sylvie abandoned,[11] implying that she views her semi-vegetarian sister-in-law as sanctimonious. Second, Mercia has recently learned that she may not only be the child's aunt, but also his half-sister. The third and final irony is that she lives in Scotland, not England. It is of the utmost importance that Sylvie simultaneously misrepresents facts about Mercia's life while being misunderstood. The implication of her insincere promise is that *both* parties are complicit in forming biases based on class, race, sex, or species terms. The fiction's experimentally styled form serves to show that worldliness inevitably involves disordered and contradictory transcultural exchanges with others in a community of human and nonhuman subjects.

The very conclusion of the novel thus resists resolution of the many ethical dilemmas which it raises. There is an ongoing negotiation between rural and urban settings, characters and imagery—but these forces do not constitute a simple binary. Rather, the cosmopolitan aspects of the text capture a variety of contradictory contemporary attitudes toward human and nonhuman others, rendered into futher complexity by the recurrence of repressed trauma and gendered abuse. Through Sylvie's defiance of her husband and his sister, it is implied that rendering carnist practices as simply "unethical" does nothing to fight the hegemonic system of binaries which has historically naturalized the oppression of poor and/or black women.

Simultaneously, however, Mercia's unsolicited sympathy merely cements barriers between social groups. To avoid both elitist moralising *and* the reinforcement of poverty cycles, therefore, we should recognize that there is no singular way to live ethically, but rather multiple "starting-points" for varying situations (Deckha 541). These exchanges will inevitably be imperfect, as transcultural living often involves miscommunication. Furthermore, it is seemingly impossible to avoid being at least partly complicit with causing suffering. Yet *October* approaches the idea of culinary hospitality with nuanced language and terms, thereby rethinking ideas of personhood in locally situated conditions. "Food relationships" between human and nonhuman subjects are troubled by the novel's form, plot, and symbolism, gesturing toward an understanding of veganism that embraces conflict, futility, and imperfection. It is suggested that the words "vegetarian" or "vegan" should not signify a singular and self-congratulatory identity. Rather, the "vegan" is a lived value that should hold practical application around the globe. Perhaps there are ways for us to replace the individualist adage "you are what you eat" with visions which are less obsessive over moral perfectionism, and more concerned with how *we* can move forward.

WORKS CITED

Adams, Carol J. *The Sexual Politics of Meat: A Feminist-Vegetarian Critical Theory*. New York: Continuum, 2010.

Armstrong, Philip. "The Postcolonial Animal." *Society & Animals* 10, no. 4 (2002): 413–19.

Bailey, Cathryn. "We Are What We Eat: Feminist Vegetarianism and the Reproduction of Racial Identity." *Hypatia* 22, no. 2 (2007): 39–59.

Crenshaw, Kimberlé. "Demarginalizing the Intersection of Race and Sex: A Black Feminist Critique of Antidiscrimination Doctrine, Feminist Theory and Antiracist Politics." *The University of Chicago Legal Forum* 140 (1989): 139–67.

Deckha, Maneesha. "Toward a Postcolonial Posthumanist Feminist Theory: Centralizing Race and Culture in Feminist Work on Nonhuman Animals." *Hypatia* 27.3 (2012): 527–45.

Dodd, Alexandra. "Thinking Outside of the Cage." *South African Vegan Society*, August 1, 2016. http://vegansociety.org.za/news/thinking-outside-of-the-cage/.

Dominick, Brian A. "Animal Liberation and Social Revolution: A Vegan Perspective on Anarchism or an Anarchist Perspective on Veganism." The Anarchist Library, August 1996. https://theanarchistlibrary.org/library/brian-a-dominick-animal-liberation-and-social-revolution.

Driver, Dorothy. "Zoë Wicomb and the Cape Cosmopolitan." *Current Writing* 23, no. 2 (2011): 93–107.

Goswami, Danavir. "Dairy Krishna." Dandavats, November 12, 2007. www.dandavats.com/?p=4745.

Hamblin, James. "1922: Strength and Vigour Depend on What You Eat." *The Atlantic*, April 1, 2014 *www.theatlantic.com/health/archive/2014/04/1922-strength-and-vigor-depend-on-what-you-eat/284604/*.

Harper, A. Breeze. *Sistah Vegan: Black Female Vegans Speak on Food, Identity, Health, and Society*. Brooklyn: Lantern, 2010. Kindle.

Joyce, James. *Ulysses*. London: Wordsworth, 2013.

Nagai, Kaori. Introduction to *Cosmopolitan Animals, 1–6*. Edited by Kaori Nagai, et al. Basingstoke: Palgrave Macmillan, 2015.

Nyman, Jopi. *Postcolonial Animal Tale from Kipling to Coetzee*. New Delhi: Atlantic, 2003.

Seneca, Lucius Annaeus. "Epistolae ad Lucilium." In *Ethical Vegetarianism: From Pythagoras to Peter Singer*. Edited by Kerry S. Walters and Lisa Portmess, 23–26. Albany: SUNY Press, 1999.

Twine, Richard. "Vegan Killjoys at the Table: Contesting Happiness and Negotiating Relationships with Food Practices." *Societies* 4 (2014): 624–39.

Van Dyke, Christina. "Manly Meat and Gendered Eating: Correcting Imbalance and Seeking Virtue." In *Philosophy Comes to Dinner: Arguments about the Ethics of Eating*. Edited by Andrew Chignell, Terence Cuneo, and Matthew C. Halteman, 39–55. New York: Routledge, 2016.

"Vegetarians Also Enjoy a Braai, Broer." *Vegetarian Society of South Africa* (2016): 22 www.vegsoc.org.za/index.php?option=com_content&task=view&id=144&Itemid=1.

Wicomb, Zoë. "Five Afrikaner Texts and the Rehabilitation of Whiteness." *Social Identities* 4, no. 3 (1998): 363–83.

——. *October : A Novel*. London: The New Press, 2014. Kindle.

Woodward, Wendy. "The Nonhuman Animal and Levinasian Otherness: Contemporary Narratives and Criticism." *Current Writing* 21, no. 1–2 (2009): 342–62.

——, and Erika Lemmer. "Figuring the Animal in Post-apartheid South Africa." *Journal of Literary Studies* 30, no. 4 (2014): 1–5.

END NOTES

1. A more detailed example is a recently published book of essays titled *Cosmopolitan Animals* (2015), which opens with the declaration that nonhuman organisms should be viewed alongside humans as experiencing subjects in contemporary contexts. Drawing on the Greek origins of the term "cosmopolitan," Kaori Nagai asserts in this collection's introduction that "we have to start by redefining 'a cosmos' as a tangled-up 'knot of species coshaping one another,' rather than as an orderly 'good world'" (2).

2. Twine's research was conducted in the United Kingdom, where poverty and food shortage are comparatively uncommon in relation to developing countries. Such findings may not be true for other regions.

3. Coined by Kimberlé Crenshaw to highlight the disjuncture between mainstream (white) feminism and the civil rights movement, "intersectionality" objects to approaching rights struggles as singular issues in a "top-down approach" (Crenshaw 167). The term has since been used to show that one must consider how subjects can fall victim to various disadvantages due to ableist, classist, heterosexist, racist, or sexist prejudices.

4. During a conference titled Towards a Vegan Theory hosted by the University of Oxford in May 2016, many delegates returned to two prominent problems. The first was that the movement's relative youth means that it remains unclear what exactly vegan studies *is*—or, rather, what it could grow to become. Second, scholars alluded to the dangers of "academic colonisation" in animal rights circles—a potentially ironic observation, given that the event took place at one of the world's most prestigious universities.

5. In South Africa, the term "coloured" is used to refer to people of mixed ethnic descent—particularly those whose ancestors were South- and Southeast Asian slaves. Even in the post-transitional democracy, such groups mostly embrace this term, viewing it as a source of "mythologised" pride (Wicomb, "Five Afrikaner Texts" 363).

6. *Boerewors* is an inexpensive form of coiled sausage which evokes references as disparate as Afrikaner nationalism, coloured cultural identity, and (in Wicomb's fiction) James Joyce's *Ulysses* (Driver 101).

7. *Roosterbrood* is traditional bread made using activated yeast, similar in consistency to sourdough.

8. The gesture also serves to implicitly highlight the mammalian connection between cows and humans: both species only produce milk to feed their young. This fact is often unaddressed by corporatized dairy farms.

9. Driver notes that in Wicomb's earlier fiction, coloured characters often refer to traditional dishes with the collective term "*ons kos*" (105; my italics), meaning "our food."

10. Mercia's reflection on interconnected species calls to mind earlier acoustic-phonetic effects, such as Jake's repetition of the phrase "Bu-ullshit" (15–16), or the young Sylvie's recurring concern that she is known as a "loose goose" (195–97).

11. Earlier in the narrative the protagonist refuses to be called by the nickname Mercy after she learns that the name Mercia refers to an English-speaking region of South Africa that was inhabited by Namaqua people (26). Therefore, it is dubious that Sylvie intends this word to be a fond diminutive.

CHAPTER 9

Estonia

The Rise of Veganism in Post-Socialist Europe: Making Sense of Emergent Vegan Practices and Identities in Estonia

Kadri Aavik

Within the emerging field of vegan studies, veganism as a cultural practice and personal identity has been explored mainly in Western societies and cultures, such as the US (Wright). However, these observations on veganism are not necessarily representative of vegan identities and practices elsewhere in the world. Veganism as an emerging social and cultural phenomenon is likely to be empirically and conceptually different in other social, cultural, and political settings. This essay explores veganism as a nascent social and cultural practice in the post-socialist context via the example of Estonia, a small EU member state, which regained its independence in 1991 after the collapse of the Soviet Union. Veganism has thus far received little scholarly attention in this region. The concept and practice began to arise and slowly enter mainstream consciousness in Estonia only since the mid-2000s. Yet particularly the last couple of years have witnessed "a vegan boom" in Estonia, with growing interest in veganism and the number of vegans rising, particularly among the younger generations.[1] Additionally, there has been a considerable increase in vegan food options, especially in bigger cities, and veganism is becoming increasingly visible in mainstream culture.

In this chapter, I unpack the politics and challenges of being vegan in contemporary Estonia—a setting where access to a vegan identity was impossible until very recently. I discuss three ways in which we could begin to study veganism in this context. My principal point is that veganism should be understood not only as a personal lifestyle choice, but also as a political practice. As such, I will argue that this duality is best understood in intersectional terms. Second, I consider veganism in Estonia vis-à-vis mainstream culture and point out some social and cultural norms that veganism disrupts. As a third and final issue, I briefly explore vegan consumption's uneasy relationship with capitalism. This chapter will argue that studying these three dimensions relating to veganism will help to paint a more nuanced and intersectional picture of veganism, one that is situated within political practice enmeshed in power relations and structures. This analysis might be useful for vegans and scholars in Estonia and in other societies where veganism is an emergent phenomenon (such as in the post-socialist countries) to reflect on the histories, current meanings, and future directions of veganism in these spaces.

Stemming from my own academic and personal situatedness as a feminist sociologist and vegan, I explore the issues introduced above through an intersectional and sociological feminist lens. In my approach to veganism, I also draw on insights from critical animal studies and ecofeminism, highlighting the interlinked nature of oppressions (see for example Glasser 53; Adams). I do not consider veganism as simply a dietary choice or lifestyle, but always a political project (Jenkins and Twine), enmeshed in various power relations, even if those who engage in it do not explicitly always see it as such. In my view, any sociological analysis should take into account this political dimension of veganism, as well as see vegan practices as situated in particular social and cultural contexts. This latter insight has implications for ways in which we conceptualize veganism and vegans. Beyond the common key commitment of abstaining from animal products, veganism is manifested differently and might mean different things to vegan individuals and communities located in various parts of the world. It might thus be more apt to speak of veganisms, to acknowledge this diversity on a global scale.

THE EMERGENCE OF THE ESTONIAN VEGAN MOVEMENT

Insofar as definitions of social movements (see for example Diani) typically entail elements such as groups of actors building and sharing a collective identity, exchanging information through (informal) networks, and a shared focus on particular political or social issues with the aim of bringing about (or resisting) social change, collective vegan practices in Estonia today can certainly be understood as a social movement.

Curiously, the escalating emergence of veganism has not been pre-ceded by a vegetarian movement, as is common in many Western societies where vegetarianism, with its more comfortable relationship to the mainstream, has paved the way and helped veganism to fight for public recognition, as Wright (32–36) has noted about American culture. Vegetarians, many of whose motivations are primarily related to health and not necessarily a clear agenda of animal justice, have not engaged in collective identity-building around their vegetarianism as mainly a dietary choice, as vegans have around veganism, which in Estonia arose out of concerns for animal lives. Even today, key vegan and animal advocacy activists work closely together, although division between those two areas is increasingly taking place.

In part, historical reasons account for the absence of a vegetarian movement and vegetarian identity in Estonia. The Soviet regime did not enable any independent social movements to emerge, including collective identity building and practices around food and consump-tion. When part of the Soviet Union, Estonia was cut off from infor-mation from the West. Furthermore, food choices were limited and people only had access to basic foods in the Soviet Union.

The first decade post-independence in the early 1990s was character-ized by major uncertainty, as the country was going through the transi-tion to democracy. Many people were struggling to establish basic levels of material security, which made it difficult for any social movements to emerge that did not concern the immediate well-being of people. Since post-independence, processes of Westernization began to take place in Estonia and the country became increasingly connected to the global flows of capital and information. Internet began to spread in Estonia during the second half of 1990s, which greatly facilitated access to infor-mation previously inaccessible to Estonians. The first information on veganism in the Estonian language started to appear online only around the mid-2000s, translated from the English language by local vegans and vegan activists.[2] While inspiration and information on veganism were (and are often still) drawn from online English-language resources and communities, to say that veganism was simply a Western import unduly simplifies the narrative of how veganism developed in Estonia and underestimates the agency of Estonian vegans in selecting and engag-ing with particular ideas deemed relevant for the local context. This representation risks reproducing the colonial discourse of the "supe-riority" of Western knowledge and its gradual but inevitable spread to other (non-Western) parts of the world as part of a "modernizing" or "civilizing" mission. It is more accurate to conceptualize the emergence of veganism in Estonia as a complex interaction between particular information and ideas borrowed from elsewhere with local knowledge, historical circumstances, traditions, and social practices. This involves active and critical engagement with these ideas, rather than their passive reception.

Vegans in Estonia began to connect, socialize, and engage in activism through online channels in the mid-2000s. In 2012, the Estonian Vegan Society was established. It has been a purely voluntary organization but has recently started taking steps to fund-raise and create paid positions. The Vegan Society and its key activists have been instrumental in bringing together vegans and those interested in veganism, establishing and maintaining the Facebook groups where Estonian vegans interact. Everyday community building and "identity work" (Snow and Anderson) is still largely taking place online, with occasional offline meet-ups.[3] For Estonian vegans and particularly the Vegan Society, this online presence has had an amplifying effect—leaving the impression that the organization is bigger than the actual small core group of volunteers.

In 2018, we can speak of an increasingly active and visible vegan community, which is gradually diversifying. It includes more and more people whose motivations are not necessarily embedded in animal ethics, but stem, for example, from health and fitness considerations. Subgroups within the movement have begun to emerge in recent years, around nodes of interest such as vegan parenting, vegan fitness, etc. Also, members of the vegan community can be differentiated according to their level of involvement—ranging from key activists for whom veganism and vegan activism forms a central part of their identity, to those more loosely associated with the movement. For example, a large proportion of participants in the popular Estonian Facebook group focused on food and food images titled "Yes, it's vegan!," including many non-vegans interested in vegan food. Hence, the boundaries of the Estonian vegan movement are rather blurry, and notions of a coherent community can be illusory.

VEGANISM AS MORE THAN IDENTITY: STRUCTURAL AND INTERSECTIONAL CONSIDERATIONS

It has become a tendency in much of contemporary sociological research to focus on identities and lifestyles. Studying identity, often conceptualized as a personal project linked to individual lifestyle choices, gives consideration to individual agency but does not often pay sufficient attention to structural limitations that individuals face. This approach risks overshadowing issues of material inequality and class, rooted in Marxist thought, and hence obscuring the fact that some individuals and groups have more limited capacity for making "lifestyle choices" than others, stemming from the way they are positioned in the social hierarchy.

Veganism, when taken up as a scholarly subject matter, can easily lend itself to the former type of analysis. Indeed, definitions of veganism, including by vegans themselves, typically conceptualize it as "a way of living," consciously chosen for ethical, health, and/or environmental reasons. In practice, it is associated primarily with making alternative consumption choices. Studying veganism as a personal identity places emphasis on individual choices (such as choices around consumption), leaving aside power relations, ways in which food choices are always political (Lavin; Jenkins and Twine), and how marginalized social groups are limited in making "lifestyle choices." To counteract the former tendency, veganism should be studied as a situated collective practice enmeshed with systems and relations of power. A good place to begin this kind of analysis would be to take an intersectional perspective on the vegan movement in Estonia and those who are part of it.

Intersectionality is an analytical framework apt for exploring social differences, identities, and power relations, originating from black feminist thought (see for example Crenshaw 1989, 1991; Hill Collins 1990, 1993). This approach emphasizes the intertwined nature of socially constructed categories of identity and difference, such as gender, race, class, age, and others. Intersections of these categories acquire meanings in relation to each other to produce social hierarchies and unique experiences (of privilege and/or disadvantage) for individuals and groups differently positioned in terms of these divisions.[4] The issue of membership of the community, particularly in terms of (invisible) barriers of participation and who gets included and excluded, is one that individuals and groups, as part of the Estonian vegan community (and indeed in many vegan movements elsewhere in the world) rarely critically reflect on. Yet this is a matter of social justice and has implications for the spread of veganism and its potential to form ties with other social movements.

Some scholarly attention has been paid to questions of privilege and inequalities in relation to animal advocacy and vegan movements, mostly in the North American context. It has been pointed out that these movements primarily consist of privileged individuals in terms of race and class (Harper; Nocella); veganism is an identity category "marked by whiteness" in the US (Wright 31). Also, gender has been examined in this context (see Gaarder). Sexist advertising used by PETA, one of the most visible organizations promoting veganism, goes against feminist commitments (Glasser). These findings suggest that intersectional sensitivities in the vegan movement could well be sharpened.

I have previously looked at membership of the animal advocacy movement in the Baltic countries from an intersectional perspective (Aavik, "The Animal Advocacy Movement"). As important parts of vegan and animal rights communities in Estonia overlap, the same insights largely apply to the Estonian vegan community as well.[5]

Similar to many Western contexts, vegans in Estonia share a familiar demographic profile: they are typically educated, urban, young, white, ethnic-majority women.[6] This has implications for the dominant representations of veganism and vegans. Below, I will briefly consider three categories—gender, class, and ethnicity—and some of their intersections in the context of veganism in Estonia.

In terms of gender, Estonia exhibits some of the largest inequalities in the EU, such as the largest gender pay gap (26.9 percent) (Eurostat 2015) as well as high gender-based employment segregation (Bettio and Verashchagina). While traditional notions of masculinity and femininity are slow to disappear, segments of the younger generation are increasingly challenging traditional ways of doing gender. In recent years, feminist ideas have started to gradually reach mainstream audiences through social media (for example, via the popular feminist blog Feministeerium.ee).

Among vegans in Estonia, one finds significantly more vegan women than men, for similar reasons as elsewhere, such as gendered socialization encouraging girls to be more emphatic than boys. Also, as in many other countries, civil society activism is underpaid and undervalued, resulting in a vegan advocacy workforce that is overwhelmingly female.

When examining gender in the context of the Estonian vegan movement, it would be fruitful to pay closer attention to masculinities, the traditionally unmarked dimension of the category of gender. Traditional anti-egalitarian masculinities are still prevalent in Estonia today, even in novel social situations (Pajumets). Veganism could largely be seen as incompatible with notions of hegemonic masculinity (Connell 1987; Connell and Messerschmidt). As in most Western societies, meat eating is an important element in the construction of masculinities (Adams) in Estonia.

Yet as in other cultures, what could be considered "alternative masculinities" are starting to emerge, under which the practices of many vegan men would fall. In this light, it would be interesting to study vegan men to understand how they negotiate vegan masculinity, as it has been already done in Western contexts (see for example Adams; Potts and Parry; Rothgerber; Wright 107–29). Further studies could focus on the following questions, among others. Whether and how does veganism encourage enacting alternative masculinities in Estonia? Whether and how do vegan masculinities disrupt traditional notions of what it means to be a man in Estonia? Whether—and in which ways—do vegan men continue to retain male privilege and benefit from the patriarchal dividend (Connell; Gender 142)? Here it is again crucial to take an intersectional perspective to appreciate how men's veganism is intertwined with their positioning in terms of ethnicity, class, age, etc., as well as their politics and practices in relation to feminism, nationalism, capitalism, etc. Indeed, going vegan might not necessarily constitute a threat to men's sense and doing of masculinity. As some exampes from Western popular culture demonstrate, vegan men might emphasize some elements of hegemonic masculinity in their everyday practices, such as bodybuilding or drinking (see, for example, Vegan Bros, veganbodybuilding.com).

The gender split in the Estonian vegan movement has implications for establishing romantic and intimate vegan partnerships. Heterosexual vegan women might find it challenging to find a vegan man as a partner. Given this reality, many are faced with a choice of whether to remain single or to enter into a relationship with non-vegan men, which many do. Hence, it becomes important to consider issues around intimate and sexual relationships, including vegansexuality—the preference of some vegans to form sexual and intimate relationships exclusively with other vegans (Potts and Parry 53). How are conflicts around veganism negotiated on a daily basis in relationships where one partner is vegan and the other is not? How are such conflicts gendered in heterosexual relationships? What does this tell us about the functioning of patriarchy, hegemonic masculinity, and the gender order?

Looking at the vegan movement in Estonia in terms of class presents a somewhat complicated picture. The category of class itself is ambiguous in the post-socialist space. The Soviet regime obliterated the class system emerging in Estonia prior to its occupation. Yet while socioeconomic inequalities in post-socialist European societies are rising, they are typically not conceptualized through the notion of class. For example, Estonia is one of the most unequal societies in Europe,[7] yet talking about inequality here is unpopular (Helemäe and Saar). This is partly due to the prevalence of neoliberal logic, which largely dismisses structural inequalities.

In Western societies, vegan identities are typically associated with privileged class positions; however, this does not necessarily apply to Estonia. While some vegans come from relatively privileged socioeconomic backgrounds, many, particularly young students, may grapple with economic insecurity. For example, most key vegan and animal advocacy activists hold full-time jobs elsewhere, which in some cases involves unskilled work. However, I argue that their ability to go vegan and engage in vegan activism is facilitated by their privileged position in terms of other social divisions—they are young, members of an ethnic-majority, educated, internet-savvy, fluent in English, and live predominantly in urban areas. Many less privileged people might not be able to afford to spend extra time and effort to go vegan. This is particularly evident for example with older Russian-speakers in rural areas lacking vegan communities and in places where information and vegan products tend to be difficult to access.

This brings me to the category of ethnicity. Social divisions in Estonia are seen primarily along ethnic, not racial, lines, with ethnicity being a politicized category. Estonia's Russian-speaking community (around 25 percent of the population) remains largely separate from Estonians. Rather meager attempts at integration of the two ethno-linguistic communities by successive governments have largely been unfruitful. Despite optimistic hopes in the public discourse that younger generations, especially with the improved Estonian-language skills of Russian-speaking youth and the generally greater open-mindedness attributed to younger generations, will be able to bridge this divide, this division has proved to be notoriously challenging to navigate.

This ethnic divide manifests itself well in the Estonian vegan community and has not shown much change over recent years. Russian-speaking people are virtually absent from Estonian vegan circles, including from the membership of the Estonian Vegan Society. This includes absence from Estonian-language social media communities focused on veganism. There is a Facebook page and a related Instagram page[8]—both with modest numbers of followers—run by a Russian-speaking vegan activist, in the Russian language, with only very few Estonian followers.

There are several reasons for a lack of Russian-speakers in the Estonian vegan community. They face some similar barriers that affect people of color in many Western countries, such as in the US: marginalization due to a stigmatized racial or ethnic identity position and/or citizenship status constitutes structural obstacles that might make going vegan difficult. For example, nearly 20 percent of Russians in Estonia do not have Estonian citizenship, or indeed the citizenship of any country.[9] The fact that white and ethnic majority groups do not have to deal with the negative consequences of racial or ethnic discrimination and issues related to equal citizenship rights makes it easier for them to consider veganism. Globally, veganism is far more common among the privileged. In part, it is the lack of discrimination that enables people to consider options outside the norm.

Also, reasons include lack of other vegans (as role models) in minority communities and poor availability of vegan food options—for example, Russian-speakers in Estonia are concentrated in Eastern Estonia and in parts of Tallinn and other cities that provide very limited vegan options when eating out.

Barriers of language and access to information are also important. While most young Russians are fluent in Estonian, their parents and grandparents (older generations) are less so. Many receive most of their information through Russian state media. This, exacerbated by spatial segregation in many cases, leaves them in a social vacuum, which prevents them from learning about veganism.

Privileges based on gender, ethnicity, and class that I have discussed here, and their intersections, generally remain invisible to those who enjoy them. Hence there is a need for more critical reflection on the membership of the Estonian vegan movement on the part of its activists and participants. This is not only important for the spread of veganism, but also an issue of social justice. Further studies on vegans and vegan identities in Estonia should therefore take into account the structural positioning of vegans. Other social categories of difference and identity, such as age, sexual orientation, and able-bodiedness, and their intersections, should also be considered. Tackling these issues is important empirically, theoretically, methodologically, as well as politically.

THE RELATION OF VEGANISM TO THE MAINSTREAM CULTURE AND INSTITUTIONS

Similar to other countries, veganism in Estonia occupies an uneasy position in relation to mainstream culture. From around ten to fifteen years ago, when the phenomenon of veganism gradually started to emerge in the public sphere, its visibility has increased significantly, facilitated by the rise of social media. Today, vegan issues frequently find their way to the mainstream media. However, most coverage in the Estonian media has been of a negative nature, highlighting the dangers of veganism to human health (particularly regarding children) and its nutritional inadequacies. The major coverage of veganism in the Estonian mainstream media in March 2017 could be understood as an episode of nationwide moral panic, which unfolded following the publication of a newspaper article quoting the head of the Estonian Pediatric Association declaring that "veganism forced on small children might be life threatening." [10] In other instances of more positive coverage, veganism is reduced to a lifestyle project or diet, as when vegan recipes are introduced to readers. As a further project in vegan studies in Estonia, a discourse analysis of media representations of veganism would be crucial.

While veganism is still marginal culturally, it is even more so in terms of its institutional reception, for example its acceptance by hegemonic institutions and bodies of knowledge, particularly by the medical and nutrition establishments. As in other cultures, traditions and social norms around what constitutes "proper eating" are deeply rooted in Estonia and are enmeshed with academic knowledge production in the discipline of nutrition. One of the biggest challenges that Estonian vegans face today concerns the virtually universal condemnation of veganism by doctors and nutritionists. This is well reflected in the national dietary guidelines, the key document establishing the country's official discourse on nutrition. My analysis of the latest nutrition guidelines from a vegan perspective (see Aavik, "Nonhuman Animals") demonstrates that eating animal-based foods is deemed essential by the authors (leading nutrition experts in Estonia) of the guidelines and veganism is declared as unsuitable for human health. Veganism is labeled a "self-restricted diet," reducing it to a personal choice without any political motives. This language of "restriction" is also problematic for other reasons. For example, it implies that one has to limit what one eats when, more often than not, becoming vegan in fact increases the diversity of one's diet (for a more extended critique of this language used in the Estonian dietary guidelines, see Aavik, "Nonhuman Animals").[11]

The implications and material consequences of these dietary guidelines for vegans are dire, affecting their lives on a daily basis. Based on the guidelines, public institutions such as schools and hospitals will compile their menus, and medical professionals will advise patients. Vegans will not receive institutional support, but will likely be ostracized. If doctors and nutritionists declare veganism as nutritionally inadequate, it will likely not be taken up by large segments of the population.

Given this state of affairs, becoming and staying vegan in Estonia is a rather disruptive and even risky move, as it means challenging established scientific discourses in nutrition and medicine and the practices following from them. This is no easy task, especially for young vegans such as teenagers, who still depend on their parents, nor for pregnant women and young mothers, who are particularly demonized.

The consumption of animal-based foods is linked to nationalist ideas around proper eating, just as Wright (39) describes the perceived sanctity of "American" food. Nationalist ideas around food are in turn intertwined with the capitalist system of production. There are state-endorsed campaigns to promote local foods and the interests of local Estonian businesses, including, notably, the dairy and meat industries, who continue to receive significant subsidies from the state. Indeed, authors of the new nutrition guidelines explicitly declare that among the factors taken into account in compiling the guidelines are Estonian large- and small-scale production, supply, and consumption patterns (Pitsi et al). Evoking elements of the capitalist system of production in this context indicates the intertwined nature of medical and nutritional knowledge and business interests. A leading Estonian nutritionist and member of the team of authors of the national nutrition guidelines is closely associated with and holds several patents in an Estonian venture where scientists and the dairy industry cooperate to create "healthy dairy products,"[12] an obvious conflict of interest that remains unproblematized by everyone except vegans. Ironically, as the promotion of (especially locally produced) meat and dairy in diet seems to originate from a "neutral position," one of genuine concern over public health, representing "proper" and "healthy" eating. This is an indication of how culturally normalized meat and dairy are in Estonia.

Given this climate, vegans find themselves with the discursively and materially difficult task of challenging these norms established and upheld by enmeshed hegemonic discourses of nutrition, nationalism, and capitalist interests.

Future research could consider, in detail, the ways in which veganism and vegans are constructed as a threat—such as to traditional eating habits, the nationalist project, gender norms, etc.—in mainstream discourses, and how vegans in fact disrupt these established norms through their everyday practices.

In a culture that marginalizes veganism, it would be crucial for vegans to form strategic alliances and intersectional coalitions (Hancock 119) with other (marginalized) groups in order to support each other and to gain public recognition on particular issues of common interest. A potentially fruitful collaboration in Estonia in this respect could be with feminist groups. While some ecofeminist thinkers have long sought to show how the oppression of women and animals is deeply intertwined (see for example Adams), the relationship between mainstream feminism and veganism has typically been ambivalent, with feminists reluctant to connect these two strands of thinking and activism (Aavik and Kase). Yet some in the emerging generation of feminists in Estonia take an intersectional perspective, which includes attention to animal lives. Vegans and feminists could engage in collaborative dismantling of nationalist, speciesist, and patriarchal discourses, which enforce traditional gender norms linked to food practices. For example, it would be in the interests of both vegans and feminists to challenge the ideal of hegemonic masculinity, which is partly constructed around eating animals. This might also help to encourage the emergence of more egalitarian masculinities.

VEGANISM, CAPITALISM, AND CONSUMPTION

Finally, I will critically examine the relationship of vegan identities and practices in Estonia to capitalism and consumption, which I already alluded to in relation to the national dietary guidelines in the previous section. While for many in the Estonian vegan community ethical considerations were central in going vegan, collective identity building typically revolves around food, eating, as well as health issues, all ultimately linked to consumption practices, as evidenced by discussions in the main Estonian vegan online communities. The most popular

Estonian vegan Facebook page, titled "Yes, it's vegan!," focuses exclusively on sharing images of food, recipes, and information on the availability of vegan products in Estonian grocery stores. Openly critical attitudes toward capitalism appear to be scarce among most vegans, although, among the diverging vegan community, one of the small subgroups includes anarchist animal-rights advocates and vegans, who approach oppressions as interlinked.

The annual key vegan event, the Estonian Vegan Fair, organized by the Estonian Vegan Society, and held for six consecutive years, focuses on the sales of vegan products and has been extremely popular. This event, while instrumental in introducing veganism to the Estonian mainstream public, is nonetheless focused almost exclusively on consumption, albeit vegan consumption. Based on major public events such as the Fair, veganism has acquired a particular image in popular imagination, one associated primarily with food and the consumption of certain products. An important question for subsequent research would be how vegan groups represent veganism and what their considerations are behind choosing these particular representations. As is typical with vegan groups elsewhere in the world, the Estonian Vegan Society tends to choose language and messaging that is rather mild, emphasizing the individual (consumption) choices of people, not politicizing food choices in their public communication and not associating them with animal rights discourses. It is widely believed that doing so would scare people away. The latest Vegan Fair was advertised with images of conspicuous health and socializing over appetizing food. Attractive, young, and fit ethnic Estonians were shown at the gym and later sharing a meal (Estonian Vegan Society, online video clip). The orientation of the ad was clearly toward presenting a certain desirable lifestyle. How does this representation speak to people who do not identify themselves with such images? Will it in their minds consolidate veganism as an unattainable endeavor, reserved for the relatively privileged?

Given the scarcity of funding sources for civil society organizations in Estonia, the Vegan Society has been considering a range of funding streams. One of these includes corporate sponsorship. Indeed, regular donations from private donors, mostly companies, are seen by the Society as the primary viable funding option. Entering into such partnerships poses a variety of ethical questions that need to be negotiated. This is a concern that NGOs face the world over.

There is a danger that as long as vegans and the vegan movement retain a largely uncritical relationship to capitalist relations of production, they are complicit in reproducing a variety of inequalities and forms of exploitation. While it is encouraging to see many vegans increasingly paying attention to the use of palm oil in some vegan-labeled products, and many preferring fair-trade products, veganism through "ethical consumerism" is unlikely to provide the societal transformation we might be looking for.

Future research needs to critically consider the entanglement of vegan identities and practices embedded within capitalism, including its relationship with what has been termed as "ethical capitalism" (Barry 195) or "humane economy" (Pacelle 248). As vegans, thinking of ourselves as "ethical consumers," capable of changing exploitative relations of production, is often misleading (see Gunderson, and Littleton for a critique), and it gives us a false sense of accomplishment each time we buy vegan products. Profound structural inequalities of capitalism remain unaddressed (Littleton). In Estonia, as elsewhere, it is important to consider how capitalism is intertwined and supported by nationalism. Indeed, the Estonian Internal Security Service lists "extremist ideologies" as threats to the nation on its website. In the list of "left-wing extremism," it identifies anti-capitalism as one of the threats.[13]

This chapter has discussed the potential for the emergence of vegan studies in post-socialist contexts, focusing on the case of Estonia, where veganism is a new and emergent social and cultural phenomenon that has thus far received no scholarly attention. I have examined various factors that shape veganism in Estonia and proposed some directions in which vegan identities and practices could be studied in subsequent research, both in terms of subject matter as well as methodologically.

I have argued that studying veganism primarily as a personal identity and lifestyle choice produces a limited and myopic understanding of veganism, sidelining its political dimensions and the ways it is enmeshed with various systems of power. I advocate for an intersectional approach, which I propose to use in the case of the thematic areas and issues around veganism that I outlined here: the membership of the vegan movement and who is left out based on their structural positioning in the social hierarchy, the relationship of veganism to mainstream culture and its potential to form alliances with other movements, and finally, its relationship to capitalism and consumption. In developing vegan studies, conceptual frameworks could be adopted from ecofeminism and the emergent discipline of critical animal studies (see for example Taylor and Twine), in part inspired by ecofeminist ideas, which embrace intersectionality.

In terms of the uniqueness of veganism and vegan studies in the post-socialist and particularly the Estonian context, there are similarities as well as important differences with the development and manifestations of veganism in Western countries. Despite the short time that Estonia has lived under democracy and capitalism, veganism here exhibits similar tendencies as in many Western countries, such as orientation to consumerism. Indeed, after the collapse of the communist system, market economy and neoliberal policies were considered by governments as well as by citizens as the only legitimate ways forward. Serious opposition to capitalism is particularly slow to emerge in post-socialist nations. While the Estonian vegan movement is difficult to access for particular social groups, with similarity to race- and class-based barriers in the US context, some unique elements stand out, such as a different relationship to the category of class. Another particularity concerns the relationship of veganism to the local nutrition and health establishment. While in most Western European and North American contexts, mainstream nutrition discourses do not necessarily endorse veganism, in Estonia, this relationship is downright hostile.

This mapping exercise has highlighted some of the more unique aspects of veganism in post-socialist Europe and in Estonia in particular. The insights I provided will hopefully set the ground for the emergence of vegan studies in this region.

This work was supported by the Kone Foundation in Finland.

WORKS CITED

Aavik, Kadri. "The Animal Advocacy Movement in the Baltic Countries." *Animal Liberation Currents*, January 23, 2017 Edited by Michael John Addario. https://www.animalliberationcurrents.com/baltic-states-animal-liberation/

———. "Nonhuman animals as 'high quality protein'. Insistence on the Consumption of 'meat' and 'dairy' in the Estonian Nutrition Recommendations." In *Capitalism and Animal Oppression. Vol. 1, The Oppression of Nonhuman Animals as Sources of Food*. Edited by David Nibert, 140–165. Santa Barbara, CA: Praeger Press, 2017.

———, and Dagmar Kase. "Challenging Sexism While Supporting Speciesism: The Views of Estonian Feminists on Animal Liberation and Its Links to Feminism." *Journal for Critical Animal Studies*, 13, no. 1 (2015) 92–127.

Adams, Carol J. *The Sexual Politics of Meat: A Feminist-Vegetarian Critical Theory*. New York: Continuum, 1990/2010.

Barry, Andrew. "Ethical Capitalism." In *Global Governmentality*. Edited by Wendy Larner and William Walters, 195–211. London: Routledge, 2004.

Bettio, Francesca, and Alina Verashchagina. "Gender segregation in the labour market. Root causes, implications and policy responses in the EU." In European Commission's Expert Group on Gender and Employment (EGGE). Luxembourg: Publications Office of the European Union, 2009.

———. 1987. *Gender and Power*. Sydney: Allen & Unwin, 1987.

Connell, Raewyn. *Gender*. Oxford: Polity Press, 2002.

———, and James W. Messerschmidt. "Hegemonic Masculinity." *Gender & Society* 19, no. 6(2005) 829–59.

Crenshaw, Kimberlé. "Demarginalizing the Intersection of Race and Sex: A Black Feminist Critique of Antidiscrimination Doctrine." *University of Chicago Legal Forum* 140 (1989): 139–67.

———. "Mapping the Margins: Intersectionality, Identity Politics, and Violence against Women of Color." *Stanford Law Review* 43, no. 6(1991): 1241–99.

Diani, Mario. "Networks and social movements: A research programme." In *Social Movements and Networks: Relational Approaches to Collective Action*. Edited by Mario Diani and Doug McAdam, 299–319. Oxford: Oxford University Press, 2003.

Education First. "English Proficiency Index," 2015. http://media.ef.com/__/~/media/centralefcom/epi/downloads/full-reports/v5/ef-epi-2015-english.pdf.

Estonian Vegan Society. "Taimetoidumess 2016." Tallinn Vegan Fair 2016 video clip. YouTube, October 25, 2016. https://www.youtube.com/watch?v=Y56RVbbssM8.

Eurostat. "Gender Pay Gap Statistics," 2015. http://ec.europa.eu/eurostat/statistics-explained/index.php/Gender_pay_gap_statistics.

Eurostat. "Gini Coefficient of Equivalised Disposable Income—EU-SILC Survey," 2017.

Gaarder, Emily. *Women and the Animal Rights Movement*. New Brunswick, NJ: Rutgers University Press, 2011.

Glasser, Carol J. "Tied Oppressions: An Analysis of How Sexist Imagery Reinforces Speciesist Sentiment." *The Brock Review* 12, no. 1 (2011): 51–68.

Gunderson, Ryan. "From Cattle to Capital: Exchange Value, Animal Commodification, and Barbarism." *Critical Sociology* 39, no. 2(2011) 259–75.

Hancock, Ange-Marie. *Solidarity Politics for Millennials: A Guide to Ending the Oppression Olympics*. New York: Palgrave Macmillan, 2011.

Harper, A. Breeze. "Race as a 'Feeble Matter' in Veganism: Interrogating Whiteness, Geopolitical Privilege, and Consumption Philosophy of 'Cruelty-Free' Products." *Journal for Critical Animal Studies* 8, no. 3 (2010): 5–27.

Hill Collins, Patricia. *Black Feminist Thought*. London: Harper-Collins, 1990.

———. "Toward a New Vision: Race, Class, and Gender as Categories of Analysis and Connection." *Race, Sex and Class* 1, no. 1 (1993): 25–45.

Jelena, Helemäe, and Ellu Saar. "Estonia—Highly Unequal but Classless?" *Studies of Transition States and Societies* 4, no. 2 (2012): 49–58.

Jenkins, Stephanie, and Richard Twine. "On the limits of food autonomy— Rethinking choice and privacy." In *The Rise of Critical Animal Studies: From the Margins to the Centre*. Edited Nik Taylor and Richard Twine, 225–40. London: Routledge, 2014.

Lavin, Chad. *Eating Anxiety: The Perils of Food Politics*. Minneapolis: University of Minnesota Press, 2013.

Littleton, Eliza. "The Inhumane Economy. How Capitalism is Hindering Real Transformation in the Lives of Other Animals." *Animal Liberation Currents*, December 3, 2016. Edited by Michael John Addario. https://www.animalliberationcurrents.com/the-inhumane-economy/.

Nocella II, Anthony J. "Challenging Whiteness in the Animal Advocacy Movement." *Journal for Critical Animal Studies* 10, no. 1 (2012): 142–52.

Pacelle, Wayne. *The Humane Economy: How Innovators and Enlightened Consumers Are Transforming the Lives of Animals*. New York, NY: William Morrow, an imprint of HarperCollins, 2016.

Pajumets, Marion. "Post-Socialist Masculinities, Identity Work, and Social Change: An Analysis of Discursive (Re)constructions of Gender Identity in Novel Social Situations." Tallinn University, 2012.

Pitsi, Tagli, et al. *Eesti toitumis- ja liikumissoovitused 2015*. Tallinn, Estonia: Tervise Arengu Instituut, 2017.

Potts, Annie, and Jovian Parry. "Vegan Sexuality: Challenging Heteronormative Masculinity through Meat-Free Sex." *Feminism & Psychology* 20, no. 1 (2010): 53–72.

Reger, Jo, et al. *Identity Work in Social Movements*. Minneapolis: University of Minnesota Press, 2008.

Rothgerber, Hank. "Real Men Don't Eat (Vegetable) Quiche: Masculinity and the Justification of Meat Consumption." *Psychology of Men & Masculinity* 14, no. 4 (2013): 363–75.

Snow, David A., and Leon Anderson. "Identity Work Among the Homeless: The Verbal Construction and Avowal of Personal Identities." *American Journal of Sociology* 92, no. 6 (1987): 1336–71.

Taylor, Nik, and Richard Twine. *The Rise of Critical Animal Studies: From the Margins to the Centre.* London: Routledge, 2014.

Twine, Richard. "Intersectional disgust? Animals and (eco)feminism." *Feminism & Psychology* 20, no. 3 (2010): 397–406.

Wright, Laura. *The Vegan Studies Project: Food, Animals, and Gender in the Age of Terror.* Athens: University of Georgia Press, 2015.

END NOTES

1. There is no official statistical data on the proportion of vegans and vegetarians among the Estonian population. The rise in the numbers of vegans and interest in veganism is evidenced for example by the growing numbers of members in Estonian-language Facebook groups dedicated to veganism. For instance, at the end of 2015, the groups titled Yes, it's vegan! and Estonian Vegans had 7,000 and 3,500 members, respectively. As of May 2018, Yes, it's vegan! had over 22,000 members and Estonian Vegans nearly 8,500 members. Google Trends shows a steady increase in the search term "vegan" in Estonia over the last five years.

2. Estonians are highly proficient in English. According to the EF English Proficiency Index (Education First 2015), Estonia ranks seventh in English proficiency among seventy countries where English is a non-native language.

3. See Reger, Myers, and Einwohner on identity work within social movements.

4. There has been considerable resistance in mainstream feminism to the inclusion of animals in intersectionality. For more on this, see for example Twine.

5. The insights I present in the rest of this section are based on an article I published at Animalliberationcurrents.com; see Aavik, "The Animal Advocacy Movement."

6. Due to lack of statistical data on the numbers of vegans in Estonia and their gender ratio, I rely here on personal experiences, observations, and data from social media. In the Facebook group Estonian Vegans, the ratio of men to women is roughly one to four.

7. Estonia's GINI index was 34.8 in 2015 (Eurostat 2017)—only 5 other countries in the EU (in total, 28 countries) display larger income inequality; the gender pay gap in Estonia is 26.9 percent—the largest in the EU (Eurostat 2015).

8. VeganBoom.ee, facebook.com/veganboom, instagram.com/vegan_boom/

9. This large number of stateless persons in Estonia is due to the fact that, after

regaining independence in 1991, Estonia did not grant automatic citizenship to Russian-speakers who migrated to Estonia in the Soviet era or to their descendants.

10. Oja, Triin. "Dr Ülle Einberg: pealesurutud veganlus võib väikelastele olla elu-ohtlik." Pealinn, March 23, 2017, http://www.pealinn.ee/tagid/koik/dr-ulle-einberg-pealesurutud-veganlus-voib-vaikelastele-olla-n189362.

11. For a discussion on the language of restriction in relation to vegan eating and identities in the US, please see Wright 89–106.

12. Bio-Competence Centre of Healthy Dairy Products http://tptak.ee/en.

13. See www.kapo.ee/et/content/äärmuslusest-üldisemalt.html.

CHAPTER 10

South Korea

Looking at the Vegetarian Body: Narrative Points of View and Blind Spots in Han Kang's *The Vegetarian*

Margarita Carretero-González

To Princesse, who was, is, and will always be

Being vegan or vegetarian in a culture where meat eating is normative comes with many challenges. Even if they vary depending on how uncommon veganism is in each particular culture, after reading about vegans' experiences in different parts of the world and comparing them to my own, I think it is safe to affirm that most vegans will face the same trials at one point or another in their lives, ranging from the material difficulty of finding any vegan option when eating out, to the hostility sometimes displayed by omnivores, even among close friends or family members. The form this hostility takes also varies: overt or veiled accusations of radicalism and narrow-mindedness, more or less innocent mockery, or even commiseration, all of which contribute to perpetuating the association of vegetarianism—and, of course, veganism—with radicalism and dissenting groups, which goes back to the very coining of the term (Thomas 295–96).

The picture for vegans and vegetarians seems to have changed in South Korea in the decade passed since *The Vegetarian* was published, even if not eating meat is "still rare enough to be subversive in itself" (Smith). According to the Korean Vegetarian Union, there are about fifty vegetarian restaurants in Seoul, and over eighty eateries that offer vegetarian dishes (Bo-eun), yet the concept is still commonly met with bafflement, particularly when ethical reasons—and not health or religious issues—are behind the choice to go vegetarian or vegan (Bo-eun, Dunbar, "Vegan in Korea").

If we add that South Korea, ranked by the World Economic Forum as the 115th out of 145 countries in gender equality, is still an "entrenched patriarchy" in which "toxic gender relations are taking a toll on society" (Koo), a woman's choice to stop eating meat or preparing it for her husband may very well raise a few eyebrows. Indeed, when Yeong-hye, the virtually voiceless protagonist of Han Kang's *The Vegetarian,* becomes vegan[1] in a society where "meat and animal products have traditionally been staples of the societal diet," her decision "rends her entire social fabric" (Fallon).

Each of the three parts that make up *The Vegetarian* presents a different narrative point of view, none of which is the protagonist's. Kang chooses a first-person narrator, Yeong-hye's insensitive husband, in part one, "The Vegetarian," whereas parts two and three, "Mongolian Mark" and "Flaming Trees," are told by a third-person limited narrator, with focalization, respectively, on Yeong-hye's unnamed brother-in-law and her elder sister, In-hye. The story of Yeong-hye is thus constructed from narrative points of view external to her own, although the reader has the advantage over the three narrators of accessing her dreams, memories, and reflections which, in italics, interrupt her husband's narrative and appear briefly in her sister's account. The result is a complex account of acts of abnegation and rebellion, of different levels of miscommunication, and, most importantly, of a woman's struggle to keep claim to her own body, vegetarianism thus losing progressively the prominence it held in the first part.

Indeed, as Clair Fallon has observed, *The Vegetarian*'s "real concerns" may be "stickier [than] the quotidian issues of vegetarianism" the novel engages with. Yet Yeong-hye's vegetarianism is what sets the plot in motion, dominates her husband's account, and acts as a guiding thread all through the book, which is a good reason to look at the way the novel reproduces or challenges cultural perceptions and representations of vegetarianism/veganism. Despite the narrative points of view that conflate on Yeong-hye, her body resists any univocal interpretation: her husband's disgust contrasts with her brother-in-law's fascination, while for her sister it ends up being a mirror that forces her to appraise her own life choices.

In the pages that follow, I will explore the issues *The Vegetarian* addresses regarding vegetarianism, gender, and the material body as they are presented through the limited point of view of its three narrators. I will also look into one aspect of the novel that I find particularly troubling: the way the narrative allows Yeong-hye's vegetarianism to be perceived as an eating disorder, originating in a determination to lead a life exempt of any sort of violence.

NONVIOLENCE AND FEMALE BREASTS: THE VEGAN BODY AS A THREAT

Once it is labeled "vegetarian," Yeong-hye's body "poses various threats to the status quo in terms of what it eats, what it wears, what it purchases, and how it chooses *not* to participate in many aspects of the mechanisms that maintain what constitutes the mainstream" (Wright 19). The threats may be different from those in the US after 9/11 pointed out by Wright, yet her change still destabilizes important pillars of Korean culture. Her husband's narrative celebrates the virtues of Yeong-hye's utter ordinariness prior to her turning vegetarian and, in so doing, lays bare to the reader his own shortcomings, providing us with a textbook case of how to deal with an inferiority complex by surrounding oneself with those considered inferior. For a man who admittedly always inclined "towards the middle course in life," a wife who is "completely unremarkable in every way" (Kang 11)—except for her refusal to wear a bra—is obviously the perfect choice to make his own mediocrity palatable. He happily traded excitement for a comfortably ordered existence, which takes an unpleasant turn the day this "most run-of-the-mill woman in the world" (Kang 12) gives up meat and all animal products, giving no further explanation when asked beyond the answer she repeats like a mantra: "I had a dream."

The inscrutability that each of the three narrators finds in Yeong-hye is textually present from the very beginning of the novel, in the most literal sense, when her husband finds her standing motionless in front of the fridge, with her face "submerged in the darkness so [he] couldn't make out her expression" (Kang 14). This impossibility of communication will be constant through the novel, working in both directions, since the narrators cannot fathom Yeong-hye, partly because she chooses not to elaborate on the reasons for her decision. Only the reader can work out the hidden narrative behind her conversion by putting together each storyteller's account with the privileged access she or he has to the protagonist's dreams and thoughts.

It is worth mentioning that Yeong-hye never introduces herself as a vegetarian or a vegan, although her refusal to eat meat leads her husband, family, and acquaintances to identify her as such. Instead of functioning as an element to help communication, the label remains the depository of all the popular connotations vegetarianism acquired almost instantly the moment the term was coined, when it became "a fixed identity—indelibly associated with crankiness" (Stuart 423), as her husband's ruminations evince:

> People turn vegetarian for all sorts of reasons: to try and alter their genetic predisposition towards certain allergies, for example, or else because it's seen as more environmentally friendly not to eat meat. Of course, Buddhist priests who have taken certain vows are morally obliged not to participate in the destruction of life, but surely not even *impressionable young girls* take it quite that far. As far as I was concerned, the only *reasonable* grounds for altering one's eating habits were the desire to lose weight, an attempt to alleviate certain physical ailments, being possessed by an evil spirit, or having your sleep disturbed by indigestion. In any other case, it was nothing but *sheer obstinacy* for a wife to go against her husband's wishes as mine had done. (Kang 21–22, my emphasis)

Apart from oozing with male chauvinism, Mr. Cheong's observations keep in tune with common perceptions and incomplete representations of vegetarianism, which reduce it to either a healthy lifestyle option or a religious imposition, thus rendering unreasonable any other motivation to embrace a vegetarian or vegan diet. Unfortunately, the views exposed by Yeong-hye's husband are far from being circumscribed to this fictional work; on the contrary, as Wright has pointed out, they have become quite prevalent "due to the current mainstream tendency to divorce veganism from animal advocacy and focus instead on the health benefits of such a lifestyle" (31). Ignoring that most people turn vegan or vegetarian out of respect for other forms of sentient life renders animals invisible, even in discourses in which they should occupy a privileged position. To the three ways in which Carol J. Adams considered animals functioning as absent referents in her seminal *The Sexual Politics of Meat*—literal, definitional, and metaphorical (66–67)—Wright has added their disappearance "from the cultural understanding of veganism" (Adams Foreword xiii).

Another example of the hostility displayed onto the vegetarian, coming most certainly from a certain fear of judgment on the omnivore's part, is offered later on in this same part of the novel, at the formal work dinner given by Mr. Cheong's boss. Very much in the same way as the vegetarian has remained virtually "absent from all human studies whether of history, science, ethics or theology," and even vegetarianism

(Linzey x), Yeong-hye is excluded from a discussion that revolves around her ethical stand. Her husband's boss launches the attack, resorting to the logic of binary opposition that separates *us* (Korean meat-eaters) from *them* (non-Korean non-meat-eaters, i.e., vegetarians), which consigns the negatively marked term to an inferior position:

> "My word, so you're *one of those* 'vegetarians,' are you? . . . Well, I knew that some people in *other* countries are strict vegetarians, of course. And even here, you know, it does seem that attitudes are beginning to change a little. Now and then there'll be someone claiming that eating meat is bad . . . after all, I suppose giving up meat in order to live a long life isn't all that unreasonable, is it?" (Kang 30, my emphasis)

Although the conversation remains centered on Yeong-hye's vegetarianism, none of the diners seem to be genuinely interested in her reasons for being one, or at least no one asks her before they have expressed their opinion about the unnaturalness, narrow-mindedness, or mental imbalance involved in "arbitrarily cut[tting] out this or that food, even though they're not actually allergic to anything" (31). When Yeong-hye's answers in the negative to her husband's boss's question about health issues being the cause, Mr. Cheong actually steals her voice, contradicts her, and blatantly lies, making everyone feel relieved for not sharing a table with "a proper vegetarian . . . who considers eating meat repulsive" glaring at the meat eater "like you were some kind of animal" (Kang 31–32). Better to feel sorry for someone who cannot enjoy a delicious twelve-course meal than having one's ethical choices questioned by their mere presence at the table.

Verbal hostility eventually turns into physical violence exerted by dominant males against the female vegan body, doubly violated with undesired penetration in the form of rape and force-feeding. Yeong-hye refuses to have sex with her husband because he smells of meat, yet Mr. Cheong justifies his forcing his way into her body, arguing that "it was no easy thing for a man in the prime of his life . . . to have his physical needs go unsatisfied for such a long period of time" (Kang 38), bragging about how much easier it becomes to violate her again after the first time. Finally, in the climactic moment in part one, her father forces a piece of meat into her mouth after slapping her face in front of the whole family, a final act of violence that leads the up-to-then pacifist Yeong-hye to fiercely claim her right to her own body in front of patriarchal authority by cutting her wrist.

As already mentioned, the details of the dream remain in the darkness for the rest of the family but are vividly conveyed to the reader in a vibrant, sensual prose that contrasts with her husband's insipid style. They are intense recollections of blood, flesh, of a face that seems to be both uncannily familiar and alien, of a dog her father had brutally killed after he had bitten her and then made everyone eat, and the more recent memory of cutting herself while chopping meat, which had led to the dream. For Yeong-hye, the accidental cutting actually dissolved the limits that separated her living flesh from that of the dead animals' on the board:

> *Murderer or murdered . . . hazy distinctions, boundaries wearing thing. Familiarity bleeds into strangeness, certainty becomes impossible. Only the violence is vivid enough to stick . . . Intolerable loathing, so long supressed . . . Perhaps I'm only now coming face-to-face with the thing that has always been there"* (Kang 35).

Her demure exterior and her progressively shrinking body contrast with the horrific images that lie buried in Yeong-hye's psyche, preventing her even from sleeping. Her breasts, always free from the restriction of a bra, become icons of nonviolence:

> *It's back—the dream. Can't even call it that now. Animal eyes gleaming wild, presence of blood, unearthed skull, again those eyes. Rising up from the pit of my stomach. Can only trust my breasts now. I like my breasts, nothing can be killed by them. Hand, food, tongue, gaze, all weapons from which nothing is safe. But not my breasts. With my round breasts, I'm okay . . . So why do they keep on shrinking? . . . Why am I changing like this? Why are my edges all sharpening—what I am going to gouge?* (Kang 41)

On the last occasion the reader has access to her thoughts in this part of the text, she does not seem to see her body as a living organism anymore, but rather as a site of death; in fact a graveyard for all the animals she has consumed through her life:

> *Yells and howls, threaded together, layer upon layer, are enmeshed to form that lump. Because of meat. I ate too much meat. The lives of the animals I ate have all lodged there. Blood and flesh, all*

those butchered bodies are scattered in every nook and cranny, and though the physical remnants were excreted, their lives still stick stubbornly to my sides. (Kang 55–56)

Becoming with other mortal beings through eating and killing them (Haraway 295) is no longer acceptable for Yeong-hye. Her vegetarianism stems for an act of atonement, which will lead her into the posthuman fantasy of eschewing not only her humanity but even her animality.

VEGETAL SEX: THE VEGAN BODY IN THE ARTIST'S GAZE

Slicing her wrist in front of her family is the powerful statement that definitely takes Yeong-hye away from her previous inconspicuousness and makes her uncomfortably visible. Unable to take her body as anything but a site of shame and disgust, her husband does not wait long to divorce her; her brother-in-law, in contrast, a video artist on a two-year fallow period, starts to envision her body as a canvas on which to express his posthuman artistic fantasies.

Before his wife tells him that her sister still has a Mongolian mark,[2] Yeong-hye's body had been for him "nothing more than an object of pity, albeit a faintly inscrutable one" (Kang 76), but after learning of the existence of this bluish spot in the form of a petal, his artist's eyes start looking at his sister-in-law's body as the subject/object in an idea for a piece of video art that had been haunting him for some time: a man and a woman, their bodies lusciously painted with flowers, having sex against a backdrop of silence. It can be argued that her Mongolian mark simply reduces Yeong-hye's body to an object, even if it is an object of beauty. Where her husband sees ordinariness, the artist sees originality—"Did that insensitive oaf know about her Mongolian mark?" (Kang 94)—declaring it in perfect harmony with her veganism: "the fact that she didn't eat meat, only vegetables and cereal grains, seemed to fit with the image of that blue petal-like mark, so much so that the one could not be disentangled from the other" (Kang 79). His is, certainly, the gaze on an artist to whom Yeong-hye has become a muse of sorts; therefore, a degree of objectification is expected together with the projection, as suggested by Anton Ehrenzweig, of the artist's fragmented parts of the self into his work (Richman 39).

However, Yeong-hye is no passive muse; the gaze of her brother-in-law and the flowers he paints on her body breathe a new life into her, to such an extent that this is the part of the book in which she is most active, fully engaging in his art. Her body not only becomes a vehicle for artistic expression, but it also allows her to open herself up to him, timidly emotionally at first, and fully physically when he becomes her artistic partner on the video. With him, Yeong-hye laughs for the first time in the text and enjoys a calm meal at a Buddhist restaurant, during which she explains to him that the flowers he has painted on her body have actually stopped the recurring dream that made her stop eating meat, telling him about the details of the blood and the haunting faces: "I thought it was all because of eating meat . . . I thought all I had to do was to stop eating meat and then the faces wouldn't come back. But it didn't work" (Kang 122). She even becomes sexually aroused during the filming of the visual artwork, which comes to an abrupt ending when her partner in the video leaves after her brother-in-law announces that he wants the sex to be real. Yeong-hye had refused to have intercourse with her husband because his body smelled of meat; her arousal now is connected to the flowers on the man's body, as she confesses to her brother-in-law: "I've never wanted it so much before. It was the flowers on his body . . . I couldn't help myself. That's all" (Kang 113). After painting flowers on his own body, he becomes her partner in the film, both engaging fully in sexual intercourse as a form of artistic expression.

At first, Yeong-hye's Mongolian mark had been connected in his mind with sexual desire, but from the moment in which he accidentally sees her naked, the narrator stresses the change in perception, maintaining that "[r]ather than provoking lust, it was a body that made one want to rest one's gaze quietly upon it" (Kang 80–81). When he finally sees the mark, instead of awakening desire, it evokes "something ancient, something pre-evolutionary, or else perhaps a mark of photosynthesis, and he realized to his surprise that there was nothing at all sexual about it; it was more vegetal than sexual" (Kang 90). Finally, when he's painting flowers on her body, he describes it as

> the body of a beautiful young woman, conventionally an object of desire, and yet . . . a body from which all desire had been eliminated[,] a body from which all superfluity had gradually been whittled away. Never before had he set eyes on such a body, a body which said so much and yet was no more than itself." (Kang 91–94)

When the anticipated moment of sexual intercourse takes place, the narrator presents it as a work of art connected to the artist's desire to express his own posthuman fantasy about hybridization, readjusting the camcorder whenever they change position, and wondering whether they would seem "like one body, a hybrid of plant, animal and human" (Kang 120). Indeed, his piece is in perfect tune with Rosi Braidotti's considerations on the artistic object as

> a combination of non-functionalism and ludic seductiveness. . . . By transposing us beyond the confines of bound identities, art becomes necessarily inhuman in the sense of nonhuman in that it connects to the animal, the vegetable, earthy and planetary forces that surround us. [I]t carries us to the limits of what our embodied selves can do or endure. (Braidotti 107)

However, the narrator makes the workings of the artist's view exclusive to the reader, while the characters act according to the blind spots caused by their necessarily limited knowledge. When In-hye drops by her sister's place unannounced and comes across the video tape, she can only see the images caught in the camera as an instance of sexual abuse, exerted by her husband on the body of her mentally weak sister, which brings their union to an end.

ANIMAL NO MORE: THE FREEDOM OF THE VEGAN BODY

For the third part of the novella, "Flaming Trees," the author chooses, as in "Mongolian Mark," a limited third-person narrator who, on this occasion, adopts the point of view of In-hye. In a narrative dominated by the male gaze up to this moment, In-hye complements her sister's fragmented discourse, which interrupted Mr. Cheong's personal account in "The Vegetarian," placing Yeong-hye's progressive descent into madness and physical deterioration in the context of a shared history of violence. Yeong-hye's earlier confession to her husband that her father "had whipped her over the calves until she was eighteen years old" (Kang 37), the episode of the dog, and the slap and force-feeding that led Yeong-hye to cut herself, are now revealed to us as just a few of the many instances of the rough treatment exerted by a "heavy-handed father" who had frequently left the girls' young cheeks throbbing with pain (Kang 135).

In this last part of the novel, actually written after the first two had been published separately, Yeong-hye is confined in a psychiatric clinic, diagnosed with anorexia nervosa and schizophrenia.

Convinced that she is becoming a plant, she has stopped eating altogether, arguing that only water and sun are necessary for her survival. In-hye is the only family member who keeps on visiting her,
making weekly her previously monthly visits after Yeong-hye goes
missing one day and is found in the woods, standing "stock-still and
soaked with rain as if she herself was one of the glistening trees"
(Kang 131). During the visit related in this part, the narrator uses
the present tense whenever dwelling on the present moment, which
alternates with a series of flashbacks as In-hye remembers her more
recent and distant past, examining her own life in connection to her
beloved younger sister, their abusive father, and her fragile husband.
Her sister's emaciated body, "her prominent cheekbones, her hollow
eyes, her sunken cheeks . . . her ragged breath" (Kang 165), stands at
first as an indecipherable riddle, to become progressively a mirror
in which In-hye is forced to look at herself and reflect upon her own
life choices. Her reflections are those of a woman who, determined
to take care of everyone else, has forgotten to take care of herself;
a woman who was on the verge of leaving her life behind, including her own child, only to go back at the last minute. In looking at
Yeong-hye's body, she even wonders whether this could be the final
stage of a journey she herself might unknowingly be embarking
upon. A part of In-hye actually envies her sister's freedom, longing
to keep her alive, but unable to forgive her for

> soaring alone over a boundary she herself could never bring her-
> self to cross, unable to forgive that magnificent irresponsibility that
> had enabled Yeong-hye to shuck off social constraints and leave her
> behind, still a prisoner. And before Yeong-hye had broken those
> bars, she'd never even known they were there. (Kang 148)

In hindsight, this final stage of Yeong-hye's arboreal transformation
has been foreshadowed to the reader in the two previous accounts.
Even her insensitive husband could hint at it when, during the dinner
with his boss, he comments on "her nipples resembling a pair of acorns
as they pushed against the fabric of her blouse" (Kang 32). As we saw
in the previous section, her brother-in-law makes constant remarks
on the vegetal traits that he perceives in her body, from the petal-like
Mongolian mark, to her obsession with baring her chest to the sunlight,
as if she were "some kind of mutant animal that had evolved to be able
to photosynthesize" (Kang 98), which leads to an erotic dream in which

Yeong-hye is a green woman whose body exudes sap during sexual intercourse. Even now her sister, with the distance of time, can appreciate the vegetal qualities of the piece of art that had destroyed her marriage, recalling now two bodies that resembled "jungle creepers," and which become less and less sexual in her regard: "Covered with flowers and leaves and twisting green stems, . . . so altered it was as though they no longer belonged to human beings. The writhing movements of those bodies made it seem as though they were trying to shuck off the human" (Kang 184). Indeed, Yeong-hye seems to believe that she has succeeded in shucking off not only her humanity, but her animality: "'I'm not an animal any more, sister. . . . I don't need to eat, not now. I can live without it. All I need is sunlight" (Kang 159).

Yeong-hye's delusion stems from a desire to reject any form of violence except, paradoxically, that which she exerts upon her own body, whether actively by cutting her wrist, or passively by refusing to nourish it. Her dreams may be filled with images of her body developing roots and sprouting leaves and flowers, but the less poetic truth, as In-hye confirms, is that her sister is dying. "Nothing else" (Kang 175).

THE VEGAN? BODY

In "Death by Veganism, Veganorexia, and Vegaphobia: Women, Choice, and the Politics of 'Disordered' Eating," the fourth chapter of her *Vegetarian Studies Project*, Laura Wright exposes the similarities in the rhetoric used to discuss vegetarianism/veganism and eating disorders, denouncing an insistence on rendering "nonnormative diets . . . as inherently disordered forms of consumption that must be kept in check" (Wright 90). Unfortunately, *The Vegetarian* ends up participating in this discourse, which makes for a disquieting reading of the novel from a vegan perspective. Although Yeong-hye's body can be considered that of an ethical vegan, given that it is an anti-speciesist reason that leads her to stop consuming animal products, the final stages of her transformation are an indication of a mental disease. Her story is not that of the female protagonist of a short story Kang published in 1997, "The Fruit of My Woman," who actually becomes a plant, tenderly looked after by her husband; it is the story of a woman on the verge of death. Yeong-hye's vegan body is, actually, a diseased one. Indeed, she only appears healthy in "Mongolian Mark": she gains weight after her stay in the hospital, she has no problem eating, provided the food does not contain animal products, and she is capable even of enjoying her body. All this comes to an end after the artistic experiment that leads to her confinement in a psychiatric hospital, where we find a delusional Yeong-hye who believes she can survive on just water and sunlight.

The Vegetarian, in fact, turns out to be not so much a story about veganism, but about abstention and atonement. Even if, as Kang admitted, Yeong-hye makes a powerful statement "against the violence humans live with and take for granted," in presenting vegetarianism as "as a perfectionist way of being pure, in that it's not committing any kind of violence" (Reynolds), she gives us a protagonist that almost confirms Harold Fromm's outlandishly reductionist views on vegans as individuals "enlisted in an open-ended but futile metaphysic of virtue and self-blamelessness that pretends to escape from the conditions of life itself."

On the other hand, the beautiful prose almost runs the risk of romanticizing a mental illness, a dangerous tendency, which Kelsey Oswood has frequently come across in narratives of anorexia (Gregory). However, there is nothing romantic about the details that the narrator does not spare concerning the horrors of having to be forcefully fed through the nose, or the vision of a body inexorably drifting into death. What the novel certainly does is vindicate a woman's right to claim ownership of her own body, when In-hye utters—unclear whether to herself or having her sister in mind: "It's your body, you can treat it however you please. The only area where you're free to do just as you like. And even that doesn't turn out how you wanted" (Kang 182).

And yet, even though Yeong-hye's veganism appears to be "an ethical response to an unethical practice, the killing and use of animals" (Adams xi), it has very little to do with the "joyful, delicious, and healthy" experience it provides. Indeed, veganism is not about longing for an unattainable form of purity, but about remaining alive and healthy by choosing not to inflict perfectly avoidable pain and suffering on other sentient beings. The last part of the novel allows for a reading of her veganism as an eating disorder rather than an ethical choice, one aspect of the novel which, as said above, I find particularly troubling. Yeong-hye may embrace the path of nonviolence toward other sentient bodies, but her decision to live on sunlight and water, as if she were a tree, does constitute an act of violence against her own body, a threat to her survival.

The Vegetarian does not really have a resolution, but its ending with its protagonist on the verge of death does not present her veganism under a very flattering light. The question remains whether the novel is just about veganism, since Yeong-hye's impossibility to thrive, even when she chooses a vegan lifestyle, seems to come from an existential angst that separates her from everyone around her, an inability to feel at home in her own skin. As she confesses to her brother-in-law, the violent dreams did not disappear after she stopped eating and wearing animal products, but only when she was covered with painted flowers. In-hye's reflections while observing her sister's body tell readers a hidden story of shared oppression and expectations, of different degrees of violence that Yeong-hye seems unwilling to tolerate. At the risk of sounding absolutist, I would conclude that choosing to give up her own life in order not to take any other, animal or vegetal, may render Yeong-hye's body that of a martyr, but not that of a vegan. Porochista Khakpour has referred to *The Vegetarian* as a "death-affirming novel." Veganism is actually about affirming life.

WORKS CITED

Adams, Carol J. *The Sexual Politics of Meat: A Feminist-Vegetarian Critical Theory.* New York, NY: Continuum, 1990.

——. Foreword to *The Vegan Studies Project: Food, Animals, and Gender in the Age of Terror,* by Laura Wright, xi-xvii. Athens, GA: University of Georgia Press, 2015 Kindle.

Bo-eun, Kim. "Embracing vegetarianism." *The Korea Times,* April 1, 2015. www.koreatimes.co.kr/www/news/nation/2016/02/654_176353.html.

Braidotti, Rosi. *The Posthuman.* Cambridge: Polity Press, 2013.

Dunbar, Jon. "Going Vegetarian in Korea." Korea.net, October 11, 2012. www.korea.net/NewsFocus/Society/view?articleId=103026.

Fallon, Claire. "The Bottom Line: *The Vegetarian* by Han Kang." *Huffington Post,* January 29, 2016. www.huffingtonpost.com/entry/the-vegetarian-han-kang_us _56abca2ae4b00b033aaf16d2.

Fromm, Harold. "Vegans and the Quest for Purity." *Chronicle of Higher Education,* July 4, 2010." www.chronicle.com/article/Vegansthe-Quest-for/66090/?sid=cr.

Gregory, Alice. "Anorexia, the Impossible Subject." *New Yorker,* December 11, 2013. www.newyorker.com/books/page-turner/anorexia-the-impossible-subject.

Haraway, Donna J. *When Species Meet.* Minneapolis: University of Minnesota Press, 2008.

Kang, Han. *The Vegetarian. A Novel.* Translated by Deborah Smith. London: Portobello Books, 2015. Kindle.

Khakpour, Porochista. "'The Vegetarian,' by Han King." *The New York Times,* February 2, 2016. www.nytimes.com/2016/02/07/books/review/the-vegetarian-by-han-kang.html?_r=0.

Kibbi, Abdul-Ghani, and Christina M. Bergqvist "Congenital Dermal Melanocytosis (Mongolian Spot)." Medscape, May 23, 2016. https://emedicine.medscape.com/article/1068732-overview. Accessed 21 August 2016.

Koo, Se-Woong. "South Korea's Misogyny." *The New York Times,* June 13, 2016. www.nytimes.com/2016/06/13/opinion/south-koreas-misogyny.html.

Linzey, Andrew. 2004. Foreword: "Veggie Pilgrim Fathers," to *Vegetarian America,* edited by Karen Iacobbo and Michael Iacobbo, ix-xi. Santa Barbara, CA: Praeger.

Reynolds, Mark. "Han Kang: To Be Human." Bookanista, n.d. bookanista.com/han-kang/.

Richman, Sophia. *Mended by the Muse: Creative Transformations of Trauma.* London: Routledge, 2014.

Smith, Deborah. "How Korean It Is." *English Pen,* January 29, 2015. www.englishpen.org/pen-atlas/how-korean-it-is/.

Stuart, Tristram. *The Bloodless Revolution: Radical Vegetarians and the Discovery of India.* London: HarperPress. 2006.

Thomas, Keith. *Man and the Natural World. Changing Attitudes in England 1500–1800*. Harmondsworth, UK: Penguin Books, 1984.

"Vegan in Korea: Living in Seoul as a Vegan." The Vegan Woman, June 8, 2013. www.theveganwoman.com/vegan-in-korea/.

Wright, Laura. *The Vegan Studies Project: Food, Animals, Kindle. and Gender in the Age of Terror*. Athens: University of Georgia Press, 2015. Kindle.

END NOTES

1. Although Yeong-hye is referred to as a "vegetarian" all through the novel, beginning with its title, she actually is a vegan, since she refuses to eat and wear all sorts of animal products.

2. A Mongolian mark, or Mongolian spot, is a bluish mark of varying sizes that appears in the back or buttocks of infants (most frequently Asian) and that usually disappears within four years, although on rare occasions it can persist for life. (Kibbi and Bergqvist).

CHAPTER 11

Nonviolence through Veganism: An Antiracist Postcolonial Strategy for Healing, Agency, and Respect

Shanti Chu

As human beings, we have a complicated relationship with food, and we cannot separate our relationship with food from our embodiment as raced, gendered, and classed beings. In fact, our relationship with food serves as a reflection of the relationships human beings have with one another. In the US, eating meat and dairy from the factory farming industry is viewed as a "normal" and "natural" form of consumption. The primary ways in which humans interact with animals is through their slaughter and consumption. Recognizing the sentience of animals—the suffering that they share with us as human beings—can be a catalyst for veganism.[1] When it comes to understanding human liberation and animal liberation, there is often a disconnect, but all liberation from oppression is interrelated, and we cannot solely focus on human liberation at the expense of animal liberation and vice versa. While veganism has the mistaken stereotype of being a white bourgeoisie privilege, forms of plant-based eating have been practiced by indigenous and native populations *prior* to colonization and are still being practiced today as revolutionary acts of self-care. Veganism can be a means of resisting the lasting violence of the oppressor insofar as it enables the oppressed to regain agency in their daily existence and interrupts the cycle of violence. More specifically, veganism can be a tool for women of color[2] to dismantle the violence of the neocolonial,[3] capitalist structure of Western society as understood through the work of critical race theorist A. Breeze Harper.

Forms of colonial resistance can still be used today to dismantle Western hegemonic capitalism on behalf of marginalized subjects.

Colonization is a violent phenomenon in every aspect; it is a metaphorical violence and a literal violence. Two main means are often conceptualized to be the correct response to this violent, inhumane process: violent revolution as experienced during the Algerian War and nonviolent resistance as experienced during India's independence movement. Martinican psychiatrist Frantz Fanon and Indian spiritual activist Mahatma Gandhi represent these two poles on a spectrum of responses to colonization. Fanon, on one hand, believed that in order to overcome colonization, it is permissible to respond with physical violence in certain contexts. Gandhi, on the other hand, was a proponent of nonviolence, which serves as a medium between passivity and active violence. While their tools are quite distinct, both Fanon and Gandhi view their tactics as a means to the same end of recognition. I would like to extend and apply this discussion of nonviolence to our relationships with animals in late capitalism[4] through Harper's work, which can bridge the gap between Fanon's and Gandhi's arguments. Harper's work illustrates that veganism can be an act of radical nonviolent resistance on behalf of the oppressed and therefore a means of decolonization.

Turning toward German philosopher G.W.F. Hegel's account of recognition in *Phenomenology of Spirit* is also helpful for examining the struggles for power and possibilities for recognition. While Hegel maintains that physical violence is necessary for self-control insofar as it *begins* the master/slave dialectic, Fanon believes that this same physical violence is also potentially necessary for *responding* to unequal power relationships such as colonization.

In contrast, I will argue that mutual recognition between the colonized and colonizer or oppressor/oppressed[5] need not require violence. Through practice of Gandhian nonviolence and *ahimsa* (embodying compassion for all sentient beings), theoretically, opposition between oppressed and oppressor is overcome because the oppressed do not consider the oppressor as pure opposition, but as having a common humanity, while still being aware of their differences. One's compassion not only extends to other human beings but also to animals who are sentient beings. A shift from viewing animals as commodities for our consumption to beings that experience suffering is required. This shift can be manifested in one's daily practices of resisting the violent, factory-farming industry and instead embodying veganism that is simultaneously a revolutionary act of self-care and a form of decolonization.

A STRUGGLE FOR RECOGNITION

The struggle between colonizer and colonized can be explained with Hegel's theoretical master-slave dialectic, which begins as a struggle revealing the necessity of metaphorical and physical violence in the dialectical progression. The outcome of this struggle is mutual recognition where both the master and the slave recognize one another in their autonomy. The slave is able to realize that the master is dependent upon him. Autonomy and self-identity can be attained through otherness, which entails struggle and ultimately transcendence beyond one's seemingly natural instincts.

In the context of colonization, Fanon captures this otherness that has been imposed through an inferiority complex. In order to overcome the violence of colonization and regain self-identity, Fanon discusses a "racialized recognition" throughout *Black Skin, White Masks* (190–97). Fanon's "racialized recognition" requires recognition of racial differences, but also transcends those differences in a way that does not reduce either individual to their race. It appears that "racialized recognition" can never be overcome in a racialized society, yet it is important to acknowledge these concepts in order to overcome the naïveté of "color-blind" forms of resistance.

In her discussion of Hegel's dialectic, Vinay Gidwani identifies a rather compatible conception of loving recognition that serves as a complement to Fanon's "racialized recognition." She describes love as the "relation in which I rediscover myself within the other—my own other—and thereby actualize my existence. To love is to alienate or lose yourself in another, but thereby to regain and actualize your own life and selfhood" (2582). To let go of oneself is indicative of how one is moving past immediate being toward a further unfolding of consciousness. This actualization of consciousness requires letting go of one's immediate being by no longer clinging to imposed social norms that usually hold beings in opposition. We can now further consider how loving recognition can be a means of resisting the inherent violence of colonization and oppression, which will be contrasted with Fanon's support of physical violence.

HEGEL AND FANON: AN ANALYSIS OF COLONIALISM AND INFERIORITY

Given the obstacles and possibilities that arise with recognition, we can now examine a historically specific master-slave relationship embodied within colonial struggle. In 1914, 85 percent of the world was colonized by Europe, which is why it is imperative to discuss the history of colonization in order to shed light on contemporary decolonization practices (Mills 29). Colonialism and capitalism also go hand in hand insofar as imperialism reveals "the true nature of capitalism . . . Finance capital is understood to exploit not only wage workers, but all consumers. . . . [which embodies] political power exercised through the state . . .; it is furthermore based on direct repression and violence . . ." (Gronow[6] 152). The capitalist state employs totalitarianism by violently repressing its domestic and global subjects while economically exploiting its workers and deceiving its consumers.

The colonizer/colonized relationship is premised upon structural power inequalities in which the colonizer imposes their culture, language, food, and economic structure upon the colonized. Colonization inherently exercises force, a lack of respect, and manipulation, making it extremely difficult to overcome this power inequality. The Hegelian master/slave and the colonizer/colonized exhibit parallel struggles insofar as their positions are arbitrary; both parties are dependent upon one another and need to go through mutual recognition in order to transcend the immediacy of natural life. The threat of physical violence with the simultaneous existence of metaphorical violence as a negation of the colonized leads the slave to be self-disciplined. Fanon recognizes the legitimacy of physical violence as a means of dismantling the master/slave relationship, which ultimately dismantles the colonizer/colonized relationship.

In *Black Skin: White Masks*, Fanon says that "all colonized people—in other words, people in whom an inferiority complex has taken root, whose local cultural originality has been committed to the grave—position themselves in relation to the civilizing language . . ." (2). Fanon is speaking from his experiences as a colonized subject from Martinique, an island colonized by France, and as someone who experienced this otherness in France as a "black" man. His experiences as a psychiatrist in Algeria also gave him further insight into the atrocious impact of colonization from both the French soldiers' perspectives (who were torturing the Algerian freedom fighters) and Algerians' perspectives. The colonized universally experience an inferiority complex, which cohabitates with their national, racial, and ethnic identity. The colonized internalize this projected inferiority that the colonizer uses as a justification for their colonization. Even further, Fanon notes that there is an "epidermalization" of this inferiority complex; it is injected into their skin (xv). Their inferiority complex cohabitates with their skin color, which cannot be separated from one's national, racial, or ethnic identity and is internalized within their being. This complex embodied by epidermalization prevents "racialized recognition" because the colonized subject's identity is reduced to their racial and ethnic identity, which is why Hegel's reciprocal recognition does not seem to be a possibility. Fanon also discusses how the "black man" wants to be like the colonizer instead of resisting the colonizer, unlike the Hegelian slave who wants to fight the master (195).

The original culture and language of the colonized is deemed "savage" and as deficient from what the colonizer introduces, which is why assimilating to the culture of the colonizer is perceived as making the colonized subject superior.[7] Katharine Bradley and Hank Herrera, in "Decolonizing Food Justice", convey how, "For over five centuries colonizing forces have included many forms of destruction, for example, through disease; economic exploitation; subjugation and enslavement of indigenous people; . . . the positional superiority of European knowledge; the dismissal of indigenous spirituality; and imposition of what is 'human' and what is 'Other'" (104). The politics of assimilation and epistemological privilege of whiteness, driven by the projected inferiority complex, is one of the reasons why the colonized do not even have the possibility of recognition like the Hegelian slave does. In "Unbounded Histories: Hegel, Fanon, and Gabriel Garcia Marquez," Alejandro Vallega describes this lack of recognition as a "blindness that dupes the white man into believing himself to be superior. . . . The colonized does not recognize his labor, but only recognizes himself in and through the image of his master"(47). The colonizer only sees the colonized as a vehicle of labor and the colonized only conceive of themselves by how the master conceives of them, which is inferior.

Furthermore, the inferiority complex and its epidermalization encourage the colonized to be dependent upon the colonizer. Fanon discusses the pernicious effects of the "white man's gaze" in terms of fragmenting the "black" individual and objectifying him specifically as a "black" man in France. This experience is described by Fanon when he says, "I came into this world anxious to uncover the meaning of things, my soul desirous to be at the origin of the world, and here I am an object among other objects" (*Black Souls, White Masks* 89). His desire to attain meaning and move beyond immediate being is prevented due to the fix of the white man's gaze. All of these instances of inferiority and being tied to one's facticity elucidate how the colonized do not even have the potential to be recognized because of their forced dependence upon the master.

VIOLENT REVOLUTION AS A NECESSARY MEANS FOR COLONIAL INDEPENDENCE

In many cases, Fanon recognizes physical violence as a solution to this inequitable, oppressive situation: violence as a means to mutual recognition. In both *A Dying Colonialism* and *Wretched of the Earth*, Fanon discusses what he refers to as the "inevitable violence" that accompanies decolonization, specifically in Algeria. Algeria serves as a contrast to the peaceful subservience of the French Antilles. While formal French colonization has ended, these countries are still permanently changed from colonialism as reflected in the French spoken throughout former French colonies in diplomatic government settings. Fanon asserts that while capitalist domination is a prevalent force in colonialism, keeping the colonized subservient by degrading their identity is just as prevalent.

Fanon believes that the colonized must engage in a life-and-death struggle *and* be self-controlled (which requires one to remain tied to one's ideals and not let anger completely take over). For Fanon, this combination of self-control *and* violence is what enables colonialism to be overcome by the Algerians. Yet using violence to attain freedom and mutual recognition does run the risk of a violent regime replacing another violent regime. Physical violence and self-discipline seem incompatible. In order to go beyond oppression, one cannot resort to the same tactics as the oppressor.

VIOLENCE: HEGEL, FANON, AND GANDHI

Clearly violence is an understandable solution from the perspective of Fanon, but it is not a holistic, long-term solution for colonization and twenty-first-century capitalist imperialism. While Hegel and Fanon believe that violence is a necessary part of the slave's independence, it is inadequate for truly changing an oppressive system. Gandhian philosophy shares a similar metaphysics of unity with Hegel's philosophy (i.e., union with the universal). More specifically, the most fundamental principle of his philosophy is the sacredness of all life. This is why active love or the "element of conscious compassion" (an identity with all living beings and service of all living beings) holds the highest place in Gandhian moral theory (Parekh 127–31). Gandhi's ahimsa seems to be a more comprehensive and long-term solution to decolonization. Not only will ahimsa negate the oppressor's power, it will enable the colonized and oppressed to heal and establish their own subjectivity. We will now explore Gandhi's reasoning for nonviolence and vegetarianism[8] in the context of British colonization.

Like Fanon, Gandhi experienced colonization as a Western-educated, Indian man occupying the spaces of the colonizer. While he grew up in India, Gandhi practiced law in South Africa and lived in London, where he experienced a racialized otherness. When Gandhi was practicing law in South Africa, he experienced the racist apartheid structure of that country when he was kicked off the train for sitting in the "whites only" first-class section. After a series of moments observing and experiencing colonial racism in South Africa, Gandhi started to see the dehumanization inherent within colonization and started to practice *satyagraha* or truth-force and eventually returned to India. For Gandhi, ahimsa is a fundamental aspect of ethical living. As discussed in "My Nonviolence," ahimsa is the abstaining from harm and ill-will of all sentient beings (15), which includes animals.

While Fanon understood the necessity of violent revolution in Algeria, he also expressed interest in nonviolent resistance at the end of *Black Skin: White Masks*. He expressed that the colonizer and colonized both need to pause; instead of experiencing feelings of disregard and contempt toward the other, Fanon asks, "Why not simply try to touch the other, feel the other, and discover each other?" (206).[9] This sounds very similar to the philosophy of nonviolence because the oppressed are recognizing the suffering of the "other."

However, Gandhi was aware of humanity's violent desires. The role of nonviolence has a twofold purpose—its main task is to resist violence in all its forms, but in a way that enables humans to sublimate these violent impulses. One must practice *satyagraha*, which is the concrete application of nonviolence in order to stand firmly with the universal truth of spiritual realization (Gandhi, "Nonviolence" 23). The *Satyāgrahi* engages in nonviolent means such as boycotting the colonizer's products (Parekh 138) or forms of noncooperation ("mass refusal to obey government authority") such as strikes, boycotts, and vegetarianism (Wiredu 377). The *Satyāgrahi* possesses humility, and most importantly self-control (Gandhi, "Satyagraha, Civil Disobedience" 40), in the face of brutal violence by the British. But nonviolence is not merely a temporary tactic, it is a way of being. In order to be truly nonviolent, we have to consider how we embody violence in our daily practices. While the type of colonization that Fanon and Gandhi were directly responding to has ended, the former European colonial powers still hold a tremendous amount of global power over formerly colonized countries and their subjects. The US occupies a unique position as a relatively "newer" country with a prodigious amount of global power. The US has been founded upon "territorial expropriation" from Native Americans and relied upon African slave labor (Mills 24). While the days of legalized slavery and Jim Crow are over, clearly, racism is still a major aspect of the daily American experience. There are many parallels between the inferiorization of the colonized and the contemporary inferiorization projected on communities of color.

HARPER'S "RACIALIZED CONSCIOUSNESS"

While African American theorist A. Breeze Harper's writings mainly focus on the contemporary American context, her work is a conceptual bridge between Fanon and Gandhi. What does it mean to decolonize? Decolonization includes embracing one's indigenous culture, language, and food, and resisting the dehumanizing notions that have been imposed by the colonizer. The colonial legacy is employed through the global North exercising power over the global South (Biel 75). Controlling a nation's food supply is necessary for exercising a neocolonial "web of power" (Biel 77). This imperial power is illustrated by the "rise of mega-corporations and speculative finance capital, which serve simultaneously as mechanisms of accumulation, and structures to smother resistance. Both the corporate and finance-capital aspects of imperialism are exemplified in the food system . . ." (Biel 75). A foundational component of the modern imperial food system is the factory-farming industry, a mode of capitalist efficiency, which must be dismantled as a component of dismantling imperialism.

While structural changes are extremely important, there are daily actions that the oppressed individual can do to decolonize, which entails reclaiming one's diet. The contemporary struggle against colonialism and neocolonialism is tightly wound with sustainability in farming (Biel 80). The political is tied to the ecological: "If you only have the politics (community autonomy, national sovereignty, etc.) without fundamentally changing the physical cultivation methods, it will be a failure . . ." (Biel 87). When you consider the logic of imperialism, which comes from the economic development of capitalism (Gronow 151), "it is profitable to sell seeds, fertilizer and pesticide. In the political logic, this builds a web of power, holding individual farmers and whole countries in thrall" (Biel 76). The mass industrial production of food is a foundational tool of imperialism and capitalism, which contributes to the exploitation of communities of color, the undocumented, and women (Biel 86). Controlling what we eat and understanding the context of our food is an extremely important piece of decolonization. Food systems include animals, human workers, human health, and the ecosystem. Harper's work is situated within the food justice movement by utilizing a critical-race lens. The food justice movement can be described as "fundamentally a social justice movement. It takes issue with inequalities in access to food, exploitive labor practices in the food system, and environmental degradation . . ." (Bradley and Herrera 100). One can see how the food justice movement is a means of resisting the colonial legacy where marginalized groups do not own the means of production. The food justice movement embodies a simultaneous consciousness of worker exploitation, environmental exploitation, and racism. However, Harper not only connects postcolonial resistance with the food justice movement, she also connects it with ethical, compassionate eating. I will discuss Harper's theory of "racialized consciousness" and what it means to decolonize the body through the nonviolent and ethical practice of veganism.

In "Going Beyond the Normative White 'Post-Racial' Vegan Epistemology," Harper illustrates that food studies help one understand the "socio-spatial epistemologies of consumption" (159). According to Harper, space is neither neutral, nor universal; it is racialized, classed, and gendered, which further complicates our identities. Since our identities are connected to our embodiment, our understanding of knowledge and our bodies in relation to these spaces is a part of this "socio-spatial epistemology." Through a "racialized consciousness," which can be a component of Fanon's "racialized recognition," individuals' consciousness—their understanding of reality and their identities within society—is filtered through their lived experiences of race in that society (Harper, "Vegans of Color" 224). A "racialized consciousness" occurs in a racialized society, and the US is a racialized space. American institutions and structures reflect this racialization where politically, socially, epistemologically, and ethically, "the white way is the right way" (Bradley and Herrera 105). These historical realities and entanglements with space impact our perception of morality and what are viewed as daily, ethical practices. Eating is a daily practice that embodies power and privilege. What we eat not only impacts our health, it impacts the lives of human workers, animals, and the ecosystem. Food is integral to understanding oppression within racialized spaces (Harper 229). Our dietary practices and sense of health have "functioned as markers of belonging" and expressions of identity (Bradley and Herrera 101). We will explore how imposing certain food systems has been a weapon of colonization.

HEGEMONIC FOOD SYSTEMS

Imposing a food system is an example of metaphorical, colonial violence. Malcolm Caldwell's "protein imperialism" illustrates how the meat industry "in the core exists only on the basis of global flows of nutrients, thus providing a model for other exploitative flows" (Biel 79). The meat industry and imperialism cohabitate with one another resulting in further exploitation of vulnerable populations. Nutrition has been constructed in an ethnocentric manner to the detriment of communities of color. For example, cow's milk has been Eurocentrically constructed as universally healthy, while African Americans, Native Americans, and Asians are more likely to be lactose intolerant ("Social Justice Beliefs" 35). Further, eating meat and dairy have historically been tied to Western male virility. The Chinese were stereotyped by Westerners as effeminate because they were not consuming cow products and were characterized as a nation of "rice eaters" along with Hindus (Currarino 480).

Food has been imposed as a weapon of colonial assimilation. For example, one of the potential catalysts to the Indian Rebellion of 1857 was how the Indian soldiers (made up of Hindus and Muslims who have sacred rules about the consumption of cows and pigs) were forced to bite the gun cartridge that was greased with a combination of beef and pig fat, which was offensive to the soldiers. Prior to colonization, various African societies had thrived on plant-based diets (Semmes 19). We can see how significant this internalized oppression is to the extent that it causes people to radically change their diets and justify their own oppression. The Western diet was supported by Western "nutritional science," which nefariously reinforced the "need" for the Western diet. Through this circular logic, people are socialized to think that meat and dairy are a necessary part of a "healthy" diet, and that if they don't eat meat and dairy, they are "unhealthy." By "institutionalizing nutritional knowledge," already marginalized groups such as women, the working poor, and people of color are further marginalized as being "unhealthy others," which is used as a justification for denying their rights and personhood (Bradley and Herrera 102). More specifically, animal protein was positively correlated with brain power and reason. Countries such as Mexico and China considered Western European cuisine as a symbol of status and culture (Laudan). In Japan, the elite were known to have eaten white rice and fish, but Emperor Meiji changed this custom in 1872 by eating beef in public (Laudan).

Many non-Western countries accepted Western diets in the midtwentieth century as a result of the "nutritional crisis" (Laudan). If these countries wanted to be accepted by the West, they needed to eat like the West. Plant-based diets were associated with sluggishness and stupidity, which were internalized by the formerly colonized subjects (Laudan). In these examples, we can see the intersectional relationship between racism, colonialism, capitalism, and speciesism. pattrice jones explains in *Sistah Vegan*, "here in the Americas, both homophobia and factory-farming are direct legacies of colonization. Often seeing themselves as superior because they ate more meat, invading Europeans brought animal captives with them" (jones 198). If one wants to be a respected person in the US—a white male—then one needs to eat meat, act "manly," and subjugate other human beings. It is historically evident how imperialism and capitalism have been inherently violent insofar as they exploit their subjects, resulting in reactive and totalitarian governments (Gronow 127–31).

"DECOLONIZING THE BODY" THROUGH HARPER

How can one resist these forms of oppression that are manifested in our everyday social structures? Nonviolent daily practices can be a means of decolonization. More specifically, women of color can decolonize their bodies through veganism as a means of resisting institutionalized racism and sexism (Harper, "Going Beyond" 157). In *Sistah Vegan*, Harper makes the explicit connections between institutionalized oppression, "unmindful consumption," and what it means to be a black female in a society founded upon the racist legacy of slavery, while at the same time being part of "an economically 'privileged' global nation where overconsumption is the norm" (xx). The US is globally privileged, yet there are exploited people within such a wealthy nation. It is this complex web of "socio-epistemologies of consumption" that must be resisted when it comes to liberation.

Veganism can challenge the practice of "unmindful consumption" and self-harm. In fact, a "nonwhite racialized consciousness" held by nonwhite vegans enables them to engage in veganism with an intersectional lens—understanding the interrelatedness of racism, colonization, capitalism, and gender (Harper, "Vegans of Color" 224). Harper discusses how 'decolonizing the body' can be a means of resisting racism, colonization, and capitalism. Many social movements throughout the past century such as the Black Panthers, the Brown Berets, and the Native American Movement have been a means of decolonization for indigenous, formerly enslaved, and colonized peoples to reclaim their land, culture, and rights (Bradley and Herrera 105). In fact, "Decolonization [is] based on mobilization, healing, transformation, and decolonization—all with political, social, spiritual and psychological dimensions—[leading] to recovery, development and ultimately self-determination" (Bradley and Herrera 105). These social movements have led to meaningful and impactful social and political changes. But one must also focus on the individual's means of healing and self-determination within their daily practices. Decolonizing the body is crucial for decolonization. It can be a means of obtaining Fanon's independent self-consciousness for transcending colonization.

How does one decolonize the body? In *Sistah Vegan*, Harper illustrates through a holistic health practitioner, Queen Afua, that veganism can decolonize the body. Queen Afua conveys that whole food veganism, racial healing, and resisting capitalism go hand-in-hand. Whole food veganism contributes to a simultaneous overcoming of bodily suffering, suffering of nonhuman animals, and the destruction of the ecosystem (Harper, "Social Justice Beliefs" 39). Queen Afua also illustrates how veganism is a way for individuals within these communities to heal from the diseases connected to the unhealthy diets that were forced upon them during slavery. The "soul food" diet or "enslaved palate" ("Social Justice Beliefs" 28) cannot be a means of liberation for these communities because it is killing them (Harper, "Going Beyond" 168). These communities of color have regained agency by developing diets separate from the Eurocentric nutrition that prescribes meat and dairy and connecting to diets *prior* to colonization and slavery (Harper, "Social Justice Beliefs" 34). By adopting plant-based diets, communities of color are not trapped within the double-consciousness that Fanon felt was an obstacle for Hegelian recognition; instead, it enables one to construct its own identity.

However, these structural inequalities cannot be ignored. The racial disparities in health within the US are reflective of these neo-colonial power structures. According to Harper, "American society is a continuum of colonialism and imperialism driven by the collective addiction of material acquisition" ("Social Justice Beliefs" 32). The society of the US represents capitalist prioritization where the inter-ests of humans and animals are subjugated for profit and efficiency. The neocolonial[10] structure of the US perpetuates racial disparities in health, wealth, and ultimately power, which further normalizes the oppression of people of color. Two foundational industries within the US, factory farming and the meat industry, constitute the embodi-ment of intersectional oppression of humans and animals. Today, individuals continue to self-inflict wounds and hurt others in ways that parallel the wounds of colonization and slavery (Harper, "Social Justice Beliefs" 23) via their addiction to meat and dairy, just as the colonizers justified their oppression and exploitation of Africans to support their "addiction" to cotton, coffee, and sugar ("Social Justice Beliefs" 32–33). Now that we have a broader picture of the contem-porary relationship between colonialism, capitalism, and racism, we can explore how veganism and ethical consumption can be a means of decolonization.

GANDHI'S AND HARPER'S THEORIES OF *AHIMSA* AND VEGANISM

Resisting and unlearning the violent practices of colonization and capitalism (e.g., the factory-farming industry) is necessary for a truly autonomous consciousness. By recognizing the speciesism of Western society, one can understand the connections between speciesism, rac-ism, classism, and sexism. For example, in the interest of the capitalist class, corporations and the entire factory-farming industry have been given a tremendous amount of freedom when it comes to polluting the air, land, and water, which demonstrates a privileging of profit over life (Schlosser 205–06). Efficiency and self-interest are hallmarks of capi-talism, which has detrimental effects on the most vulnerable popula-tions (Lazear 101). Additionally, the human beings that are the most negatively impacted by these unchecked corporate actions are poorer communities of color that do not possess the economic means to leave the polluted areas nor have access to plant-based foods. We can see the simultaneous exploitation of humans, animals, and the environment as a consequence of how capitalist consumerism has been implemented within the US. Veganism can be a means of rejecting capitalist consumerism, racial exploitation, and sexual exploitation.

Contrary to the stereotype of veganism being a white bourgeois practice, if one is a woman of color living in a Western, capitalist society, she can make the connections between her sexual objectification and her projected "exoticism" and the objectification of animals and their reduction to being a "tasty piece of meat" (Adams 51). Violations of autonomy and consent are manifested in these relationships of power inequality. By no longer consuming animals, humans are eliminating a pervasive, violent force that is also a major contributor to climate change, as factory-farming emits a significant amount of methane and CO_2 (Koneswaran and Nierenberg 579). None of our social justice efforts will matter if we will no longer have an Earth to sustain life, which is why we need to be conscious of how our consumer habits also impact the environment.

Nonviolent resistance allows for the possibility of mutual recognition and loving recognition in a situation where it seems bleak (i.e., colonialism and capitalism), which also requires being completely nonviolent in one's daily life and no longer perpetuating violence against animals. If the oppressed respond to the oppressor with ahimsa and remain courageous in the face of possibly losing physical life, the oppressor could be baffled. Ahimsa can be a means of mutual recognition that Fanon believed was impossible within certain colonial contexts.

It is crucial to extend this recognition beyond human beings and consider this notion of "racialized recognition" to a "speciesized recognition" for animals insofar as we live in a speciesist world. Instead of reducing animals to objects for our consumption, we can recognize the transcendent aspects of animals and their role in the larger ecosystem. We can see how speciesism is used to justify exploiting and torturing animals. Humans pride themselves on their ability to be more rational. Such a worldview uniquely privileges rationality over the ability to run fast or have a very delicate sense of smell. It moreover demonstrates human bias toward human abilities. This lack of rationality and self-consciousness has been used as a justification for animal torture and consumption. Yet one could believe in the superiority of humans and still justify the dignified treatment of animals. Humans can be thought of as moral agents[11] insofar as they are rational beings that can make moral decisions, whereas animals can be thought of as moral patients who lack agency, but can still be respected in terms of their sentience. Understanding animals as moral patients helps us move beyond our oppositional thinking of us versus them. Instead, this recognition emphasizes our *relationship* to animals. Being able to resist this oppositional thinking is a means of achieving self-actualization when one is in a marginalized position. Losing yourself in another being dismantles the rigid, oppositional thinking of "us" versus "them." One lets go of their egocentrism by fully embracing "the other" and recognizing their common suffering. One is able to empathize with the "other," one is able to truly love the "other." Love requires sacrifice by not clinging to differences that lead to domination. This love of the "other"—or the animal—requires one to make sacrifices such as no longer consuming animal products within a society that normalizes their commodification and consumption.

We can draw some parallels here between how the colonized are treated and how animals[12] are treated. The projected inferiority of animals is used as a justification for their oppression. Both the colonized and animals are forced into positions of dependency through their perceived inferiority, yet they are both dependent upon one another not only through their interconnectedness through ecology but also in their mutual exploitation. Women, people of color, the working class, animals, etc. are all exploited within the puzzle of modern day capitalism. In our contemporary society, veganism can be a means of subverting this economic and cultural domination since it makes one less dependent upon the violent factory-farming industry, a hallmark of American capitalism.

People of color are on the "front lines" of the suffering that comes with the factory-farming and meat industries because of how institutionalized colonialism and racism function, making it even more imperative that they resist these exploitative systems (Harper, "Social Justice Beliefs" 29). Consuming meat is a means of engaging in violence within one's daily practices, given the reality of the factory-farming industry, where sentient animals are mercilessly tortured and human beings are exploited. Given the prominence of the "enslaved diet" within American communities of color, eating unhealthy food that has come from the torture of animals has become an integral part of the African American community's very own destruction (Jones 192). By resisting this violent practice and "dietary colonialism" (Jones 196), the oppressed individual is able to heal and embody agency while subverting neocolonialism.

Refusing to eat meat can challenge the factory-farming industry, which in turn challenges the larger oppressive structure of Western society. As Gandhi states in "The Moral Basis of Vegetarianism," "food is life" (3). Gandhi saw vegetarianism as an embodiment of ahimsa as animals are living beings that have been severely exploited through industrialization. One cannot be nonviolent while contributing to the slaughter of animals since nonviolence involves recognizing others as suffering beings, which requires compassion and self-alienation (Presbey). Vegetarianism is an expression of compassion toward all sentient beings and serves as a daily revolutionary force that subverts the violence of colonization and capitalism. One must dismantle the "dietary colonialism" "that began when Europeans forcibly replaced subsistence crops with cash crops . . . that make it cheaper for poor people to eat [at] fast-food restaurants owned by multinational corporations than to buy healthy food from local farmers" (jones 196). The struggle for economic, political, and social justice is not possible without personal transformation and an awareness of food production (Danielle 51), which requires a movement towards food sovereignty.

Food sovereignty is the gradual process of "land reform, indigenous struggles, food networks . . . community supported small farms, [etc.]. Such movements, generated by the reality of alienation and dispossession, are descendants of struggles going back to the origins of colonialism and class society, and the point now is to bring them together . . ." (Biel 89). As a human community, we must bring an end to all of these inequalities, not just ones that we see as directly impacting us (jones 98). To understand the intersectionality of oppression, capitalism, and colonization is "to begin the painful, agonizing process of . . . healing [from] the historical trauma" that has been caused by the violence of colonization (Bradley and Herrera 104). The legacy of colonization is still a prevalent force within American society, which is why decolonization is a gradual process. Decolonization requires one to decolonize desires that are hurtful to others (jones 197), which will enable one to regain an independent consciousness and agency.

Veganism can be a means of resisting oppression within the context of Western hegemonic capitalism. It disrupts the violence of the oppressor, whether it is the violence of colonization or the structural violence of contemporary racism and capitalism. Colonialism and capitalism are governed by a similar logic of profit and efficiency over life and compassion. The factory-farming industry, which is married to both the meat and fast-food industries in the US are integral parts of daily life, especially for poorer communities of color, which are disproportionately suffering from obesity and heart disease. Veganism can be a powerful tool for oppressed individuals, especially for women of color, whose bodies have been marked by the social and historical context of colonization, slavery, sexism, capitalism, and racism. Veganism can be a radical act of self-love. In fact, decolonizing the body, decolonizing desire, and decolonizing nutrition are a powerful means of gaining agency within one's everyday life as illustrated through Harper.

Nevertheless, it is helpful to look back on theories of colonial resistance through examining Hegel's master/slave dialectic and Fanon's analysis of colonized subjects. Both Hegel and Fanon believe violence to be a necessary component of independence, yet it seems contradictory to Fanon's self-control and Hegel's loving-recognition. Using the "master's tools to dismantle the master's house" will not result in structural change, it will only perpetuate the violent, oppressive structure (Lorde). However, Harper's "racialized consciousness" and Fanon's "racialized recognition" elucidate the reality of "socio-spatial epistemologies of consumption" in how racialized individuals perceive their reality, knowledge, and identities, which cannot be transcended in a racialized society. But loving recognition through Harper's veganism can transcend the oppressor/oppressed dichotomy, leaving the oppressed with agency, as her work provides a conceptual bridge between Fanon and Gandhi's solutions.

Both Gandhi's vegetarianism and Harper's veganism provide powerful tools for subverting historical and contemporary oppressor/oppressed relationships. Their views are rooted in ahimsa, which requires one to refrain from harming living beings. As a human community, we need to recognize the interconnectivity of racism, sexism, heterosexism, classism, speciesism, etc. They are governed by the logic of violence and domination. Decolonizing one's desire from attaining pleasure in other beings' suffering is imperative for decolonizing one's body. By shifting our daily practices from exploiting and torturing animals to respecting them and preserving their existence, not only will our society be transformed as a whole, but marginalized subjects will be revolutionary in cultivating their own agency. Oppressed individuals can heal and engage in self-love through veganism. Although veganism has the unfortunate reputation of being for the privileged in the West, it has been a way of life for many indigenous and pre-colonized populations and can still be used today as a means of resisting the Eurocentric, capitalist patriarchy. Such revolutionary ways of existing are even more of a necessity within the current politically tumultuous context and the reality of climate change.

WORKS CITED

Adams, Carol. *The Sexual Politics of Meat: A Feminist-Vegetarian Critical Theory.* New York, NY: Continuum, 2000.

Biel, Robert. *Sustainable Food Systems: The Role of the City.* London: UCL Press, 2016. E-book.

Bradley, Katherine, and Hank Herrera. "Decolonizing Food Justice: Naming, Resisting, and Researching Colonizing Forces in the Movement." *Antipode* 48, no. 1 (2015): 100–05.

Currarino, Rosanne. "Meat vs. Rice: The Idea of Manly Labor and Anti-Chinese Hysteria in Nineteenth Century America." *Men and Masculinities* 9, no. 4(2007) 476–90.

Danielle, Melissa. "Nutrition Liberation: Plant-based Diets as a Tool for Healing, Resistance, and Self-Reliance." In *Sistah Vegan.* Edited by A. Breeze Harper, 47–53. Brooklyn: Lantern Books. 2009. E-book.

Fanon, Frantz. *A Dying Colonialism.* New York, NY: Grove Press, 1965.

———. *Black Skin, White Masks.* New York: Grove Press, 2008.

———. *The Wretched of the Earth.* New York: Grove Press, 1963.

Gandhi, Mahatma. *My Nonviolence.* Ahmedabad, India: Navajivan Publishing House, 1959. E-book.

———. "Nonviolence." In *Selected Political Writings.* Edited by Dennis Dalton. Indianapolis: Hackett Publishing Company, 1996.

———. "Satyagraha, Civil Disobedience." *Selected Political Writings.* Edited by Dennis Dalton. Indianapolis: Hackett Publishing Company, 1996.

———. *The Moral Basis of Vegetarianism.* Ahmedabad, India: Navajivan Publishing House, 1959. E-book.

Gibson, Nigel. "Dialectical Impasses: Turning the Table on Hegel and the Black." *Parallax* 8, no. 2 (2002): 30–45.

Gidwani, Vinay. "The Subaltern Moment in Hegel's Dialectic." *Environment and Planning* 40, no. 11 (2008): 2578–87.

Gronow, Julia. *On the Formation of Marxism.* Boston: Brill, 2016.

Harper, A. Breeze. "Going Beyond the Normative White 'Post-Racial' Vegan Epistemology." In *Taking Food Public.* Edited by Psyche Williams-Forson and Carol Counihan, 155–74. New York, NY: Routledge. 2012.

———. Introduction, "The Birth of the *Sistah Vegan Project*, to *Sistah Vegan,* xiii-1. Edited by A. Breeze Harper,. Brooklyn: Lantern Books, 2009. E-book.

———. "Race as a 'Feeble Matter' in Veganism: Interrogating Whiteness, Geopolitical Privilege, and Consumption Philosophy of 'Cruelty-Free' Products." *Journal for Critical Animal Studies* 7, no. 3 (2010): 5–27.

——. "Social Justice Beliefs." In *Sistah Vegan*. Edited by A. Breeze Harper, 20–41. Brooklyn: Lantern Books, 2009. E-book.

——. "Vegans of Color, Racialized Embodiment, and Problematics of the 'Exotic.'" In *Cultivating Food Justice: Race, Class, and Sustainability*. Edited by Alison Alkon and Julian Agyeman, 221–38. Cambridge, MA: MIT Press, 2011.

Hegel, G. W. F. *Phenomenology of Spirit*. Oxford: Oxford University Press, 1977.

jones, pattrice. "Afterword: Liberation as Connection and the Decolonization of Desire." In *Sistah Vega*. Edited by A. Breeze Harper, 187–202. Brooklyn: Lantern Books, 2009. E-book.

Koneswaran, Gowri, and Danielle Nierenberg "Global Farm Animal Production and Global Warming: Impacting and Mitigating Climate Change." *Environmental Health Perspectives* 116, no. 5 (2008): 578–82.

Laudan, Rachel. "Power Cuisines, Dietary Determinism and Nutritional Crisis: The Origins of the Globalization of the Western Diet." Conference Proceedings February 3, 2001. http://webdoc.sub.gwdg.de/ebook/p/2005/history_cooperative/ www.historycooperative.org/proceedings/interactions/laudan.html

Lazear, Edward P. "Economic Imperialism." *The Quarterly Journal of Economics* vol. 115, no. 1(2000): 99–146.

Lorde, Audre. "The Master's Tools Will Never Dismantle the Master's House." In *Sister Outsider: Essays and Speeches,* 110–14. Berkeley, CA: Crossing Press, 1984.

Mills, Charles. *Racial Contract*. Ithaca, NY: Cornell University Press, 1997.

Norcross, Alastair "Puppies, Pigs, and People: Eating Meat and Marginal Cases." *Philosophical Perspectives* 18, no. 1 (2004): 229–45.

Parekh, Bhikhu. *Colonialism, Tradition and Reform: An Analysis of Gandhi's Political Discourse*. Thousand Oaks, CA: Sage Publications, 1999.

Presbey, Gail. "Fanon on the Role of Violence in Liberation: A Comparison with Gandhi and Mandela." In *Fanon: A Critical Reader*. Edited by Lewis Gordon, T. Denean Sharpley-Whiting, and Renee T. White, 340–57. Hoboken, NJ: Wiley-Blackwell, 1996.

Schlosser, Eric. *Fast Food Nation*. Wilmington, MA: Mariner Books, 2012.

Semmes, Clovis. *Racism, Health, and Post-Industrialism*. Santa Barbara, CA: Praeger, 1996.

Vallega, Alejandro. "Unbounded Histories: Hegel, Fanon, and Gabriel Garcia Marquez." *Idealistic Studies*. 38, no. 1–2 (2008): 41–54.

Wiredu, Kwasi. "The Question of Violence in Contemporary African Political Thought." *Praxis International* 6, no. 3 (1986): 373–81.

Young, Iris M. "Five Faces of Oppression." In *Rethinking Power*. Edited by T. Wartenberg. Albany: SUNY Press 1992.

END NOTES

1. Veganism requires one to abstain from harming animals by not consuming them, wearing them, etc. One no longer objectifies animals as commodities, but recognizes their intrinsic value.

2. I am referring here to any woman who identifies as "nonwhite" within a white-supremacist society.

3. While formal colonization is said to have ended, the former colonial powers still dominate the global landscape. Europe and North America (descendants of colonizers) reign supreme in world affairs with the exception of Japan and China (Mills 127–32). More specifically, the global North controls the food supply of the global South (Biel 75).

4. In these later stages of capitalism, we are experiencing an epidemic of global overproduction, which has contributed to climate change.

5. I will work with Iris Marion Young's definition of oppression being a situation where a group is inhibited "through a vast network of everyday practices, attitudes, assumptions and behaviors" (5). This is an unfortunate consequence of the violence exercised during colonialism and now upheld in a capitalist, neocolonial country like the US.

6. In the book *On the Formation of Marxism,* Jukka Gronow provides a critique of capitalism and imperialism through the lens of Lenin and Kautsky (126–33, 151–56). Their argument elucidates how capitalism and imperialism are interwoven through the logic of power and exploitation. Imperialism is an extension of capitalism.

7. Nigel Gibson in "Dialectical Impasses: Turning the Table on Hegel and the Black" elucidates how the colonizers only speak the language of violence because they do not respect the "others'" culture. Violence is marked by an avid lack of understanding on the master's side.

8. While Gandhi admired veganism, he ate dairy products because he thought they kept him "perfectly fit" while recognizing the drawbacks of consuming them ("The Moral Basis of Vegetarianism" 2).

9. This is rather contradictory to what he asserts in *Wretched of the Earth* with respect to violence alone being necessary for independence, but it seems that Fanon himself was conflicted also about the necessity of violence.

10. As Charles Mills discusses in *The Racial Contract,* we currently live in a newer era of imperialism where Europe and the US have disproportionate amounts of power relative to the rest of the globe (31). This power is manifested through an imposition of Eurocentric ideals (e.g., beauty ideals, economic and political systems, etc.) upon the rest of the world. The world is centered around the norm of whiteness (31).

11. Alastair Norcross in "Puppies, Pigs, and People: Eating Meat and Marginal Cases" argues for how animals' lack of moral agency is not relevant to their status as moral patients and draws the comparison between human beings (e.g., the elderly, young children, etc.) who lack moral agency but are still treated with respect and dignity as moral patients (243).

12. I am not equivocating between how slaves were treated and how animals are treated. I am merely drawing a comparison between the mind-set that perpetuates such atrocious actions.

PART IV

HYPOCRITES AND HIPSTERS; MEAT AND MEATLESSNESS

CHAPTER 12

H Is for Hypocrite: Reading "New Nature Writing" Through the Lens of Vegan Theory

Alex Lockwood

For social scientist Dinesh Wadiwel, whose scholarship over the last fifteen years has been grounded in theories of violence, critical animal studies, and disability rights, a first step to ending our principally exploitative relationship with nonhumans is to create "spaces of truce" where we can pause our "war against animals" and so begin the process of relating differently to those with whom we share this planet. Only once we have suspended our ongoing mistreatment of nonhuman others, says Wadiwel, can we attempt to foster "new forms of connection, friendship, topography, love and living-together that have been previously unimaginable" (8–9). Wadiwel makes these arguments in his book *The War Against Animals*, and it is clear that these spaces are not only physical but also epistemological. Drawing upon Foucauldian interpretations of Locke and Marx to explore the ways in which human superiority over nonhuman others is founded on violence, Wadiwel illustrates how these spaces of truce, in which knowledge turns on the idea of what is imaginable, are places where we can come to understand and then redefine "the 'animal' as a discursive category that is opposed and subordinated to the 'human'" (9). Wadiwel's argument is that not only throughout human history have we, in regards to nonhuman animals, overwhelmingly created spaces and institutions of violence, rather than of kindness; but what's worse is that we don't even recognize this, and "miss the nature of institutional violence, which is hidden not because it isn't in sight, but because our knowledge systems do not allow us to see this as violence" (32).

One means of seeing what is "hidden in plain sight" when it comes to the violence committed against nonhuman animals is to turn to the emerging field of vegan studies. Veganism, its study and application as a "space of truce," where questions of practical lifestyles lived from the "political and ethical rejection of the use of animals" (Adams xiii) for human benefit, has the potential to reorient us to violence that is otherwise seen through normative lenses as acceptable, even desirable, or in some cases as entertainment. That is, in its radical rejection of the "war against animals" as a form of institutional violence, veganism as a practice and theory, has, says Laura Wright, the potential to "provide a frame of reference from which to deconstruct the mainstream and media-based discourse that often depends upon and reinforces a singular yet constantly shifting conception of veganism" (23) which, in its "stark opposition to the consumer mandate of US capitalism . . . pose[s] a substantial—if symbolic—threat to such a paradigm" (22).

It might seem natural to assume that "nature writing"—the often creative, generally nonfictional, usually sympathetic accounts of human belonging in and with ecosystems and nonhumans that is commonly conceived of as American, or at least Anglo-American, in its historical emergence and current orientation—is an area of discursive world-making that allows for these epistemological spaces of truce to emerge. Nature writers since Thoreau have come to closely inhabit, care for, or at least look at, the "natural world" and its nonhuman inhabitants with more attention than those of us who lead less nature-connected lives. Nature writers take our relations with the nonhuman world as their material, forging crafts of observation, dialogue, and experimentation with the nonhuman to recognize and revalue a world outside the anthropocentric, usually as a means to engender a more compassionate and balanced way of being in the world.

But what if these works fall well short of Wadiwel's hope of spaces in which we can reimagine equitable and caring relations to the actual majority of nonhuman others alive today? My argument is that many of the works of "nature writing," and particularly of what has come to be known as the "new nature writing," often held up as exemplary "spaces of truce" for human relations with nonhuman species, fail to do this; and that this failure undermines the largely explicit pro-environmental messages of the texts. Much of our ecocriticism of nature writing has also failed to provide adequate attention to the anthropocentric shape of these texts, which reinforces existing power relations between human and nonhuman. As Jos Smith admits in (his thoughtful and cogent) *The New Nature Writing: Rethinking Place in Contemporary Literature*, perhaps the first major exploration of the field, with a specific focus on place, the theme of animals and human/ animal relationships often "falls outside of the discussion" (5), due in Smith's case to its sheer size, leaving much critical work to be done.

This work has begun with the relatively recent growth in interest in the nonhuman that has been labeled the "animal turn" within the social sciences and humanities subjects. This turn has been toward the study of the interactions between humans and nonhumans and the meanings we identify in and ascribe to them. The general field of human–animal studies (or anthrozoology, as some call it) does not approach the use or exploitation of nonhumans by humans as essentially problematic—or indeed sees it as exploitation—whereas the field of critical animal studies (and its subsidiaries, such as critical animal and media studies)—works in the tradition of other critical philosophies, identifying existing relations between groups as problematic, and seeking resolutions for change. As Nik Taylor and Richard Twine suggest, a field such as critical animal studies is not only interested in the "question of the animal" but also with the "*condition* of the animal" (1), and this sets it apart from traditional human–animal studies. Far from being a wholly new or evenly spread phenomenon, this "animal turn" is perhaps best described separately by each field's participants; for example, as Julie Urbanik notes, the field of animal geographies is in its "third wave," the difference being that animal geographies after the "animal turn" is now grappling with questions of "matter and meaning" (Gillespie and Collard 7) to do with the human–animal divide that were absent in animal geographies' two previous waves of studying the nonhuman.

But neither human–animal studies or critical animal studies is Vegan Studies. Vegan Studies engages with vegan praxis: the "matter and meaning" of what it is to both create, and act in response to, vegan identifications in our complex human cultures and more-than-human ecologies. In her introduction to the special cluster of articles on vegan studies in *ISLE: Interdisciplinary Studies in Literature and Environment*, Wright explains how vegan studies is "situated within and outside of extant conceptions of animal studies, animal welfare/rights/liberation, and ecofeminism" (3), and offers the concept of "enmeshed subjections" as a way to approach this necessarily inside/outside position of messy human and nonhuman animal relations that forms a vegan

praxis. In particular, I agree with Wright that "Vegan Studies constitute a lived and embodied ethic that impacts one's scholarly trajectory
. . . for vegan theorists, the world and all of its many texts have long
been read through the lens of the bodily choices that we make as vegans" (8). And as Traci Warkentin (2012) argued in her contribution to
a *Hypatia*-invited symposium, it is problematic to uncritically assume
that every animal studies, human–animal studies, or even critical
animal studies scholar is vegan, and so are operating from a position
of this "lived and embodied ethic." My embodied affective reactions,
as a vegan, to certain pieces of nature writing that are full of blind
spots to their continued support for the exoticization of some species of animals and the exploitation of some others, is part and par-
cel of my scholarly work, which shifts it—messily—into this domain
of vegan studies more appropriately, perhaps, than holding a critical
animal studies position. Smith's "critical work to be done," however,
applies equally to vegan studies, and here includes reading (and writing) these texts of nature writing through the lens of emerging vegan
theory to identify where they fail to acknowledge the nonhuman, and
especially those nonhumans we currently exploit most: for our food,
goods, clothing, and entertainment. This chapter explores how applying a vegan lens to nature writing can further the field of ecocritical
studies, as well as be of use to nature writers in spreading the impact
of their work to be of benefit to broader nonhuman as well as human
communities. Exploring nature writing through a vegan lens is essential to avoid the trap of failing to engage with the environmental and
moral crises of this century, which, if there is any claim to be made for
contemporary nature writing, must be its mandate.

For Wadiwel, a truce in the war waged by humans against animals
"needs not be predetermined by an existing relation of violence" (293).
"War" here can be a troubling term, implying an attempt to remove
power from invading or immoral entities, and no doubt Wadiwel considered the connotations before setting out to write a book with the
word "war" in its title. For example, how are animals construed as
combatants, particularly when set against other conceptions of how
we make meaning out of nonhuman existence and experience such as
that proposed by Anat Pick. She has argued that nonhuman animals,
especially those within the animal agricultural complex, exist within
"an exemplary 'state of exception' of species sovereignty. To speak
of animals' vulnerability in this context is to draw attention to their
outstanding position in the judicial, political, and moral orders" (15).

That is, nonhumans are exemplary in their vulnerability: not enemy combatants at all, but "first and foremost [living bodies]—material, temporal, and vulnerable" (5).

However, the use of "war" in relation to animals is not new—Jacques Derrida used the term over a decade before Wadiwel—and the way in which Wadiwel employs the term to bring forth and theorize the concept of "spaces of truce" perhaps gives us some remedy, an end point even, to the application of "war" as a metaphor in relation to fellow species. The concept of the truce is, I suggest, employed to make abundantly clear that what is needed is not simply a new ethics, but also political strategies that have a shape and can be implemented. A truce is a cessation of violence between parties. It is not immediately about redistributing power, nor about rebalancing equality—two objectives that are seen by some, including Peter Singer, as often overambitious and responsible for limiting change. Rather, this chapter makes a case for vegan readings of nature writing as a way of critiquing the genre constructively, providing directions for ecologically minded literature to fulfill its potential in creating space where, as Wadiwel says, we can "begin the work of imagining what a world beyond the war against animals might look like" (292).

THE NEW NATURE WRITING

The "new nature writing" is a contested term (as is "nature writing"), but is often pinned to the masthead of issue 102 of *Granta* magazine in summer 2008 as the moment it became a genre. "New nature writing" breaks with traditional writing about the environment and the human place within it by challenging previous practices; of decrying, as Becky Ayre writes, "earlier nature writing's belief in nature as a wholly redemptive force."[1] For "new nature writers" such as Alice Oswald, Kathleen Jamie, and Robert MacFarlane, this thing called "nature" and by extension the nonhuman is often ambivalent, brutal, something that we cannot know even as we are charged with finding ways to reconnect.

For Jason Cowley, editor of that 2008 edition of *Granta*, new nature writing separated itself from more traditional forms by being performed by writers "who approached their subject in heterodox and experimental ways" (10). Unfortunately, as Smith points out, this "claim suggests rather erroneously that 'old nature writing' was not heterodox or experimental" (9). For Smith the best examples of this

new form of writing have a "self-reflexive dialogue with the longer tradition" (27). What *new* nature writing may be most useful for, suggests
Smith, is that its authors have "come to recognize that the planet is
now in a volatile state of change on a trajectory that will be disastrous
for the sustainability of ecosystems and the future of biological life if
it continues" (13). In acknowledging this reality, these writings offer
us a "recognition of the Anthropocene [that] forces us to look very
carefully at our cultures of 'Nature' and ask if they too, however well
intentioned, are part of the problem. Is there, enshrined within them,
a belief that 'Nature' is 'eternal and separate'?" (13–14). What does this
mean, Smith asks, for "our cultural understanding of 'Nature'?

> First perhaps, it puts the word in inverted commas or gives it a
> capital letter: that is to say, it estranges us from what we have,
> for a long time, taken for granted. Attention has been drawn to
> the way the naming of 'Nature' as an object establishes a distance
> between us and it, a distance characteristic of, and symptomatic
> of, the continuous exploitation that has led to such vast anthro-
> pogenic disruption. (13)

Many nature writers have seemingly taken up the challenge of reori-
enting our knowledge systems to undo this "continuous exploitation
[and] vast anthropogenic disruption." Biocentric poetry, essays, and
fiction could, perhaps should, be seen as spaces of truce, or as elements shaping such places. At its most impactful, such writings do
not work simply as metaphor, argues the writer Richard Mabey, but
in their diversity are "the nano-bricks for rebuilding things" (qtd. in
Smith 5) in the face of the ongoing loss of wildlife and species extinction, the moral crimes of animal agriculture, and environmental
devastation. This approach is what Smith calls a "microcosmic view"
(7) of how we can reconfigure human-centric knowledge systems,
through "fresh and innovative writing" that "is alert to the subtle,
ongoing dialogues between layers of history, and layers of genre that
have lodged themselves in our expectations and in our ways of looking" (26) at animals and the broader environmental world.

A familiar trope of new nature writing is the (often traumatic) emotional experiences of the author: here is Helen Macdonald's grief at her
father's death in the award-winning *H Is for Hawk* ("one cannot think of
this new genre without recalling that book," writes Ayre); here, in *Being a
Beast*, is Charles Foster's not-quite-admitted guilt at once being a prolific

hunter; here, in *Feral*, is George Monbiot's "ecological boredom" and the desire to live a rewilded life; here, in *Great Tide Rising*, is Kathleen Dean Moore's anger at climate devastation, the loss of wildlife and habitat that her grandchildren may never have the pleasure to discover.

There is much to champion here, even if many authors refuse such a label as "new nature writers." Yet the contrast between the field's aims and the failures of much new nature writing to take *all* nonhuman life into account asks us to question why these writers ignore deeper questions of animal otherness, and the resultant inequalities and environmental impacts such ignorance brings forth. For example, re-viewing the texts above through a vegan lens would begin to reveal that the environmentally responsible actions these narratives urge us toward are problematized by this failure of attention to the exploitation of nonhuman bodies for human consumption practices. To begin with:

Feral: The opening page sees Monbiot pick up the larva of a cockchafer. "I watched it twitching for a moment, then I put it in my mouth."[2]

Great Tide Rising: Dean Moore laments the climate-change-induced sickening of starfish, is shaken by the Stanford scientists who call for all nations to take immediate action against fossil fuels, then takes her family home for dinner and, ignoring industrial agriculture's carbon footprint, cooks them roast beef.

Being a Beast: Taylor lives like five nonhumans: a badger, an otter, a fox, a swift, and a deer. Quite typically he writes: "Red deer are victims," erasing the other side of that asymmetric equation sustaining the myth of humans as innate hunters. "Their landscape is the landscape of victims, and invisible except through victims' eyes."

H Is for Hawk: "'Come on, Mabel!'" writes Macdonald. "I'm kneeling on the carpet and holding out a dead day-old cockerel chick. My freezer is packed with their sad, fluffy corpses, by-products of industrial egg production. Mabel loves them."

To put it more bluntly: why are only the lives of some animals worth "thinking with" in this new nature writing, and not others? And why do the authors not recognize this blindness as anthropocentric violence? As Erika Cudworth suggests, one way of approaching this set of questions is to consider "human relations with nonhuman animals . . . as a system of social institutions and practices that have their own conceptual repertoire. This involves different degrees of domination of other animals by humans" (28). Cudworth uses the concepts of oppression, exploitation, and marginalization in order to describe this domination. One social practice that wields such concepts in the repertoire of human domination is discourse: the texts of culture that shape how we see and think about the other, human and nonhuman. It is clear that the abuses of these other, less important, consumable nonhuman animals in what are otherwise compassionate and environmentally concerned texts, contributes to the reinforcement of human dominance over other species.

However, how does this all-too-common carelessness in relation to the exploitation and suffering of some (indeed, most) nonhuman animals result in the texts' failures to achieve what they explicitly set out to do: encourage a change in the readers' attitudes and behaviors towards "Nature?" It is with concern for this question that I approach the last book listed above.

H IS FOR HAWK

Macdonald's *H Is for Hawk* has held readers in thrall since its publication in July 2014. The book won that year's Samuel Johnson Prize for nonfiction and the Costa Book of the Year award. *Hawk* has been praised for the quality of writing and embodied engagement with the nonhuman, specifically the goshawk that Macdonald buys, domesticates, and trains. The underlying theme of the book pronounces a need to steward our environmental commons better, and to do this Macdonald puts forward a nostalgic conservancy ethic of intimately "knowing nature" as the best means of protection. It has spent months on best-seller lists on both sides of the Atlantic and propelled Macdonald into the glare of global writerly popularity.

Not bad for the diary of a blood sport.

Of course, *H Is for Hawk* is much more than that; the emotional center of the book is an honest account of how Macdonald processes grief at her father's death. Yet in doing so, *Hawk* retells the usual tale of human dominance. It is the breaking of a wild goshawk, Mabel, and their subsequent trips into the countryside to kill. (Macdonald grew up with birds, and especially falcons and birds of prey, and in 2006

wrote *Falcon* in the Reaktion series.) Macdonald and Mabel hunt rabbits and pheasants, the narrative repeating and reasserting particular
social relations to other species: here, between moral agent (human),
exotic addendum (the hawk), wild victim (pheasant, rabbit), or
domestic product (dead day-old chick). Such repetition is the basis of
identity formation—our identities, and the identities of others. It's not
wholly Macdonald's fault, circumscribed as she is by a society-wide
speciesist structure of perception. How Macdonald relates to others,
suggest sociologists Matthew Cole and Kate Stewart, is (as for the rest
of us) strictly controlled by societal pressures and norms, especially in
childhood, channeling our experiences of other animals into precise
categories: vermin, wildlife, pets, companions, food. Arnold Arluke
suggests that this process, by which most of us look at animals not
through a phylogenetic scale but through what he calls the "sociozoologic scale" (qtd. in Herzog 48) is learned psychological behavior.
Or as Hal Herzog frames it: "Culture plays a major role in how we
construct the sociozoologic scale . . . based on the roles animals play
in our lives" (48). This process of cultural categorization is intimately
bound up with the language we use about animals, making the role of
writers, cultural producers of such language, critical to these categories' reinforcement.

But it is not good enough to uncritically reinforce these categories
through discourse; this is perhaps especially the case when, as Macdonald
does, an author uses their (highly successful and widely read) narrative
to call for taking greater responsibility for "Nature" in protest at humanity's destruction of the environment.

"One of the biggest themes of my book is the way we think about
the natural world," Macdonald told the *Washington Post*. "We use it as
a mirror of ourselves. It's important to consider how and why we do
that. We must look past that and see the world itself."[3]

But which world? And critically, which nonhumans are allowed to
appear in the mirror? The anthrozoologist James Serpell suggests that
we respond to animals through a combination of attaching to them
varying levels of emotion in two dimensions: affect and utility. Some
are loved, some are loathed; some are useless, and some are useful.
While *H Is for Hawk* is often seen as the flag bearer for this new nature
writing, it is also at work fetishizing some animals into categories worthy of our love and protection (hawks, humans) while at the same time
reinforcing and naturalizing the subordination of other beleaguered
nonhumans as merely useful as "game" or food (pheasants, rabbits,

dead day-old chicks). This matters, and not only when such a lack of attention to these subjugated forms of nonhuman life undermines the environmental message of the author and text.

But sometimes these other creatures won't stay silent. A bird has already appeared in *Hawk* quite literally by a sleight of hand, as if the author doesn't want us to see it and certainly refuses to take careful note of it herself. But we do see it, and it betrays Macdonald's failure of vulnerable nonhumanity; it is the abject object of human hubris and the hell of domestication *par excellence*: it is the dead day-old cockerel chick she feeds Mabel during her training.

In numbers, the chicken is the most abused land animal in history. "Broiler" chickens live to around forty-five days old, their bodies pushed beyond limits to grow at a rate that maximizes bodily flesh at the cost of suffering from broken limbs and other ailments. Other chickens get to live less than one day. These are what Macdonald calls "by-products of industrial egg production," the male chicks who are economically useless because they cannot lay eggs. Many are macerated for pet food or fishmeal. Others are gassed in plastic bags or left to die in bins. One outlet the industry has found for them is as food for exotic pets such as snakes, other reptiles, and birds of prey.

"When [Mabel's] head is up swallowing a mouthful of chick," writes Macdonald,

> I tug its remains through my palm and spirit it away. She looks down, then behind her, then at the floor. *Where did it go?* I persuade her to step back onto her perch. Then I hold the chick out once more, and further away. Instantly I feel that terrible blow. It is a killing blow, but there is something about the force of it that reminds me that I am alive. (108)

Macdonald hides the chick behind her back to train Mabel to take food from her hand, as a way of controlling Mabel for hawking. Later when Macdonald has *manned* Mabel (the term for the training to hunt) and they go out, the act spurs Macdonald to reflect on the act of killing. Hunting is "not a 'high-intensity birdwatching' [. . .] What I had done was nothing like birdwatching. It was more like gambling, though the stakes were infinitely bloodier. At its heart was a willed loss of control" (177). But who loses in this gamble? They chase a rabbit that gets away. Macdonald is "crestfallen too. It's not that I'm baying for blood. But I don't want Mabel to get discouraged" (179).

Mabel finally makes a kill:

> I stare at the hawk as she grips the dead pheasant, and her mad
> eyes stare right back at me. I'm amazed. I don't know what I
> expected to feel. Bloodlust? Brutality? No. Nothing like that.
> . . . I look at the hawk, the pheasant, the hawk. And everything
> changes. The hawk stops being a thing of violent death. She
> becomes a child. It shakes me to the core. She is a child. A baby
> hawk that's just worked out who she is. What she's for. I reach and
> start, unconsciously as a mother helping a child with her dinner,
> plucking the pheasant with the hawk. For the hawk. (184)

Macdonald collapses the species boundaries between human and
hawk into generic terms of mother and child. But the work being
done by such a collapse of categories is to normalize the consumption of meat by both bird and human. Indeed, for Macdonald, the
eating of flesh is not only normal but also formative of an essential
nature that is shared across species lines. In many ways, this position
reverses that put forward by many advocates for veganism in asking
people to consider shared characteristics across nonhuman species
("Why love one but eat the other?") and between humans and nonhumans. Examining how the hawk "becomes a child" through the lens
of a vegan theory highlights how, as Cole and Stewart argue, a human
child *also* "becomes a child" through the careful manipulation of categories to which she is exposed and into which she is placed.

A few pages later, Macdonald adds:

> I hate killing things. I'm loath to tread on spiders and get laughed
> at for rescuing flies. But now I understood for the first time what
> bloodthirstiness was all about. . . . Hunting took me to the very
> edge of being a human. Then it took me past that place to some-
> where I wasn't human at all. (195)

Can we take the author's word for it? Perhaps my discomfort with *H Is
for Hawk* was exacerbated when I met the author after a book reading
and was invited to join her and the organizers for dinner. At a restaurant that had a separate vegan menu (but which they had to print off
fresh for me, as it had never been asked for before), Macdonald ordered
leg of duck. Over dinner I told Macdonald that I felt sorry for the pheasants in the book. "Oh, so do I," Macdonald answered. I looked down

at her dinner, the dead leg of a "game" bird corpse on her plate and was unsure of her felicity. Did she truly feel for the pheasants as I did? If she did, would she not reject, as I was doing, their consumption by humans, and as such, her part in the blood sport of falconry, of hunting with hawks? This visceral disgust I felt at her choice of meal, part of what Wright names as a vegan scholar's "non-normative embodied status," (8) has, I know, framed my scholarship toward Macdonald's work. But is that any different for a carnivorous scholar or reader, framed, as he will be, by his "normative embodied status"?

In this speciesist social practice of killing, Macdonald has found her avatar in the goshawk Mabel to do her killing for her. This is not only a metaphor for the way that humans live in the Western world: We *do* have proxies (other human proxies) to do our killing for us, those slaughterhouse workers who are as hidden to us as the animals they kill—the pigs, cows, ducks, pheasants, or chickens (see Eisnitz, Pachirat). Macdonald is smack in the middle of a "meat paradox"— how we often claim we "hate killing things" and yet outsource our killing in efforts to assuage our guilt over what we eat. We do not want to be seen as killing animals (in both senses). Yet Macdonald seems to be arguing that it is exactly by killing and consuming others that we come closer to our humanity. As she concludes:

> Of all the lessons I've learned in my months with Mabel this is the greatest of all: that there is a world of things out there—rocks and trees and stones and grass and all the things that crawl and run and fly. They are all things in themselves, but we make them sensible to us by giving them meanings that shore up our own views of the world. In my time with Mabel I've learned how you feel more human once you have known, even in your imagination, what it is like to be not. (275)

Yet the stretch of Macdonald's imagination is limited by her own speciesist practices. What is most problematic about *Hawk*, common across new nature writing, are the tears that Macdonald sheds "for the pheasant, for the hawk, for Dad and for all his patience, for that little girl who stood by a fence and waited for the hawks to come home" (184) while the dead day-old chick (or the leg of duck) arouses nothing about the value of "Nature" or "wildness" or the "nonhuman." The pheasant is mourned because of its status as another person's property: "I am guilty. I've poached a pheasant from someone's shoot. I didn't mean to, I almost say out loud" (237–38). Neither does Macdonald take responsibility for the killing of the chick. It's a "by-product," as if her responsibility for this consumption stands outside of her considerations in how we "protect nature." Her use of the term "by-product" suggests that *no one* needs take responsibility for the killing of the chick at all. Is the chick, then, not nature/Nature? How does this sit with Macdonald's assertion that we (re)discover our connections with nature as a means of understanding our place in the world and therefore, she hopes, our willingness to protect it? The dead chick is the absented victim in this story, hidden twice, first by Macdonald's sleight of hand and then by her sleight of words.

This absence matters beyond the chick's own life. As the 2006 UN report *Livestock's Long Shadow* identified, animal agriculture is the foremost contributing industry to the greenhouse gas emissions that lead to dangerous climate change.[4] For *Hawk* to bring the "by-product of industrial egg production" into the narrative, only to spirit it away again behind the back, lets neoliberal capitalism's rapacious animal consumption off the hook. That is, to bear no responsibility for the dead day-old chick (*only* a "by-product") undermines *H Is for Hawk's* environmental call-to-arms. Despite her claims to look beyond the mirror, Macdonald glamorizes two species—the hawk, the human—while actively killing or ignoring others, seemingly blind to the threat that continued abuse of nonhuman others poses to the animals themselves, and our planet.

Earlier in *Hawk*, Macdonald writes that,

> To train a hawk . . . You are exercising what the poet Keats called your chameleon quality, the ability to "tolerate a loss of self and a loss of rationality by trusting in the capacity to recreate oneself in another character or another environment." Such a feat of imaginative recreation has always come easily to me. Too easily. It's part of being a watcher, forgetting who you are and putting yourself in the thing you are watching. That is why the girl who was me when I was small loved watching birds. (86)

Such a claim is hubristic when placed against the image of Macdonald blithely reaching into the fridge freezer to pull out the bag of frozen chicks or tucking into a leg of duck. Macdonald turns herself into the victim; it is *her* vulnerability as a young girl that feeds her ability to watch, bond with, write about, and profit from the birds. But which birds? Those she watches: wildlife, the hawk. But not the chicken? It is *not* the little girl who has disappeared in this story, but the suffering of the chicken behind the adult's back, at whom the human *never* looks. Why is the chick worth so little of her imagination? Her empathy? If Macdonald is practicing empathy here, it is lacking of what philosopher Lori Gruen calls "entangled empathy," a kind of moral attention enthused with what longtime animal activist Kim Stallwood has called "The Magical Connection"—an altruistic love for nonhuman individuals, allowing us to recalibrate the categories into which we place other species. It is far from a full engagement with Wright's concept of "enmeshed subjections" and even farther from the "tactical, categorical unravelling" (5) that such messy enmeshment calls for.

On these grounds, I strongly refute Macdonald's claim that she finds the ability to "tolerate a loss of self and a loss of rationality by trusting in the capacity to recreate oneself in another" . . . "too easy" at all. Rather, such claims merely reinforce the need to reveal further the value of taking all nonhuman life into account when asking fundamental questions such as not only "what is a human?" but also "what is an animal?" and indeed "how can both coexist on this planet?" Macdonald's conservancy ethics based on a "love" and "connection" with one singular animal, and the places to which this connection takes them both, fails to address the structural causes of the devastation to nonhuman bodies and environmental systems that appall the author (and most of her readers). Rather, *Hawk* reinforces an outdated paradigm of relating to the nonhuman that remains based on speciesist valuations, with the human as hierarchically superior—the one who values. Such works foreclose an opportunity for a radical revision of affective knowledge, gained through an embodied engagement with other species. This is what, on the surface, Macdonald seems to advocate. But instead of offering us a "space of truce," *Hawk* remains rooted in a historical relation to knowing nature that is wilfully blind to the systems of exploitation that such knowledge shores up and sustains, such as, perhaps most of all, animal agriculture. Applying a vegan lens reveals Macdonald's writing practice to be constitutive of, rather than in opposition to, many of the worst ways in which humans continue to deracinate the planet through often-overlooked practical and daily food choices.

Following Warkentin, I agree that it would be problematic to suggest that all nature writers should be vegan. But as Wadiwel suggests, and this is relevant for nature writers too, "Humans declare themselves exceptionally intelligent, but only after they have prevailed over other animals with violence" (27). And it is this violence that structures our institutions and knowledge systems that in the end leads to devastating environmental and biodiversity destruction, climate change, and the threat to our very social systems. When considered through this new lens of vegan theory, perhaps *H* is not for *Hawk* at all, but for *Hypocrite*.

A vegan lens offers us the tools, as with the aligned critical animal studies, write Amy Fitzgerald and Nik Taylor, to "analyze normalization discourses surrounding the consumption of animal products" so that the ways in which "power plays out and manifests itself through discourse" (166) is revealed. What a specifically vegan lens offers us in theoretical work and creative endeavours is a radical and more ecologically coherent way of ensuring the present experiences of all beings are taken into account when examining the ways in which discourse shapes power. In particular, the "non-normative embodied status" of the vegan scholar or reader should be afforded credibility for the role it plays in the composition of such questions. Many of the most abundant nonhuman animal life forms on the planet are those we breed to kill—over eighty billion land mammals each year. Critiquing such texts with the conceptual tools of vegan studies means that such imaginative operations as those at work in Macdonald's *H Is for Hawk* can be tested for salience and efficacy against these numbers: asking if such human praxis is constitutive of oppression or equality; asking whether such writing takes these usually ignored nonhumans into account; and determining whether such accounts then achieve their overarching aims to bring about more ecologically sustainable and compassionate practices.

In an interview with *Electric Literature*, Macdonald responds to the question *Is wildness what is not human?* by suggesting, "Ultimately, yes, but in that sense, a chicken is wild. I think pretty much everything that isn't human is a wild thing."[5]

Why the "but"? This abrogation of the chicken's tendencies and desires for life in a derogatory comment that pits humanity against wildness is a complicated and yet depressing synecdoche of all that is wrong with the way we have normalized the un-wildness of the chicken and the un-wildness of the human. In this paradigm, hawks are worth our imaginative work and protection. Chickens, it seems, are not. For Macdonald, perhaps the imaginative leap into the mind of other birds is only "too easy" if that bird is exotic enough a metaphor for her grief.

In the end, *H Is for Hawk* fails to create a "space of truce" because it does not take into account the war being waged against *all* animals. *Hawk,* as exemplar of new nature writing, fails the abused, exploited, eaten, and tested upon at the expense of the exotic and anthropocentric. It falls short of its potential: to reveal the full range of "enmeshed subjections" and bodily entanglements we have with a nonhuman world.

Rather, to create such "spaces of truce" calls for writing that offers a radical revision of the knowledge systems that we humans have fashioned in our colonization of the Earth. Vegan theory offers a way toward this goal. A truce in our "war against animals" will provide time and space—just as it would in a conventional military war—to reconfigure how we perceive others and our entanglements with them; indeed, such a timeout would allow the nonhuman animals' own entanglements with the world and with each other to emerge and be respected, outside of a human-centered view. Such a process encourages "new forms of connection" to be proposed and shared for the benefit of all species, and our fragile ecosystems.

WORKS CITED

Adams, Carol J. Foreword to *The Vegan Studies Project: Food, Animals, and Gender in the Age of Terror,* by Laura Wright. Athens: University of Georgia Press, 2016.

Cole, Matthew, and Kate Stewart. *Our Children and Other Animals: The Cultural Construction of Human-Animal Relations in Childhood.* London: Routledge, 2014.

Cudworth, Erika. "Beyond Speciesism: Intersectionality, Critical Sociology and the Human Domination of Other Animals." In *The Rise of Critical Animal Studies: From the Margins to the Center.* Edited by Nik Taylor and Richard Twine, 19–35. London: Routledge, 2014.

Eisnitz, Gail. *Slaughterhouse: The Shocking Story of Greed, Neglect, and Inhumane Treatment Inside the US Meat Industry.* Amherst, NY: Prometheus, 2006.

Fitzgerald, Amy, and Nik Taylor. "The Cultural Hegemony of Meat and the Animal Industrial Complex." In *The Rise of Critical Animal Studies: From the Margins to the Center.* Edited by Nik Taylor and Richard Twine, 165–82. London: Routledge, 2014.

Foster, Charles. *Being a Beast.* London: Profile Books, 2016.

Gillespie, Kathryn, and Rosemary-Claire Collard. *Introduction to Critical Animal Geographies: Politics, Intersections, and Hierarchies in a Multispecies World,* 1–16. Edited by Kathryn Gillespie and Rosemary-Claire Collard. London: Routledge, 2015.

Gruen, Lori. *Entangled Empathy.* Brooklyn: Lantern Books, 2015.

Herzog, Hal. *Some We Love, Some We Hate, Some We Eat.* New York, NY: Harper Perennial, 2011.

Macdonald, Helen. *H Is for Hawk.* London: Jonathan Cape, 2014.

Monbiot, George. *Feral: Rewilding the Land, the Sea, and Human Life.* London: Penguin, 2014.

Moore, Kathleen Dean. *Great Tide Rising: Toward Clarity and Moral Courage in a Time of Planetary Change.* Berkeley, CA: Counterpoint, 2016.

Pachirat, Timothy. *Every Twelve Seconds: Industrialized Slaughter and the Politics of Sight.* New Haven and London: Yale University Press, 2011.

Pick, Anat. *Creaturely Poetics: Animality and Vulnerability in Literature and Film.* New York: Columbia University Press, 2011.

Serpell, James. "Anthropomorphism and Anthropomorphic Selection: Beyond the 'Cute Response.'" *Society & Animals* 11, no. 1 (2002): 83–100.

Singer, Peter. *Practical Ethics.* 3rd edition. Cambridge: Cambridge University Press 2011.

Smith, Jos. *The New Nature Writing: Rethinking Place in Contemporary Literature.* London: Bloomsbury, 2017. Pre-publication manuscript.

Stallwood, Kim. "Animal Lovers and Animal Rights." In *Animal Lovers: An Exhibition*. Berlin: nGbK Gallery, 2016.

Taylor, Nik, and Richard Twine. "Locating the 'Critical' in Critical Animal Studies," in *The Rise of Critical Animal Studies: From the Margins to the Center*, 1–15. Edited by Nik Taylor and Richard Twine. London: Routledge, 2014.

Urbanik, Julie. *Placing Animals: An Introduction to the Geography of Human-Animal Relations*. Lanham, MD: Rowman & Littlefield, 2012.

Wadiwel, Dinesh. *The War Against Animals*. Leiden and Boston: Brill-Rodopi, 2015.

Warkentin, Traci. "Must Every Animal Studies Scholar Be Vegan?," *Hypatia* 27, no. 3 (2012): 499–504.

Wright, Laura. "Introducing Vegan Studies," in *ISLE: Interdisciplinary Studies in Literature and Environment*, 2018. Draft.

———. *The Vegan Studies Project: Food, Animals, and Gender in the Age of Terror*. Athens: University of Georgia Press, 2015.

END NOTES

1. http://www.litro.co.uk/2016/08/amy-liptrots-outrun-new-nature-writing/
2. George Monbiot has altered his diet to be vegan out of environmental concerns; see https://www.theguardian.com/commentisfree/2018/jun/08/save-planet-meat-dairy-livestock-food-free-range-steak.
3. https://www.washingtonpost.com/express/wp/2016/03/17/whats-next-for-helen-macdonald-author-of-h-is-for-hawk/
4. http://www.fao.org/docrep/010/a0701e/a0701e00.HTM
5. https://electricliterature.com/the-great-natural-drama-an-interview-with-helen-macdonald-author-of-h-is-for-hawk-5d50980b4c9a#.frfg7qmaq

CHAPTER 13

The Best Little Slaughterhouse in Portland: Hipsters and the Rhetoric of Meat

D. Gilson

"Today, at stake in the question of eating animals is not only our basic ability to respond to sentient life, but our ability to respond to parts of our own (animal) being."

—*Jonathan Safran Foer*

In "Farm," the premier episode of *Portlandia*, "A well-intentioned Portland couple wants to know if the chicken they are ordering for dinner had a nice life."[1] We watch *Portlandia*'s stars, Carrie Brownstein and Fred Armisen, order dinner at The Gilt Club, a hip café: "I guess I do have a question about the chicken," Brownstein tells Dana, their server. "Can you just tell me a little bit more about it?" Dana answers in all seriousness: "Yes, the chicken is a heritage breed, woodland-raised chicken that's been fed a diet of sheep's milk, soy, and hazelnuts." Dana's answer spurs a chorus of questions: "Okay, this is local? Is that USDA Organic, or Oregon Organic, or Portland Organic . . . and the hazelnuts, are those local? How big is the area where the chickens are able to roam free?"

Dana steps away from the table as Brownstein assures Armisen, "We're doing the right thing." When Dana returns, she presents the couple with a portfolio. "All right, so here is the chicken you'll be enjoying tonight . . . his name was Colin, here are his papers . . . they do a lot to make sure that their chickens are, uh, happy." Brownstein presses the issue. "When you say 'they,' who are these people raising Colin?" In suppressed frustration, Dana responds, "It's a farm about thirty miles south of Portland." Armisen retorts, "You have a good relationship with this farm? It's not some guy on a yacht who lives in Miami?" "Oh no," Dana assures them, and this seems to please Brownstein, who adds, "It just tears at the core of my being the idea of someone just cashing in on a trend like *organic*." Tellingly, rhetoric slips in the scene, from care for and of the animal, to the highest concern for what is about to be consumed by the caricatured hipster body, and how that body labels the food it consumes for approval or disapproval. Or perhaps better said: the white hipster is masking its privileged demand for pleasure by transferring its (over-) concern for the self onto a seeming concern for the objects of violent consumption.

This essay explores how hipsters eat meat, questioning particularly how hipster omnivores—those in a position of relative wealth allowing them to make a variety of food choices—rhetorically defend their consumption of nonhuman animals. More specifically, I focus on the Portland Meat Collective (PMC), a butchery training business, and Camas Davis, its founder, as indicative of the dystopic hipster rhetoric that neoliberal politics offers as deceptively radical (in the formerly whites-only "utopia" of Oregon, no less). Here, I contend with the popular view of the hipster as a whiney, spoiled brat whose cultural performances provide victimhood to the political project(s) of whiteness, while also hindering the emergence of a more diverse and progressive mainstream coalition.[2] In her foundational 2015 study *The Vegan Studies Project*, Laura Wright playfully places "veganism in the category of study or scholarly inquiry," thus "indicating that veganism and vegan identity, as well as the popular and academic discourse that constructs those categories, need to be explored, understood, and challenged" (1). Wright goes on to explain that her work, and the nascent field of vegan studies more broadly, "constitutes a cultural studies analysis," an analysis which should examine "the mainstream discourse surrounding and connecting animal rights to (or omitting animal rights from) veganism, with specific attention to the construction and depiction of the US vegan body—both male and female—as a contested site manifest in contemporary works of literature, popular cultural representations, advertising, and news media" (19). In studying the specific site of Camas Davis and her Portland Meat Collective, indicative of hipster omnivore food politics more broadly, it might seem as if my mission is antithetical to the field of vegan studies. I argue, however, that to understand the call to veganism, both theoretically and in practice, we must also understand how and why omnivores—especially those like Davis who might otherwise share both our progressive politics and privileged ability to make a variety of food choices—defend their consumption of animals. As critical whiteness studies has become an important part of the critical race theoretical project more broadly, so must a diligent, thoughtful, and constant critique of omnivores be undertaken to understand the vegan corollary.

THE DREAM OF THE NINETIES IS ALIVE IN PORTLAND

Explaining why she chose Portland for her butchery cooperative to Marnie Hanel of *The New York Times*, Camas Davis contends, "Here, it's been pretty easy to create an alternate economy." Indeed, Portland comically represents darker specters of what alternatives are feasible (for upwardlymobile whites) under neoliberalism. "Portland is a city where young people go to retire," Armisen tells Brownstein during the opening credits of *Portlandia*'s "Farm." In an opening sequence that is part theme song, part sketch, and fully thesis statement for the show's satirical approach, Armisen explains all the ways in which Portland is a utopia. "Remember the nineties," he pleads, "when they'd encourage you to be weird? It was just an amazing time where people would go to see something like the Jim Rose Sideshow Circus and watch someone hang something from their penis? You could grow up to want to be a clown. People went to clown school!" Brownstein responds, "I gave up clowning years ago!" and Armisen assures her, "In Portland, you don't have to." *Portlandia* provides a useful entry into discussing contemporary Portland for what it is: a utopia for the white American bourgeoisie such as Davis and her cooperative. A white-topia.

Because geopolitical context is crucial to understanding such do-it-yourself entrepreneurial endeavors, I want to pause and consider the specifically neoliberal Portland in which Davis sets up (chop) shop. Sian Rowe offers that contemporary Portland "is the closest thing the US has to a bohemian theme park; a chic, eclectic and, above all, affordable hipster enclave, where outsiders are drawn by its music scene, vintage clothing stores, microbreweries and zero sales tax." Even this brief description begins to reveal the hipster wonderland, the neo-bohemia, being one of overwrought consumption, from artisan beers to carefullycurated vintage clothing upsold from thrift shops—and further, with no sales tax! Portland, which is now the whitest city in the US, with over 75 percent of the population identifying as such in the 2010 census,[3] may well have an underlying sentiment to how it sells itself: "You, too, can lead the ultimate neoliberal life with none of the guilt." It is easy to feel good about one's purchasing choices as a radical politic when one is not surrounded by those who literally cannot afford to make such "radical" choices to begin with. In short: radical politics are easy in a homogenous population that allows the political aims themselves to be markers of one's citizenship within a homogenous sub-culture-cum-dominant-culture.

But this is all to speak somewhat coyly of Portland as a laughable enclave; there is a deeper cost to the white-topia of Portland and the hipster politic it reflects in other places across the US. Hipsters' involvement in urban gentrification practices as "early adopters" within US cities places them firmly within larger strategies of neoliberal caitalism.[4] Susan Schweik aptly examines Portland's implementation of nineteenth-century "ugly laws" in the name of neoliberal progress. Citing the Americans with Disabilities Act mandate for navigable sidewalks, the city of Portland has displaced its homeless population by outlawing their congregation on public sidewalks, literally pushing them to the curbs; the city does this not to clear the way for disabled citizens, but rather to allow food trucks the space to serve their hipster consumer base without the discomfort of these primarily white and middle- or upper-class consumers having to eat in front of homeless people. More seriously mirroring Rowe, Schweik describes "Portland's downtown trouble: the consolidation and ongoing crises of global neoliberal capitalism; the dismantling of already diminished social welfare mechanisms; increasing gentrification; racism; [and] the ongoing effects of deinstitutionalization" (12).

Again, poverty, racism, and disability do not seem social injustices in need of political action if they are quite literally, and most-often violently, erased from public life. In a 2012 report analyzing the most recent US Census data, urban studies researchers from Portland State University found troubling, though not surprising, side effects of white hipster gentrification, in large part what satirical comedy like *Portlandia* lampoons. Shandas and Dann explain that, regarding the already-small African American population in Portland, they find

an overall reduction in concentration across the region and within census block groups. These results may not be surprising because they corroborate earlier findings by other reports, including the *State of Black Oregon* (2010), the *Regional Equity Atlas* (2009), and several *Oregonian* articles on the topic of neighborhood change. . . . Indeed, we see fewer block groups with a majority of African Americans overall. (16–17)

If white hipsters so often appear to lead day-glo lives relatively free of social injustice (prompting the question *why are they so sad?*), it is because their relative privilege allows them to live in white-topias: neighborhoods reclaimed from working-class people of color or whole cities, of which Portland is exemplar, which had very few people of color in need of removal to begin with.[5]

By the point Davis paints Portland as a haven for alternative economies, Hanel has already portrayed Portland as a type of utopia for the aesthetically minded consumer who wants to feel better about needless animal consumption: "In this farm-to-table era, community-supported-agriculture shares—in which families purchase farm goods through a weekly subscription—have become increasingly popular. Nowhere is that more true than in Portland, where people take their food ethics, among other things, very seriously." Neither Davis nor Hanel speak, however, of the economic prowess—both actual capital and an economics of time—necessary for such food "ethics" to arise. Davis wears her consumption and business tactics as a badge of radical honor, and Hanel does nothing to complicate this self-congratulatory gesture; they thus participate in a game of "good consumer versus bad consumer," a game that white liberals almost always, by design, win. Consumerism might have some room for political radicalism,[6] but the PMC, which represents not only a larger specter of hipster business practices, but also a specific business model that arises so prominently in Portland and similar American white-topias under neoliberalism, is not such an instance. By misrepresenting their slaughter as both necessary and humane, participants conveniently wash over the very real violence they regularly enact on nonhuman animals, while also alienating Other humans who might be organic political allies.

MEAT BY ANY OTHER NAME

According to their website (pdxmeat.com), "The Portland Meat Collective brings local meat to local people." This sounds innocent enough, as the locavore movement does have direct benefits, both of health—the food is fresher, thus fewer nutrients are destroyed in the processes required by shipping—and more obviously, economic—local food purchasing supports local farming, which in and of itself might be a worthwhile joint producer-consumer protest of agribusiness conglomerates.[7] In part, the PMC's stated philosophy reflects this seemingly neo-Marxist notion of reconnecting people with the production of their food: "We at the PMC believe that everyone is entitled to a thorough understanding of the myriad, and often complicated and confusing, ways that our food gets to our tables."[8] The "everyone" of this philosophy, however, is deceptive. "Everyone" might mean any combination of farmers, slaughterhouse workers, butchers, or instructors at the PMC, who ultimately cut out the need for outsourced slaughtering and butchery; we can assume, however, that the "everyone" does not include the nonhuman animals who will be murdered for the gastronomical pleasure of the PMC's clients.

"Heifer whines could be human cries," Morrissey opines in The Smiths' now-famous 1985 hit "Meat is Murder," until "closer comes the screaming knife, [because] this beautiful creature must die." His is an uncomfortable comparison hinging on our cross-cultural contract that anyone except sociopaths agrees the murder of other people is innately wrong; Morrissey replies that likewise, "meat is murder." On a very literal level, he is right, of course: the optional slaughter of nonhuman animals is by definition murder, even if we are ourselves removed from the process.[9] The PMC deploys two basic rhetorical strategies to distance participating omnivores from the label of murderer. Primarily, the PMC adopts a self-victimizing schema, the focus of this essay's remainder, to offer that in choosing to consume animals, humans are making themselves very sad indeed. First, however, I want to bring attention to the linguistic finessing the PMC, alongside the rhetoric of other white liberal omnivores, regularly deploys to mask murder as something else entirely.

At the most basic level, the PMC overextends the delineation between human and nonhuman animals: "The Portland Meat Collective not only helps consumers procure whole steers, pigs, or lambs directly from small Oregon farms. We also provide butchery and charcuterie classes for the proud new owners of those animals, so that they can learn how to transform those sides of pork into chops, bacon and ham roasts" (pdxmeat.com). A few subtle but important affects arise here. First, that (human) consumers purchase whole animals and become their "proud new owners"; by marking nonhuman animals as property, omnivores appeal to the attendant rights private property affords its "owners" under neoliberal capitalism (or liberalism more generally). Similar linguistic appeals were used throughout the eighteenth and nineteenth centuries in the United States, from Thomas Jefferson[10] to plantation owners in the Deep South, to legitimize the institution of slavery and all the violence allowed therein.[11] The result is painting certain (privileged, middle- and upper-class) omnivores with the ability to be "proud new owners" of thus "happy" animals-awaiting-slaughter, in a light similar to the benevolent slave owner (such as Thomas Jefferson himself). Armen A. Alchian contends that "one of the most fundamental requirements of a capitalist economic system . . . is a strong system of property rights," frighteningly adding, "but the purported conflict between property rights and human rights is a mirage. *Property rights are human rights.*"[12] Given the PMC's general philosophy, this is also to say that human rights include the right to dispatch the unnecessary slaughter of nonhuman animals at will. As such, meat might be murder, but it is the inalienable right of the animal's owner to do with that animal as he pleases.

Secondly, the PMC uses language that distances animals from their own identity as sentient beings. By teaching students "how to transform those sides of pork into chops, bacon and ham roasts," Davis teaches the art of identity-stripping, or what Carol Adams calls the process of rendering animals "absent referents" (xxiv); that is, taking claims of sentience away from animals by teaching humans not only to slaughter them, but also to think of them in different forms, not as a pig, but "sides," which eventually become "chops, bacon and ham roasts."[13] In a horrifying photograph that accompanies the aforementioned *New York Times* interview—an article frustratingly titled "The Proper Way to Eat a Pig"—Davis stands at the head of a table splayed with pig parts, ranging from dissected hooves to meaty ribs. She holds the only part we might think of as *the* pig, its head, though even here, its eyes have been gouged out and its eyelids "sliced off during an inspection for parasites." A group of high school students and teachers from the Oregon Episcopal School look longingly toward the mutilated pig parts lain before them, not in horror, but in genuine self-satisfaction. The photograph becomes a communion scene, not entirely unlike The Last Supper. Unless, of course, you are the pig, whose body is taken without consent for Davis and her students.

In describing a group of rabbits she and her students will use as subjects during another class on *This American Life*, Davis admits the rabbits are nearing an end to their lives, though she (over-)complicates the linguistic marker this act is given: "Some people call this slaughter. Some people call it dispatching. Some people call it killing. Some call it murder. Some call it torture. Some call it vulgar. Some call it food" ("Animal Sacrifice"). Davis's turn here—from *slaughter* to *murder* to finally *food*—serves to neutralize then naturalize the act; she implies the "sacrifice" is necessary, and thus natural, imploring that as her audience, we, too, consider how seemingly complicated this choice is, thus nullifying the position any outside observer might take against the act of animal butchery. Davis's personal narrative mirrors this linguistic journey from murder (bad) to meat (good): In her *New York Times* interview, Davis claims: "I turned vegetarian for 10 years, and then ate meat without thinking about why or from whence it came for another 10 years. The Portland Meat Collective is where I stand now, I say. It feels honest and blatant, respectful and messy." One can read this trajectory as a narrative bound to the drive for pleasure—a pleasure queer theory, especially, might otherwise uphold if the pleasure was derived from mutual consent. However, it isn't a narrative fully invested in consensual pleasure, but rather one masked in respectability politics, in themes of situational human-animal ethics and environmental sustainability, which cover over Davis ultimately saying, *Meat is delicious and I don't want to live without it.* Instead, she argues that her business *feels* respectful; that is, unless you are one of the nonhuman animals about to die. Though this is not the primary narrative concern of Davis or other hip omnivores like her; rather, they want you to know how utterly sad they are rendered by their choice, and it is in almost every instance ultimately a choice, to murder.

SLAUGHTER MAKES ME SAD

On "Animal Sacrifice," episode 480 of *This American Life*, Camas Davis explains what led her to found the PMC: "In 2009, after ten years of working as a magazine editor in New York and then Portland, I was laid off for the first time in my life. Like so many victims of the recession, I pouted for a while and then decided to completely reinvent myself, this time as a butcher." Let us pause briefly to consider the affective politics of this rhetoric: Davis's self-identification as a "victim" of the burst economy, an economy which, throughout the

1990s and into the early days of the Global War on Terror, allowed upwardlymobile whites to accumulate and overextend their economic prowess, while simultaneously white populist administrations (Clinton and Bush) gutted, in Lisa Duggan's words, the "already limited American welfare state" (xi). This socio-politic continues to disproportionately displace poor people of color and rural whites, both groups of which we should begin to think of as the perpetual victims under neoliberal prosperity *and* recession, instead of self-identifying white "victims" in the hip-ly reimagined urban core (like Davis) and those who might quite grossly slum to such a linguistic marker in order to garner sympathy or acquire cultural capital.

Momentarily putting this self-aggrandizement aside, I want to point to the egregious turn in Davis's comment: [I] "decided to completely reinvent myself, this time as a butcher." The move from journalist to butcher seems quite a leap, the type of narrative upon which *Portlandia* or *Saturday Night Live* producers would rightfully pounce (and like many featured regularly on *This American Life*). But this statement also implies a type of leisure one is afforded to learn a trade instead of immediately securing gainful employment. Davis goes on to explain she moved to France to learn the Art of Butchery:

> Through a friend of a friend, I found the Chapolards, a French family of four brothers who, with two of their wives, own and operate a farm in southwestern France where they handle every aspect of getting pork to dinner tables. I bought a plane ticket. I spoke no French. The Chapolards spoke little English. They handed me knives and pointed to pork legs and bellies and heads and shoulders and trusted I would find my way.
>
> I returned to Oregon wanting to learn more. I told all those chefs and butchers who wouldn't teach me before that I'd find students to pay them to teach the art of butchery. The Portland Meat Collective was born. I had no idea that classes would sell out.

Listening to Davis describe (on National Public Radio, no less[14]) her journey to France and then back to Portland, as if this was obviously the only sensible career option, reveals a lack of perspective in the white hipster experience; like many of her brethren in the hipster subculture, Davis disregards the extremely privileged ability to travel freely as the supposedly "downtrodden, jobless vagabond" she was. Who, after all, gets to spend months in the French countryside, unemployed and "discovering onself," if not the already upwardly mobile or secure. Indeed, hipsters say the darndest things. But by portraying herself as a victim in this scenario, Davis obfuscates the group who is the actual (needless) victim: the animals she teaches people how to murder.

Introducing Davis for Act Two of the show, a segment titled "Run Rabbit. No, Really, Run!," Ira Glass maintains, "Today's program, 'Animal Sacrifice,' [includes] stories about what other creatures give up for us." "Animal Sacrifice" is not meant to be a show about human omnivores, but rather the nonhuman animals in our lives, and Davis opines to *This American Life* listeners:

> Sometime between 1:30 and 8:00 AM on January 8, 2012, five adults, including a nursing mother and 13 juveniles, vanished from their cages in a Portland backyard. 10 one-day-old babies were left behind and subsequently died. We're talking rabbits here, compact, cute, furry, doe-eyed, white, brown, and black little hopping animals that were being bred and raised for meat, meat that would feed the rabbits' owners and a few of their friends.

These rabbits were stolen not to feed humans, but as a protest against the PMC's practices. Thus this segment begins as a story not about Davis, but about the rabbits from that backyard; Davis explains that, thankfully, she was scheduled to teach the course "Basic Rabbit Butchery & Charcuterie" on the morning of January 8, so the rabbits she and her students would use had already been taken to the classroom before the theft. Davis admits they still died, and in the most transparent portion of the story she weaves, explains how: "Within the span of one second, we broke their necks. Within the span of another second, their eyes closed, their nervous systems shut down, their brains went dark. That was it. They were alive one minute, gone the next, vanished." Conversely, Davis goes on to explain "how the 10 day-old rabbits without the warmth or sustenance of their [stolen] nursing mothers died. They suffered from hypothermia, they slowly starved to death, or they did both." Davis begins to illustrate here the divide upon which her business is predicated: there are humane ways for animals to be killed, which she teaches her students, and there are inhumane ways for animals to be killed (in this case, as a result of animal rights protest, but more broadly, we can imagine Davis making a case for all the animals slaughtered in our nation's factory-farming complex). There is good meat, and there is bad meat; there is murder justified by its methodology, and there is murder horrific by its methodology. Davis revises Morrissey to argue, "Meat might be murder, but sometimes that murder is okay."

The narrative Davis chooses in this instance, which reflects the general approach she has taken in venues from *Oregon Humanities* to *The New York Times*, moves quickly beyond telling the story of nonhuman animals, instead opting for those who might, via consumption or protest, kill them. What becomes clear: Davis is not invested in the narrative of the slaughtered nonhuman animals, but rather in the narratives of those who choose to murder them unnecessarily for their own pleasure. And more specifically, in how she is ultimately a victim, both at the hands of her attackers[15] and via her own reticence to eat meat in the first place. The turn is slight, easy to miss, but once more closely examined, evident and, regarding my argument here, disgusting. Davis wisely anticipates and preempts this reception:

> Media often question whether the Portland Meat Collective is just a bunch of privileged hipsters worshipping at the feet of the bacon gods. I usually tell them this: I am not obsessed with bacon.
>
> I do not growl and flex my muscles after breaking down a whole pig. I do not have a tattoo of a pig head on my bicep, nor do I have boning knife tattooed on my calf. I abhor the term "meat head," and for the most part, so do my students.

Ironically, in an August 25, 2015, picture posted to the PMC's Facebook page (below), Davis is pictured butchering alongside Jason French, a top Portland chef, who does have butchery tools tattooed prominently on his arms. But key to this passage, and the messaging of the PMC and other hipster omnivore texts more generally,[16] Davis turns to a type of deceptive bifurcation: hipsters who love bacon (bad) and hipsters (like herself) who want to tell you how hard the decision to eat meat is (the good guys).

∽

In public discussions of personal diet, progressives often fall short of calling for vegetarianism or veganism because they argue these choices are not viable for those of a lower socioeconomic position. This is a legitimate concern,[17] as Alison Hope Alkon and Julian Agyeman argue that "the food movement narrative is largely created by, and resonates most deeply, with white and middle-class individuals" (3). Sunaura Taylor further explains, "There are many pressing issues that face individuals who would perhaps otherwise choose to try to become vegetarian or vegan, such as the reality of food deserts in low-income, often largely people of color neighborhoods and a government that subsidizes and promotes animal- and fat-heavy diets" (758). This calls for our advocacy to continue to address systemic problems with wealth distribution, food production, and urban planning. Such advocacy can and should fit into a larger framework of economic, environmental, and social justice movements because, despite popularly held myths, Lusk and Norwood "show (i) that it is much more costly to produce energy and protein from animal-based sources than from some plant-based sources, [and] (ii) that sizable demand shifts away from meat consumption would result in significantly lower corn prices and production," which would balance a market demand for vegetables and other sources of non-animal protein (109). But for those who have access to non-animal proteins, such as middle- and upper-class whites in the white-topia of Portland, economic cost and access are not legitimate excuses to maintain an animal-based diet.

Certainly the answer is not for middle-class whites to (i) train others how to become more "conscientious omnivores" at the expense of training them to simply not eat meat, and (ii) wax poetically about how they are the victims of an oppressive system, and that it pains them to think about the animals they are about to slaughter. On *This American Life*, which became less an episode about animal sacrifice and more about what emotional well-being humans sacrifice to fill their own desire, not need, to murder and eat animals, Davis concludes:

> For those of us who choose to raise and kill animals for food, it's anything but a simple choice. In fact, it's hard and complicated every time. I look the animal in the eye as we breathe the same air. The same tree shades us. The world slows just long enough for us to see our shared place within it.

The decision she ultimately makes is to look that rabbit in the eyes and exert power over the nonhuman in order to kill and then consume, a consumption for which, more often than not, there are viable, perhaps even healthier, alternatives.

The choice here is actually rather simple: do not murder (slaughter, dispatch) the animal you need not. More critically to the task at hand, Davis comes to represent the worst of hipster identity politics. As Mark Greif contends, "The hipster represents what can happen to middle-class whites, particularly, and to all elites, generally, when they focus on the struggles for their own pleasures and luxuries—seeing these as daring and confrontational—rather than asking what makes their sort of people entitled to them, [and] who else suffers for their pleasures" (xvi). Choosing homespun animal slaughter is not daring; additionally, it further embeds permissive and unquestioned white consumption in the rhetoric of progressive public life, and more importantly, continues the murder of sentient beings: the nonhuman animals we are not required, by health or by economics, to eat.

WORKS CITED

Adams, Carol J. *The Sexual Politics of Meat: A Feminist-Vegetarian Critical Theory.* 20th anniversary edition. New York: Bloomsbury, 2015.

Alchian, Armen A. "Property Rights." In *The Concise Encyclopedia of Economics*, 2nd ed., 2008. Library of Economics and Liberty. http://www.econlib.org/library/Enc/PropertyRights.html.

Alkon, Alison Hope, and Julian Agyeman, eds. *Cultivating Food Justice: Race, Class, and Sustainability.* Cambridge: MIT, 2011.

Armisen, Fred, Carrie Brownstein, et al. *Portlandia.* "Farm," series premier. IFC, January 21, 2011.

Duggan, Lisa. *The Twilight of Equality? Neoliberalism, Cultural Politics, and the Attack on Democracy.* Boston: Beacon, 2003.

Glass, Ira, host and producer. *This American Life.* "Animal Sacrifice." Chicago: WBEZ, November 30, 2012.

Greif, Mark. *What Was the Hipster? A Sociological Explanation.* New York: n+1 Foundation, 2010.

Hanel, Marnie. "The Proper Way to Eat a Pig." *The New York Times*, 4 April 2013.

Lusk, Jayson L., and F. Bailey Norwood. "Some Economic Benefits and Costs of Vegetarianism." *Agricultural and Resource Economics Review* 38, no. 2 (2009): 109–24.

Morrissey. "Meat Is Murder." *Meat Is Murder.* The Smiths, Rough Trade, compact disc, 2014. Originally released 1985.

Novak, Matt. "Oregon Was Founded as a Racist Utopia." *Gizmodo*, January 21, 2015.

Osman, Suleiman. *The Invention of Brownstone Brooklyn: Gentrification and the Search for Authenticity in Postwar New York.* Oxford: Oxford University Press 2012.

Rowe, Sian. "Portlandia, Welcome to the Hipster Capital of the Muesli Belt." *Guardian,* May 11, 2012.

Safran Foer, Jonathan. *Eating Animals.* New York: Little, Brown, 2009.

Schweik, Susan. "Kicked to the Curb: Ugly Law Then and Now." *Harvard Civil Rights-Civil Liberties Law Review* 46, no. 1 (2011): 1–16.

Shandas, Vivek, and Ryan Dann. "The Dream of the 90s is Alive in Portland. Really?" In *Periodic Atlas of the Metroscape.* Portland: Institute of Portland Metropolitan Studies Publications, 2012, 13–19.

Taylor, Sunaura. "Vegans, Freaks, and Animals: Toward a New Table Fellowship." *American Quarterly* 65, no. 3 (2013): 757–64.

"Would We Be Healthier With a Vegan Diet?" *Wall Street Journal*, September 18, 2012.

Wright, Laura. *The Vegan Studies Project: Food, Animals, and Gender in the Age of Terror.* Athens: University of Georgia Press, 2015.

END NOTES

1. "Farm," Season 1, Episode 1, *Portlandia*. IMDb.com. *Portlandia* is a sketch comedy sitcom starring Fred Armisen and Carrie Brownstein; the show's lead executive producer, Lorne Michaels, is best known for creating and producing *Saturday Night Live*. A flagship original series for indie-focused network IFC, *Portlandia* digs deeply "into the absurdities of modern life" by specifically lampooning white hipsters, from their demand to "know" their food to their love of driving Subarus.

2 At their worst, this is a typical hipster rhetorical strategy, and though Brownstein and Armisen are brilliantly parodying this strategy in a long tradition of satirical comedy, the scene described here is all too familiar, oddly accurate, for anyone who has sat down to break bread with the hipster omnivore. Building upon scholarship investigating critical race and neoliberalism, the hipster, for me, represents liberal white angst manifested during neoliberalism's early twenty-first century ruptures—specifically, the Global War on Terror following the terrorist attacks on September 11, 2001, and the Global Economic Crisis of 2008 and beyond. As hipsters subconsciously mourn the perceived loss of white power (under attack, deindustrialized, and shipped abroad), they cling onto melancholic rhetorical strategies (whininess) and aesthetics, such as woodland flannels or home-brewed beer, cultural objects not innately problematic in and of themselves, but ones certainly recalling a conservative white masculine bootstrapism known colloquially as "Americana." For the purposes of this essay, I place Camas Davis in a lineage of white hipsters that reaches back to the mid-twentieth century, when the term hipster initially comes to linguistic prominence (largely through Norman Mailer's 1957 essay, "The White Negro: Superficial Reflections on the Hipster") in describing the phenomenon of urban whites appropriating black cultural productions. I have written about this emergence in "The Revolution in Our Pants: Hipsters, Race, and American Fashion" (*International Journal of Fashion Studies* 4 no. 1 [June 2017]: 35-49.

3. The US Census Bureau sources report that in 2010 Portland was 76.1 percent white (State and County QuickFacts. Data derived from Population Estimates, American Community Survey, Census of Population and Housing, County Business Patterns, Economic Census, Survey of Business Owners, Building Permits, Census of Governments. Last revised May 28, 2015).

4. See Suleiman Osman's *The Invention of Brownstone Brooklyn: Gentrification and the Search for Authenticity in Postwar New York*. Osman describes a group of white-collar gentrifiers who began buying up decaying Victorian brownstones in various Brooklyn enclaves in the late 1940s; similar to how I theorize the contemporary hipster as positioning his aesthetic as both aesthetic and politic, Osman contends Brownstoners "believed they were involved in

something more than a renovation fad. Brownstoning was a cultural revolt against sameness, conformity, and bureaucracy" (5).

5. Indeed, contemporary Portland as a white-topia fits the model provided by the state of Oregon's history. Matt Novak explains, "When Oregon was granted statehood in 1859, it was the only state in the Union admitted with a constitution that forbade black people from living, working, or owning property there. It was illegal for black people even to *move* to the state until 1926." My partial concern here is that a seemingly progressive food politic might serve to cover over this horrifying past.

6. See Sarah Banet-Weiser's *Authentic™: The Politics of Ambivalence in a Brand Culture* (NYU 2012).

7. In fact, food studies has generally made more progress in revealing the devastations of such large-scale agribusiness, colloquially referred to as *factory farming*, than it has in definitively questioning humans' supposed rights to slaughter and consume nonhuman animals. From popular practioners (such as Michael Pollan and Jonathan Safran Foer) to academics (such as Alison Hope Alkon and Julian Agyeman), almost all writers agree that such farming practices are unhealthy, environmentally dangerous, and cruel to the nonhuman animals involved.

8. See pdxmeat.com.

9. The *Oxford English Dictionary* confirms this reasoning, placing "to kill or slaughter (an animal or animals)" as one of its primary and oldest definitions of "murder." In Shakespeare's 1600 play *Henry IV*, for instance, the title character pontificates: "When, like the bee, culling from every flower / The virtuous sweets, / Our thighs pack'd with wax, our mouths with honey, / We bring it to the hive, and, like the bees, / Are murdered for our pains."

10. Who, in his *Notes on the State of Virginia*, lists slaves alongside counts of cattle, horses, and pigs.

11. I am leery of taking this comparison further, lest I over-collapse the lives of black slaves of the past with the current use of nonhuman animals. Though animal studies scholars rightfully deconstruct the line between human and nonhuman animalities, that very line also has a long history of making unacceptable violence towards black and other enslaved peoples. For more on this important debate, see Mel Y. Chen's *Animacies: Biopolitics, Racial Mattering, and Queer Affect* (Duke 2012) and Marjorie Spiegel's *The Dreaded Comparison: Human and Animal Slavery* (Mirror Books, 3rd ed., 1997). My goal here is to merely point to the slippery nature of rhetoric connected to nonhuman animals as private property.

12. Emphasis added.

13. In her quintessential study *The Sexual Politics of Meat: A Feminist-Vegetarian Critical Theory*, Carol Adams explains the phenomenon of "the 'absent referent' is that which separates the meat eater from the animal and the animal from

the end product [such as "chops, bacon and ham roasts"]. The function of the absent referent is to keep our 'meat' separated from any idea that she or he was once an animal, to keep the 'moo' or 'cluck' or 'baa' away from the meat, to keep *something* from being seen as having been someone" (xxiv). Despite her participation in a lyric self-victimization of "having" to slaughter animals and the typical hipster whitewashing of maintaining certain slaughters as humane and others as un-, Davis perpetuates the absent referent by ultimately deploying a rhetoric of de-animalized butchery.

14. For a thoughtful perspective on the whiteness of NPR, see Chenjerai Kumanyika's essay "Vocal Color in Public Radio" (*Transom*, January 22, 2015).

15. Regarding the rabbit theft specifically, Davis explains, "When the rabbits vanished, Levi, Chris, and I chose to publicize it, to try and get the rabbits back and in hopes of finding the person or people who took the rabbits. Stories appeared in local and national newspapers. Sometimes I woke up to emails like this: 'Things you should do today. Number one, get cancer. Number two, rot slowly and painfully.' Others imagined my demise in more inventive ways: 'You are chicken shit. I'd love to see you in a lion's cage and see what you think of butchery then.'"

16. Davis is not alone among hipster royalty who wax poetically over the decision to eat meat (a euphemism itself for *choosing* to murder nonhuman animals). In his wildly popular 2009 tome *Eating Animals*, Jonathan Safran Foer paints a compelling picture of what actually complicates the food politics we all might hold, including the lies we willingly tell ourselves, arguing for food as a social act of storytelling, but falling short of calling for vegan- or vegetarianism. Similarly, the documentary *Food, Inc.* (2008) and Michael Pollan's best-selling book *The Omnivore's Dilemma: A Natural History of Four Meals* (2007) advocate not for the sustainable act of eating a plant-based diet, but for the supposedly "humane" and unsustainable slaughter of nonhuman animals.

17. Though it strikes me this is perhaps most often just an excuse to continue eating animals. An institution as conservative as the *Wall Street Journal* admits that most people don't turn to vegetarianism because of "convenience, habit and taste." Through systemic changes we might imagine changing the excuse of convenience, but habit and taste are only excuses to put off progressive policy on the individual level. This is also connected to the argument that eating animals holds a key cultural component for certain peoples and groups; but as Jonathan Safran Foer, whose work is largely tied to his Jewish identity, admits, "something having been done just about everywhere just about always is no kind of justification for doing it now" (26).

CHAPTER 14

Meatless Mondays?: A Vegan Studies Approach to Resistance in the College Classroom

Natalie M. Dorfeld

When I was fifteen years old, I completed a book report on animal abuse, which awakened my soul to the cruelties of factory farming. Being an animal lover, I literally could not stomach being part of the carnivore movement, so I quit eating meat cold turkey (no pun intended). Raised in northwestern Pennsylvania all my life, with a farm literally across the road, this decision was met with opposition and endless questioning by friends and family members. "Are you sure this isn't just a phase?" "What about your protein? Where will you get it?" "You know, you are an athlete. You cannot run long distances on rabbit food." Twenty-six years later, I am still a vegetarian, and I have found that little has changed in terms of obsolete mind-sets.

In the spring of 2016, I was fortunate enough to teach my first Environmental Literature class at the Florida Institute of Technology, which is located in Melbourne, Florida. The class covered ecological writers from Henry David Thoreau to Michael Pollan, and the overall theme examined what each one of us could do to reduce our carbon footprint. For their final project, which included a twenty-page essay and ten-to-fifteen-minute presentation, students were asked to present a sustainable proposal in order to do just that.

While many were more than excited to participate in beach clean-ups, wildlife rehabilitation, and oyster restoration projects, 92 percent put on the brakes at the suggestion of limiting meat intake, despite the fact we covered the topic for quite some time in the classroom. Documentaries—such as *Cowspiracy: The Sustainability Secret*, *Food*,

Inc., and *Forks Over Knives*—shed light on the negative effects live-stock farming poses to the environment. Students were very receptive and vocal in their support of meat-free Mondays . . . at least in theory. However, at the end of the day, the notion was met with overwhelming reluctance.

My question is this: if students can all agree that they want to improve our environment, and one of the major ways they can accomplish this feat is by limiting the amount of animal products in their diets, why is decreasing meat consumption met with such resistance? The reasons must run deeper and more ingrained than bacon is simply tasty. This chapter will focus on three key areas: a brief history of Meatless Mondays, a breakdown of my class in terms of student demographics, and a vegan studies approach to how I will address the topic in the future, based on what I learned on the first go-round. Individually and collectively, I hope to dissect what influences a young person's attitude toward vegetarianism and veganism.

HISTORY

Before delving into the subject matter, a historical perspective may be beneficial. Meatless Mondays actually began around World War I. Prior to his presidency, Herbert Hoover asked Americans to limit their meat, fat, and sugar consumption on Tuesday and wheat consumption on Wednesday. Tori Avey, author of "Discover the History of Meatless Mondays," states,

> by the time the United States entered World War I, citizens of allied countries, including Belgium and France, were left starving. Much of the farmland of Western Europe was turned to battlefields and the farmers themselves became soldiers. Women, children and the elderly had no choice but to tend the remaining land themselves. In an effort to care for struggling Allies and nourish US soldiers overseas, Hoover and the US Food Administration coined a slogan: *Food will win the war.* (3)

The undertaking paid off in dividends. During the twelve-month period between 1918–19, there was a 15 percent reduction in home food consumption (Avey 3).

Fast-forwarding a few years, in the 1930s during the Great Depression and right before World War II, my grandparents would often share melancholy stories with one common thread: limitations. Beans, potatoes, and eggs were quite popular, but unless the meat was coming from one's own farm or that of a family friend, it was considered a rare treat during this period. According to Lizzie Collingham, author of *The Taste of War: WWII and the Battle for Food*:

> The food around which American civilians' dissatisfaction with rationing centered was red meat. Red meat, preferably beef, was highly valued as a prime source of energy, especially for the working man, and its presence on a plate helped to define the food as a proper meal. But during the war most red meat, and especially steak, disappeared into the army bases. (4)

Even Eleanor Roosevelt sympathized with the American public at the time, saying the president's lunches consisted of "fish four days in a row," and she bemoaned the absence of his beloved coffee after dinner (Collingham 4).

More recently, the meat-free Monday movement has become more about health and the environment as opposed to rationing in times of need. In 2003, Sid Lerner, in association with the Johns Hopkins Bloomberg School of Public Health and Johns Hopkins Center for a Livable Future, founded "Meatless Mondays." The campaign has since expanded into thirty-six countries globally from Hong Kong to the United Kingdom (Vasi 1–2). Vasi adds,

> The goal of the campaign is to reduce meat consumption by 15 percent in order to improve personal health and the health of the planet. This goal recognizes the association between high meat consumption and chronic diseases, such as heart disease and diabetes, as well as environmental impacts like rain forest deforestation, water shortages, and climate change. (1–2)

According to the campaign's website, "it is an easy way for individuals to start off their week in a healthy and environmentally-conscious fashion" (Vasi 1–2).

In summary, for those who don't want to jump headfirst into vegetarianism or veganism, Meatless Mondays provide a nice trial run. Regarding the health aspect, a meatless diet lowers the risk of various forms of cancer, heart attacks, obesity, and type 2 diabetes ("Global Meatless Monday—for Health and Wellness" 4). Environmentally, such a diet reduces our dependence on water for the animals, thus eliminating some of the contamination produced by manure runoff, as "livestock is the world's largest human-related land user, taking up 30 percent of the Earth's entire land surface, including 33 percent of the global arable land for animal feed production." When this need increases, so does "land degradation, deforestation, and the accelerated loss of rainforests" ("Global Meatless Monday—for the Environment" 9–10).

ENVIRONMENTAL LITERATURE / CLASS STATISTICS

As stated briefly in the introduction, I taught an Environmental Literature class at the Florida Institute of Technology. According to *U.S. News and World Report*, Florida Tech is ranked number one in the nation for fostering international student experiences. Likewise, according to *Times Higher Education*, we are one of the top two hundred universities in the world. We have two things going for us right off the bat: diversity (around 35 percent of our students are international) and extremely bright men and women ("Rankings & Accolades" 1).

Environmental Literature's grand debut took place in the spring of 2016. I was very excited to teach it because it was my first elective, a newly created course, and we are located one mile from the Indian River Lagoon and two miles from the Atlantic Ocean, which provided opportunities for field trips and local activism. (Brevard County recently made the national news due to massive and unexplained fish kills.) I was also semi-confident that the course would fill due to our environmental science, sustainability, and marine biology/oceanography majors.

In terms of demographics, the course was somewhat unique for two reasons. First, I had more females than males, which is quite rare at an engineering school. Our overall ratio is 70 percent male to 30 percent female. Second, I only had two humanities majors in the class. The others were predominately engineers with a few environmental studies majors thrown in for good measure.

Out of the twenty-five students, two said they would give Meatless Mondays a try. One was a female engineer. She was an athlete, so she had reservations, but the inhumane practices of factory farming bothered her. The other was a male student with a strong interest in sustainability, which is an environmentally friendly major. His concern was more based on deforestation and the negative pollutant effects farm animals contribute to runoff. Concerning the rest of the class, the statistical data broke down as follows:

Table 14.1: Meatless Mondays Experiment	
Students	25
Females	15
Males	10
Athletes Non-athletes	17 8
International US	13 12
Socioeconomic	Middle to upper class
Non-majors Majors	23 2

All were middle-to upper-class students.

FINDINGS

Perhaps naively, I thought the idea of Meatless Mondays would be welcomed with open arms. The consensus among the students was, yes, it was a good idea in theory. Abstaining from meat one day a week would give the body a break and help reduce our carbon footprint. However, when it came down to the physical act of doing so, there was much resistance. I have three newly formed theories—based on the athletic, international, and socioeconomic statuses of my students—as to why there was a pushback.

Athletes vs. non-athletes

While the female-to-male ratio was split in the class (fifteen females and ten males), an overwhelming majority of my students were varsity athletes (seventeen athletes and eight non-athletes). Of those eight non-athletes, some of them could have played for intramural teams, but I did not ask. I simply went by the roster for excused team absences. Of those said athletes, many competed in either endurance sports (rowing and swimming) or sports known for their explosive strength (football and track and field, with an emphasis on throwing events). When they began to talk about narratives, specifically eating habits, I began to understand their resistance, as they expressed the belief that the absence of flesh was somehow equated with weakness.

Regarding the females in the class, when I said I was a vegetarian, they had well-meaning but offensive comments: "Well, you don't look like one. You're not white. You're not super skinny. In fact, you have muscles." Corey Wrenn, author of "The Weight of Veganism," addresses the criticism and the myths of inadequacies of a vegetarian diet. She states:

> I am very aware of the stereotypes against vegans: we are supposed to be pale, thin, and sickly. When I am accused of such, I often jokingly grab my gut and give it a wobble, "Do I look malnourished to you?" It usually gets a laugh. But I was seriously never aware of any eating disorder associated with veganism until my experiences with my friend and later my research into vegan and vegetarian literature. Looking back on those experiences today, my perspective is distinctly more critical. (qtd. in Wright 165)

As for men who are vegetarian, they are often viewed as lesser, feminine, or even gay (not that there is anything wrong with that). Meat is closely associated with strength, power, and bulking up. Laura Wright says,

> The discourse of this backlash, unsurprisingly, mandates that meat is an essential, primal, and inescapable component of heterosexual masculinity, that male refusal to eat meat signals weakness, emasculation, and un-American values. Melanie Joy, who coined the term "carnism" as essentially the adverse of veganism, notes that keeping animals and animal agriculture invisible in the production of meat allows us to care about certain animals (e.g., dogs) and eat others, simply because we believe that this is "just the way things are." (109)

Therefore, couple these two negative mind-sets (weakness and un-American values) and place them in an arena that thrives on strength and competitiveness (sports), and it is easy to see why the movement was met with reluctance in my class.

Dr. Susan Kleiner, author of "SSE #58: The Role of Red Meat in an Athlete's Diet," adds one more precautionary warning concerning deficiencies, particularly iron and zinc. She says, "Suboptimal dietary intakes of iron and zinc resulting in decreased nutritional status have been observed in athletes who have eliminated meat. Marginal iron or zinc status may negatively affect exercise performance. Full-blown iron or zinc deficiency will definitely have a negative effect upon exercise performance" (1). An athlete needs to feel full in order to perform, so adding other nutrients almost becomes a necessity.

To many coaches, and for a consumer media touting products, it is simply unthinkable to some that high-functioning vegetarian athletes can compete without some form of "vitamin deficiency, decreased brain volume, fatigue, and confusion" (Araki 1). These myths reinforce the unknown, risky mentality of restricting animal products. Is the mind-set changing? It is hard to say. Perhaps it is with well-known athletes in the media, like ultra-marathoner and vegan Scott Jurek, but the shift will take time and a plethora of educational resources.

International vs. US Students

At the beginning of the semester, I asked each student to introduce themselves, to tell me where they were from, what hobbies they enjoy, what sports they played, etc. I had thirteen international students to twelve US students in the class. My students' bases included Germany, Israel, New Zealand, Trinidad, Greece, and Italy. Two things struck me immediately about our international population. First, fast-food restaurants are less prevalent in their hometowns. As such, when they tend to think of meat, it is with great fondness. Many students wrote narratives about the friendly local butcher down the street, who knew them by name and had their order prewrapped. Second, particularly in French, Greek, and Italian communities, food is more than just nourishment. Families come together. Meal preparation can take hours, and the dining experience may last into the night. Eating is an "experience" and clearly not the same as the American grab-and-go mentality.

The European Union, for instance, does not allow the use of hormones in cattle, and it has prohibited imports that do since 1988, especially from the US and UK. These banned hormones—including "testosterone, progesterone, trenbolone acetate, zeranol and melengestrol acetate—will continue" (Elliot 4). Ian Elliot states,

> The European Commission said its scientists are convinced that the use of these hormones to promote growth poses a threat to human health. "The measure is based on the repeatedly confirmed scientific opinion of the Scientific Committee on Veterinary Measures Relating to Public Health and maintains the current prohibition of the use of all hormones for growth promotion. . . . One of the hormones under the scrutiny of the scientific committee, estradiol 17-beta, has been evaluated as a complete carcinogen with both tumor-initiating and tumor-promoting effects," it said. (4)

Students from non-European countries added that meat from their country was "less disgusting." When I pressed what that meant, they said it came from down the road. It was fresh—not frozen. Not only did it taste better, it wasn't pumped full of unnatural chemicals to preserve it. Additionally, the portion sizes were smaller. They are continually amazed at America's "Super Size" obsession.

Secondly, I am reminded of a student from Italy named Carlos. He was kind enough to share a PowerPoint, which included many highlights of food in his hometown. He spoke whimsically about how his mother would walk to the deli everyday to pick up different meats and smoke/spice them to everyone's liking. Bresaola was his favorite. Eating, especially at night, was an event. Rick Steves, who wrote "Why I Love Eating in Italy," states,

> Italians tend to linger over each course, and dinner is the evening's entertainment. When you enjoy a full-blown Italian dinner, you don't get out until midnight; a three-hour meal is common. And when you leave, the table is a mess, with plenty of evidence of high-calorie fun with a firewater finale. Waiters provide lots of drinks that seem designed to keep you from leaving. When you want the bill, you'll have to ask for it (possibly more than once). To "eat and run" is seen as a lost opportunity. (2)

From a vegetarian perspective, I can understand the international mentality. The animals Europeans consume are healthier, and they eat less of them, at least portion-wise. Also, Americans eat differently:

we scarf down our food and run off to a meeting, the kids' soccer practice, or to pick up dry cleaning. In other countries, meals are to be savored. That is not to say that meals do not include vegetarian dishes, but meat is often a staple. When I asked Carlos if Italians could go meatless, he said it would be difficult, adding, "I don't think I could feel full, and my mom's cooking is just too good."

Socioeconomic Status

Students at Florida Tech, for the most part, come from middle-to-upper-class backgrounds. In fact, there's a running joke on campus concerning our clientele—"Q: How do you know you work at Florida Tech? A: When you drive a Honda, and your students drive a Jaguar." How does a privileged status affect their eating habits? For starters, they're not accustomed to limitations.

According to Norman Myers and Jennifer Kent, authors of *The New Consumers: The Influence of Affluence on the Environment*, this well-to-do generation (post-1990) has a voracious appetite for meat. The authors state,

> Whereas their fellow citizens enjoy pork, beef, or poultry only once a week at best, the new consumers mostly eat it once a day at least. During the 1990s when the world's meat consumption grew by 30 percent, the new-consumer countries' consumption grew by twice as much, the bulk of the meat going down the throats of the new consumers. . . . I noticed that when there was a gathering of relatives and friends, they would eat as much meat as they could, and then some more. (38)

The days of rationing are long gone. Limiting one's diet was something their grandparents' generation did, when times were harder. As people became better off, "they began to eat more and more meat. Since 1950 and as the developed countries entered economic boom times, they have generally seen meat consumption grow twice as fast as population" (Myers and Kent 39). And much of this trend in the past decade has been due to the "surging demand for meat" due to the advent of the new consumers (39).

A. Breeze Harper also touches upon this issue in *Sistah Vegan: Black Female Vegans Speak on Food, Identity, Heath, and Society*. She states that she grew up in a working-class blue-collar town. As a result, she became very passionate about antiracism and anticlassism. She adds,

> I was never able to understand how eco-sustainability, animal rights, and plant-based diets could be integral to my work. I honestly thought that these issues were the domain of the privileged, white, middle and upper-class people of America. *Sure, it was easy for them*, I had thought with ignorance and prejudice. *Race and class struggle is not a reality for them, so they can "waste" their time on saving dolphins, whining about recycling cans, and persevering the Redwood trees while my Black and brown brothas continue to be denied "human rights" because of the color of our skin.* (20)

She goes on to say how socioeconomic status plays a huge role in consumption choices, dietary and nondietary, and how that outlook hinders our outlook on social justice and animal/environmental activism.

Recommendations

It was an honor to teach a class like this, and I am still stopped on campus by students who are downright giddy to show off their new (reusable) glass bottles versus disposable plastic bottles. Likewise, it brings me joy when they e-mail me photos of their beach cleanups and volunteering efforts with local wildlife associations. Given the opportunity to do it again, I would do three things differently.

One, I would teach the book in chunks versus chronologically. I chose *American Earth: Environmental Writing Since Thoreau*, which was edited by Bill McKibben, with a forward written by Al Gore. Overall, the students enjoyed the book and its inexpensive price. According to Amazon.com, the text

> . . . offers this unprecedented, provocative, and timely anthology, gathering the best and most significant American environmental writing from the last two centuries . . . the essays of Henry David Thoreau, John Muir, John Burroughs, Aldo Leopold, and Rachel Carson are set against the inspiring story of an emerging activist movement, as revealed by newly uncovered reports of pioneering campaigns for conservation, passages from landmark legal opinions and legislation, and searing protest speeches. (1)

The book began with writings from Thoreau and took us up to Michael Pollan, who wrote the bestseller *The Omnivore's Dilemma: A Natural History of Four Meals*. His mantra? "Eat food, not too much, mostly plants" ("How to Eat" 1).

Regarding the layout, I simply went from the front to the back and supplemented the corresponding chapters with guest speakers and documentaries. The next time around, I would break the class into four distinct themes, one theme for each month: air, land, water, and self. By doing so, we could spend more time on the subject matter, thoroughly dissecting it, and spread out group projects more evenly. This approach could involve local field trips and taste-testing opportunities, which could promote vegan studies.

As for the "self" aspect, I would dedicate that section to how we impact the environment with our choices and bring into the discussion such issues, as are raised by Harper, as poor nutrition, health inequities, discernments of social justice, rights of animals, environmental racism, and race theory (Harper 21). Harper states,

> I have experienced personally over the past few years how a purity of diet and thought are interrelated. And when Americans become truly concerned with the purity of the food that enters their personal systems, when they learn to eat properly, we can expect to see profound changes effected in the social and political system of this nation. These two systems are inseparable. (21)

I wish to delve deeper into the interconnectedness of diet and politics. It's obvious that meat produced by factory farming is unhealthy for us and the environment, but I want to introduce my students to terms with which they may not be familiar, such as environmental discrimination, sustainable health practices, ecofeminism, feminist-vegetarian critical theory, addiction, ecocide, and overconsumption (Harper 29–30).

Secondly, I think I have to be more attuned to the late adolescent mind-set, specifically that of eighteen- to twenty-two-year-olds. Namely, I must be aware that my students are deeply concerned with the answer to the question—"What's in it for me?" While that may come across as cruel or disrespectful, it is not meant to be. Jennifer Silva, author of "Slight Expectations: Making Sense of the 'Me Me Me' Generation," claims that today's adolescents are more self-absorbed and lack a collective sense of responsibility as compared to one gen-eration ago. Thus, they often fail to take into account larger cultural and social contexts (1388). While saving the animals and preserving the environment are noble causes, I need to look at ways doing so will benefit the students in an immediate, tactile sense.

Benefits of a meatless diet, or in this case a reduction, include a decreased risk of heart disease, cancer, blood pressure, and other chronic diseases (Mangels 20). This is all well and good, but most col-lege students don't think about such things. They're too far off in the distance. Instead, I could package the instantaneous benefits as the following:

- **Increased energy**. The body is given a much-needed break. Breaking down animal proteins is taxing for the digestive sys-tem and saps the body of energy. By removing meat one day a week, the body is naturally detoxing itself and increasing nutri-ent absorption (Ure 1). Also, on average, vegetarians tend to be leaner than their meat-eating counterparts.

- **Clearer skin**. Another major benefit is increased skin health. In addition to consuming larger quantities of nuts (healthful oils), Meatless Monday participants will consume more fruits and veg-etables, which are rich in essential vitamins A and E and linked to a glowing complexion ("Health Benefits of a Vegetarian Diet" 1).

- **Sexual potency**. According to author Diane Vukovic's "Six Scientific Reasons that Vegetarians Make Better Lovers," reducing one's meat intake could provide the following ben-efits: less erectile dysfunction, more stamina in bed, bet-ter-tasting semen, better-smelling body odor, soy isoflavones for women (vaginal lubrication), and increased libido (1).

Could such a presentation of the material be labeled as pandering? Perhaps. But it is safe to say that most eighteen- to twenty-two-year-olds are not thinking about heart disease. They are thinking about the here and now: more energy to get through their classes, a clearer complexion—with which many Asian students grapple when intro-duced to greasy American foods—and getting it on. If all of these things can be improved, and the by-product is less animal consump-tion, deforestation, and a reduction of the carbon footprint, so be it.

Third, as a sensitive woman, I believe I look at this issue (vegetarianism) emotionally instead of logically. As briefly stated in the beginning, I became a vegetarian when I was fifteen years old due to a book report on factory farming. The photos and videos struck me on a primal, gut level. Even today, as Greta Gaard states in "Vegetarian Ecofeminism: A Review Essay," mine was more of a compassionate response:

> Most people who are not born into a vegetarian culture but become vegetarians by choice do so based on their sympathy for other animals. Today the facts of animal suffering are well known. In US laboratories between seventeen million and seventy million animals are killed every year. In factory farming operations six billion animals suffer and die annually—sixteen million each day. Dairy cows are regularly separated from newborn calves so that their milk can go to humans while their infants are chained in tightly fitting crates for four months and fed an iron-deficient diet until they are slaughtered. Chickens are debeaked and crowded five to each sixteen-by-eighteen-inch cage, their natural life spans of fifteen to twenty years shortened to two. Pigs are confined in narrow steel stalls with concrete floors, while sows are kept in a continual cycle of pregnancy, birth, and artificial insemination, their piglets taken away from them before they have even had the chance to suckle. (117)

By teaching an environmental literature class, I realized that while people tend to care about animals, most are not affected in the way that I was by writing my report. For most people, there is still a glaring disconnect between the farm and the plate; animals are still viewed as food to a majority of Americans, simply put here for us to enjoy.

I have come to realize documentaries showing animal cruelty may not be highly effective at a male-dominated engineering school, where students are regularly taught to find solutions. In fact, most engineers adhere to the five-step process when solving any quandary: "Given, Find, Equations, Diagram, Solution" (Downey et al. 110). Instead, a twofold logical approach may be more beneficial.

1. Immediacy: You are what you eat. While most students enjoy a tasty burger, do they really know what's in it? According to *Science News*, 80 percent of all US feedlot cattle are injected with

hormones: "these six hormones include three that are naturally occurring—Oestradiol, Progesterone and Testosterone—and three that are synthetic—Zeranol, Trenbolone, and Melengestrol" ("Hormones" 1). And let's not forget tasty antibiotics and steroids to keep these cows from becoming sickly in cramped environments. While animal welfare may not be on the radar, it is hoped that students can logically deduce this is not their grandfather's cow. It is instead an animal pumped full of unnatural chemicals, which are then in turn going into their bodies.

2. What will your quality of life be? Deforestation that comes from making space for animals and/or access to forest products presents a double-edged sword for these engineering students in a global economy. On one hand, they will have work due to the expansion of "roads, houses, commercial centers, industrial facilities, among other impervious surfaces" (Clement et al. 630–31). One the other, their work comes with a price, including a negative impact on biodiversity and the planet's carbon cycle, polluted air, and rising temperatures due to global warming. I have numerous students from China who all express a desire to find work in America after their graduation due to air pollution in their cities. While many have expressed homesickness, they added they don't want to raise children in such an unhealthy environment. With progress comes consequences.

When I became a vegetarian at fifteen years old, the pickings were slimmer. At restaurants, I usually had a choice of salad, salad, and coleslaw. These days, with the advent of Amy's, Boca, Gardein, Veestro, and other accessible vegetarian options, it is easier and more convenient than ever to go meatless on Mondays. More cafeterias and restaurants are offering alternatives for those with dietary concerns, including gluten-free, heart-healthy, and low-sodium options. Still, when it comes to any type of alteration, old habits die hard.

I have discovered the reasons why people are resistant to change run much deeper than the surface, visceral response of "Well, BLT sandwiches are tasty." Limiting meat often "constitutes a direct challenge to the dominant affective community that celebrates the pleasure of consuming animals. It questions the assumption of shared happiness around such consumption raising the prospect of a cruel commensality" (Twine 628). This type of direct and incidental questioning affects students based on their socioeconomic and international status, as well as their athlete status. Add in contradictory "personal narratives about [vegetarianism's] history, politics, health benefits, and ethical consideration," and it is easy to see how cultural shifts influence a young person's attitude toward vegetarianism (Wright 174).

The way a meatless lifestyle is taught or presented matters, too. (Admittedly, because of the time crunch, I didn't spend more than a week on the topic. In the future, I would like to change that.) And while some have a very emotional response to animal suffering, others can watch a violent factory-farming documentary and have a double cheeseburger for lunch. To alter that mind-set, or at least crack the door open, may require different approaches. Many young people don't think thirty years into the future but are concerned with the here and now, and that includes chemicals that can alter their appearance, moods, and concentration. Furthermore, with development comes setbacks. These students may acquire good engineering jobs but in undesirable locales due to the large carbon footprints of pollution and congestion.

The Meatless Monday/vegetarian movement has a long way to go, as it is still pigeonholed as a crusade for young, white, college-aged females who love animals (Hoffman et al. 139). Likewise, others view it as the bumper sticker of the week, a sort of "youthful rebellion" commonly found on radical campuses (Merriman 6). Despite these stereotypes, I am very hopeful. As the world population grows, diabetes/obesity rates rise yearly, and our natural resources shrink, I think it will become more an inevitability than a crusade (Hendrick 1). Change, indeed, is hard. But it can lead to healthier, more humane choices, which can alter the lives of every living entity on the planet.

WORKS CITED

Araki, Kadya. "Why All Humans Need to Eat Meat for Health." Breaking Muscle, n.d. http://breakingmuscle.com/fuel/why-all-humans-need-to-eat-meat-for-health. Accessed December 26, 2016.

Avey, Tori. "Discover the History of Meatless Mondays." PBS, August 16, 2013. http://www.pbs.org/food/the-history-kitchen/history-meatless-mondays/. Accessed March 21, 2017.

Clement, Matthew T., Guangqing Chi, and Hung C. Ho. "Urbanization and Land-Use Change: A Human Ecology of Deforestation Across the United States, 2001–2006." *Sociological Inquiry* 85, no. 4 (2015): 628–53. doi:10.1111/soin.12097.

Collingham, Lizzie. "How World War II Changed the Way Americans Ate." *Huffington Post*, April 3, 2012. http://www.huffingtonpost.com/2012/04/03/wwii-food-america_n_1398132.html.

Downey, Gary Lee, et al. "The Globally Competent Engineer: Working Effectively with People Who Define Problems Differently." *Journal of Engineering Education* 95, no. 2 (2006): 107–22, https://digitalcommons.calpoly.edu/cgi/viewcontent.cgi?referer=&httpsredir=1&article=1008&context=eth_fac.

Elliott, Ian. "European Union tightens ban on growth hormones." *Feedstuffs*, December 23, 2002 *General Reference Center GOLD*. portal.lib.fit.edu/login?url=http://go.galegroup.com.portal.lib.fit.edu/ps/i.do?p=GRGM&sw=w&u=melb26933&v=2.1&it=r&id=GALE%7CA96210837&sid=summon&asid=655ca36ae-c04ba94264d18cc539174c9.

Gaard, Greta. "Vegetarian Ecofeminism: A Review Essay." *Frontiers: A Journal of Women's Studies* 23, no. 3(2002): 117+. *General Reference Center GOLD*, portal.lib.fit.edu/login?url=http://go.galegroup.com.portal.lib.fit.edu/ps/i.do?p=GRGM&sw=w&u=melb26933&v=2.1&it=r&id=GALE%7CA99555567&-sid=summon&asid=dcfe4806612373b5328b30cf22065c07.

"Global Meatless Monday—for Health and Wellness." Johns Hopkins Center for a Livable Future, 2016. http://www.meatlessmonday.com/images/photos/2016/09/meatless-monday-global-toolkit.pdf.

Harper, A. Breeze, ed. *Sistah Vegan: Black Female Vegans Speak on Food, Identity, Health, and Society*. Brooklyn: Lantern Books, 2010.

"Health Benefits of a Vegetarian Diet." *vegetarianvegan.com, n.d.* https://www.vegetarianvegan.com/Vegetarian_Benefit.html

Hendrick, Bill. "Diabetes on the Rise in US: Survey Shows about 26 Million Americans Have Diabetes." WebMD. October 28, 2009. https://www.webmd.com/diabetes/news/20091028/diabetes-on-the-rise-in-us.

Hoffman, Sarah R., et al. "Differences between Health and Ethical Vegetarians. Strength of Conviction, Nutrition Knowledge, Dietary Restriction, and Duration of Adherence." *Appetite* 65 (2013): 139–44.

"Hormones." *Grace Communications Project*, n.d. http://www.sustainabletable. org/258/hormones. Accessed March 28, 2017.

"How to Eat." Michael Pollan, 23 January 2010. http://michaelpollan.com/reviews/ how-to-eat/. Accessed March 23, 2017.

Kleiner, Susan. "SSE #58: The Role of Red Meat in an Athlete's Diet." *Gatorade Sports Science Institute* 8, no. 5 (1995): 1–7. https://www.gssiweb.org/en-ca/Article/ sse-58-the-role-of-red-meat-in-an-athlete's-diet.

Mangels, Reed. "Vegan Diet Offers Health Benefits." *Vegetarian Journal*, General OneFile, October-December 2008. portal.lib.fit.edu/login?url=http://go.galegroup.com/ps/i. do?p=ITOF&sw=w&u=melb26933&v=2.1&id=GALE%7CA188350432&it=r&asid=- 349c356ab97ccb374efcb9f110b85f84. Accessed 23 Mar. 2017.

Merriman, Ben, and Sarah Wilson-Merriman. "Radical Ethical Commitments on Campus: Results of Interviews with College-Aged Vegetarians." *Journal of College and Character* 10, no. 4 (2009): 8.

Myers, Norman, and Jennifer Kent. 2004. *The New Consumers: The Influence of Affluence on the Environment*. Washington, DC: Island Press, 2004. EBSCOhost, search.

"Rankings & Accolades." *Florida Institute of Technology*, n.d. https://www.fit.edu/ about/rankings-and-accolades/

Silva, Jennifer M. "Slight Expectations: Making Sense of the 'Me Me Me' Generation." *Sociology Compass* 8, no. 12 (Dec. 2014): 1388–97. EBSCOhost, doi: 10.1111/soc4.12227.

Steves, Rick. "Why I Love Eating in Italy." Rick Steves' Europe, n.d. https://www.ricksteves. com/watch-read listen/read/articles/why-i-love-eating-in-italy. Accessed 30 March 2017.

"Summary of *American Earth: Environmental Writing Since Thoreau*." Amazon.com, n.d. https://www.amazon.com/American-Earth-Environmental-Writing-Thoreau/ dp/1598530208. Accessed March 23, 2017.

Twine, Richard. "Vegan Killjoys at the Table—Contesting Happiness and Negotiating Relationships with Food Practices." *Societies* 4, no. 4 (2014): 623–39, doi:10.3390/ soc4040623.

Ure, Delfina. "Five Benefits of Going Meatless on Mondays." *Muscle & Fitness Magazine*, n.d. http://www.muscleandfitness.com/nutrition/meal-plans/5-bene- fits-going-meatless-Mondays. Accessed March 23, 2017.

Vasi, Amanda. "What's Up with Meatless Monday: The History Behind the Program." *University Wire*, February 7, 2017, *https://search-proquestcom.portal.lib.fit.edu* / docview/1763842132?accountid=27313. Accessed March 21, 2017.

Vukovic, Diane. "Six Scientific Reasons that Vegetarians Make Better Lovers." PlenteousVeg December 26, 2017 http://plenteousveg.com/vegetarians-better-lovers/.

Wright, Laura. 2015. *The Vegan Studies Project: Food, Animals, and Gender in the Age of Terror*. Athens: University of Georgia Press.

CONCLUSION

Dinner with Beatriz: The Enmeshed Rhetoric of Vegan Studies

Laura Wright

"That man killed my goat."—Beatriz, *Beatriz at Dinner*, 2017

As the essays in this volume demonstrate, there has been thoughtful debate over the past decade or so with regard to trying to square veganism, vegan-inflected theory, and lived vegan experience with animal studies—and the field of "animal studies" is still a work in progress; as Robert McKay points out, in 2000 or so, he "proposed an edited collection of essays to a UK press analyzing the representation of animals in twentieth-century literature in English," yet his proposal was "rejected—on the grounds that it would not find a wide readership" (636), a circumstance that has changed considerably since that time. McKay's 2014 review essay of new works by Mary Bryden and Juliana Schiesari indicates that both of these contemporary animal studies texts—Bryden's *Beckett and Animals* and Schiesari's *Domesticities: Pets, Bodies, and Desire in Four Modern Writers*—present a feminist view that gestures toward a world in which "animal agencies and affectivities would . . . destabilize every supposedly natural categorization of bodily morphologies," but he ends his essay with a question: "what kind of literature, what kind of literary animal studies, might tell and read its story?" (643). In McKay's conception, the search for what future, destabilizing yet inclusive, deconstructive yet material, animal studies might look like remains somewhat still out of reach, but McKay does recognize the importance of "leverage[ing] feminist models" in its construction. Similarly, in the introduction to their invited symposium "Feminists Encountering Animals," published in 2012 in *Hypatia*, Lori Gruen and Kari Weil note that "one clear commonality" among all the essays that they included "is the need to maintain feminist, ethical, and political commitments within animal studies—commitments to reflexivity, responsibility, engagement with the experiences of other animals, and sensitivity to the intersectional contexts in which we encounter them," and they explain that a secondary area of concern is the often fraught "relationship between theory and practice" (493). The work of the authors included in this issue of *Hypatia* is varied and important, but veganism's place within animal studies, as discussed in these essays, again remains a point of some contention.

In the same issue of *Hypatia*, Stephanie Jenkins responds to the "gap between theory and practice in the philosophical investigation of nonhuman animals" with the assertion that "the division between the human and the animal will always be incomplete, fluid, and indefensible" (505). In turn, she calls very clearly for "a vegan, feminist ethics of nonviolence" (505) as a means of addressing the "hypo-critical project of animal studies," which she characterizes as "understanding the being of the human, even if it marks itself as posthumanist" (506). Jenkins points to Donna Haraway, who is not vegan, as an example of such hypocrisy. Of veganism, Haraway said in 2017, "I now have a profound respect for veganism as a kind of witness, as a kind of No, a kind of loud No! as well as an affirmative politics. I am not a vegan, and I remain committed to sustainable animal agriculture for many reasons" (qtd. in Franklin). Preceding Jenkins's essay, Traci Warkentin asks the question, "Must Every Animal Studies Scholar Be Vegan?," concluding that the answer might be "no," and she thoughtfully examines the often-unquestioned maxim that "if we care about animals . . . we must adopt veganism as a strict moral imperative" (499). Warkentin situates her analysis in the locus of her discomfort with the recent trend of all animal studies conferences switching to serving only vegan fare, a reality that she claims generates "a troubling rift . . . made visible in the way that participants appear to feel the need to confess whether they are a 'vegan' or a 'carnivore,'" and she seeks to unpack the underlying assumption in such instances that "a vegan lifestyle is unquestionably good, and perhaps, the only ethical choice among animal studies scholars" (501). Warkentin asserts that what has been missing from the uncritical acceptance—and I would argue the alternate dismissive rejection—of veganism as the only ethical route available to animal studies scholars is a rigorous ecofeminist analysis that has over the last two decades or so fallen "off the radar" (503).

I could not agree more. My assertion of the need for and the establishment of a fully vegan studies approach came about in large part as a result of viewing extant animal studies debates about animals in general and veganism more specifically through an intentionally and explicitly ecofeminist framework—a framework that has been in many senses disavowed, misunderstood, and in some very real ways undermined by the often more masculinist rhetorical approaches taken by the so-called leading voices in animal studies. Vegan studies constitutes work that scholars like Jenkins and Warkentin were already gesturing toward, and it is a theoretical approach the foundations of which lie specifically in the work of theorists like Carol Adams, Josephine Donovan, Greta Gaard, Lori Gruen, A. Breeze Harper, pattrice jones, Richard Twine, and Kari Weil (to name just a few), whose analyses have always examined intersectional enmeshments and who consider themselves to varying degrees ecofeminist activist scholars. An ecofeminist vegan studies approach is theoretical, but it engages a lived politics of listening, care, emotion, and the empathetic imagination. For example, the absence of an engaged analysis of veganism as both a theoretical position and an identity category within animal studies is what made it possible for Jacques Derrida to speak "animatedly about carnophallocentrism while eating with gusto a plate of steak tartare" (Attridge 54), allows Donna Haraway to write passionately about our relationships with dogs and still advocate for the eating of "responsibly" sourced meat, and allows Cary Wolfe to claim that doing animal studies has nothing to do with "whether or not you like animals" (567). Indeed, Wolfe's coining of "posthumanism" shifts the focus of animal studies from the "animal" to the human. Such a move takes animals out of a discourse that has taken us from Peter Singer's *Animal Liberation* in 1975 to a moment during which animals are essentially erased from the theories that seek to explain them. But, then again, in many ways animal studies has always been about us, human animals, as we seek to understand ourselves in relation to the nonhuman others with whom we share the planet; in this sense, animal studies might be good for *us*, but it is not necessarily good for the nonhuman animals about which it theorizes.

In "Speaking of Animal Bodies," Greta Gaard challenges the situation of the human as the true subject of animal studies, asserting that "when feminists attend to 'the question of the animal,' they do so from a standpoint that centers other animals, makes connections among diverse forms of oppression, and seeks to put an end to animal suffering—in other words, to benefit the subject of the research" (521). But she also recognizes the incredibly important and troubling reality that within the academy, "feminist empathy for animal suffering was soon feminized, and women's activism for animal rights was mocked as a movement of 'emotional little old ladies in tennis shoes': in male-supremacist (patriarchal) cultures, the association of women and animals reinforces their subordinate status" (521–22). Many contemporary animal studies theorists—often following without acknowledging the work of their ecofeminist counterparts and predecessors—have effectively erased work that has historically investigated and understood the significance of a critically rigorous and astutely interrogated veganism in terms of its engagement with and service to the interests of animals. As Gaard asserts,

> If animal ecofeminists and vegan feminists have been speaking and acting in ways that articulate a feminist animal studies approach, the absence of their scholarship from the foundations and development of animal studies indicates that the academic elite have not been listening. Not surprisingly, feminist methodology emphasizes listening as a hallmark of good scholarship. (523)

Perhaps there has never been a better time, particularly in the US, for ecofeminist vegan scholarly voices to be heard; at present, women's utterances of displacement, abuse, and unequal treatment are entering mainstream discourse in ways that heretofore have been unrecognized and unacknowledged.[1] We are in a feminist moment during which women are being heard, and women (and men) are asserting within the public sphere a tacit vegan studies approach to enmeshed oppressions; for example, during the Women's March of 2017, marchers carried signs with such slogans as "misogyny always accompanies systemic violence. Be vegan. Make peace" and "Color, gender, species. Peace and freedom for all" (Plotczyk).[2] My hope is that vegan studies is a part of this intersectional cultural articulation and conversation about oppression, as vegan studies constitutes an articulation that insists upon inclusion and that refuses to leave as *un*heard the displacement, abuse, and mistreatment of nonhuman animals. As Gaard says, both of ecofeminist vegans and of animals, "let's start listening" (524).

❧

In this brief concluding essay, I offer an ecofeminist vegan analysis of Mike White and Miguel Arteta's 2017 film *Beatriz at Dinner*, which

White claims was inspired by his outrage over American dentist Walter Palmer's killing of Cecil the Lion in Zimbabwe in 2015. In an interview with Samuel R. Murrian, White says, "I'd heard about that story, and it just hit me in the gut. I had thought to myself: If I was at a dinner party with a guy like that, and he told me he was going to Africa and hunt a lion, what would I do? Would I flip out on him? Grab a butter knife and leap across the table?" The film stars Salma Hayek as Beatriz Luna, a masseuse and healer in California and a refugee from Mexico who, as a child, had to flee after the village where she lived was overtaken by an American real estate developer. John Lithgow plays Doug Strutt, an affluent blowhard of a businessman who, among other things, hunts big game in Africa. When Beatriz's car will not start as she leaves an appointment with her client Kathy (Connie Britton), Kathy invites Beatriz to stay and attend a dinner party while Beatriz waits for a friend to come get her. What follows is a (tragi-)comedy of manners between the earnest, compassionate, and vegan Beatriz and Kathy's guests, a group of entitled, soulless carnivores who treat her by turns with amusement, disdain, and condescension. In the *Los Angeles Times*, Mark Olsen calls the film a "Trump-era allegory," and in a review in *Vanity Fair*, Richard Lawson reads the film as "perfect . . . for the Trump era," a film "about the struggle for humanity's conscience. Beatriz feels deeply that we have to care for the world, to try to heal it and make it better if we can. . . . Doug takes the opportunist's approach, figuring that everything is dying anyway, so we might as well take what we can get while we can still enjoy it." In the film, the enmeshed elements that underscore the refugee tragedy in Austria that I discussed at the beginning of this book—climate change, corporate greed, human migration, and animal exploitation—are read through a vegan lens by Beatriz, arguably the most ecofeminist character in contemporary film, a character informed by Mike White's own status as an ethical vegan and animal rights advocate.

In 2004, Mike White suffered a nervous breakdown after which he "became vegan and taught himself to meditate" (Bennett). Katherine Sullivan, in an article for *PETA*, thanks the filmmaker for his work with the activist organization and notes that "we can't help adoring the vegan writer for his inclusion—yet again!—of underlying animal rights messaging" in *Beatriz at Dinner*. In an article about White's HBO series *Enlightened,* which premiered in 2011, Laura Bennett discusses White's body of work, which includes *Chuck and Buck* (2000), *The Good Girl* (2002), and *The Year of the Dog* (2007)—a film with an animal activist, vegan protagonist—and notes White's characters "are losers and oddballs, guilty of trying too hard and caring too much, perpetually pining at a distance for the life they want. Existential disappointment is a quiet, deep current. But there is hope, too: in the distant possibility of escape, in a world of imagined alternatives." In many ways, Beatriz certainly fits this description. Profoundly empathetic, she is also deeply sad, longing for a past and a place that no longer exist, even as she maintains a peaceful stoicism that allows her to heal those around her despite the toll that doing so takes on her. We enter the film inside of Beatriz's dream of herself as a child rowing a boat through a mangrove forest as she comes upon a white goat. The camera does not show us the young Beatriz but rather provides a first-person point of view; we are seeing through her eyes, and via this device, the viewer is forced to view the world from Beatriz's perspective, that of a displaced refugee and woman of color in the contemporary US version of this scene replays throughout the film, and we learn that Beatriz had to leave her village and was separated from her family when the Mexican government took their land and sold it to an American real estate developer. The villagers were promised jobs in the hotel and golf course that would be built, but the resort remained open only for one year, and the police killed the people who protested and tried to make claims to the land that had been taken from them.

When she is massaging Kathy, we learn that Beatriz's neighbor has killed Geronimo, one of her two goats, in a fit of rage over the animal's bleating, and Beatriz mentions the death of the goat three times during the film, in the first instance identifying the man specifically: "*my neighbor* . . . killed my goat" (my emphasis). She is deeply connected to the suffering of animals and claims that she could feel the goat's pain, as well as the pain of a white octopus that her father caught and then kicked, ordering Beatriz to kill it when she was a child. When she meets Doug Strutt at the dinner party, he at first mistakes her for the hired help and asks her to get him a drink. She asks him, "Do I know you? I don't know why, I think I know you." During the meal, while everyone eats either beef or fish, Kathy notes that Beatriz is a vegetarian and asks that the staff fix her vegetables for dinner and give her sorbet for dessert—a clear indication that she also eschews dairy. Beatriz speaks of Kathy's daughter, who she treated at a "food-centered" cancer facility, and Beatriz interjects, "the first time I met her, I recognized her," claiming that the girl is an old soul, and "the earth needs old souls because it is very sick." Doug asks if she immigrated to the US legally, and when she answers yes, he congratulates her for having a job. He and the other guests consistently cut her off mid-sentence or change the subject when she is speaking, clearly uninterested in what she has to say; this dinner is about negotiating a business deal, and we learn that Doug is a developer who refuses to be hindered by environmental regulations, opting to clear the land first and deal with wildlife advocates after the fact. After dinner, Doug talks about going to South Africa to hunt big game and passes around a cell phone photo of a rhino he killed, claiming "I don't consider it murder," but rather an "original dance between man and beast, man and nature." When the phone reaches Beatriz, she pronounces Doug, like the planet, "sick," hurls the phone back at him, and storms out of the room.

In reading this scene, it is important to acknowledge and address that a vegan studies position must be culturally literate in order to recognize that the value that many of us in the West place on the lives of certain animals, yet not on others, often results in cultural insensitivity when we attempt to carry those values beyond the West. The selective outrage over the treatment of the animals killed and eaten at the China Yulin Dog Festival, for example, is often expressed by Americans who eat *different* animals killed in equally barbaric ways. Further, in the wake of the takedown of the aforementioned Walter Palmer for killing Cecil in 2015—during which outraged Americans posted his address and telephone number online, vandalized his house, and chased him out of town—I posted on Facebook that I was going to go stand outside of Whole Foods and post pictures and contact information for everyone I saw leaving with the dead carcass of an animal in their grocery bags. I posted such a thing because to my mind—and to the minds of many ethical vegans—the suffering of the animals that become food in our culture is as unconscionable as the murder of Zimbabwe's beloved lion. I was not, of course, serious, but I wanted to make a point.

In addition to the value placed on Cecil the Lion but not on animals that we typically eat, there is very often also an erasure of the people who are displaced in order to create hunting preserves in African countries. According to Martha Honey, when the Ndumo Game Reserve was established in 1924, the Tonga people of South Africa were forced to leave the area and were denied access to water within the reserve (367). In the late 1980s, when the Ndumo and Tembe reserves planned to merge so that the Tembe elephants could access water in Ndumo, the Tonga were once again threatened with the possibility of relocating but, "in the mid-1990s, the villagers, with the assistance of rural development workers, struck a deal whereby they agreed to move farther south" (367). Currently, according to John Vidal's 2016 article "The Tribes Paying the Brutal Price for Conservation" in the *Guardian,* "for the past 20 years, the San have been systematically stripped of their homes, land and culture. In a series of heavy-handed evictions, houses have been burned, schools and health centers closed, and water supplies cut off." As a result, the San now live "dispossessed, on the edge of the huge [Central Kalahari] game park, forbidden to hunt in or enter the land they have lived on sustainably for centuries"; they are displaced refugees in their own homeland.

In the West, we have mythologized lions and other "exotic" big game animals that exist in Africa. The image of Africa that we have bought into is of a place devoid of human life (or filled with warring, starving, diseased human life) and instead populated with lions, elephants, and other large regal creatures that we feel should be preserved and conserved. This image ignores the reality that actual Africans are often displaced from their homelands in the service of creating wildlife preserves and that sport hunting—sustained primarily by white men from the U.S—provides substantial financial benefits to the economies of the countries that allow such hunts to continue.[3] The outrage over the murder of Cecil looks a lot like the familiar narrative of the Concerned White Person seeking to help Africa even as the legacy of colonization by white peoples is the cause of what's wrong in the first place. It is so much easier to call out Walter Palmer than to consider our own complicated roles with regard to the suffering of the animals that we murder in multitudes in our country everyday so that we can eat them. For many people, those animals do not register, because we would never afford a chicken (or a cow, or a pig, or a fish) the same sort of misplaced reverence we ascribe to an apex predator like Cecil. And this is in no way to suggest that Cecil does not deserve that reverence and that his death doesn't warrant our outrage. It is, however, to suggest that we'd do well to recognize the hypocrisy of that outrage. The danger of these two approaches—comparing human suffering to the suffering of animals in order to make a pro-vegan argument, and of ignoring human displacement while arguing for the preservation of *specific* animals—is that both fail to fully investigate, in ways that are culturally sensitive, the more complex and enmeshed politics of oppression that should inform a truly vegan theoretical approach.

Beatriz, however, is as invested with the life of her goat—and with the lives of the other animals that she refuses to eat—as she is with the life of the rhino shot and killed by Doug. The moment that Beatriz looks at the picture of the dead animal on Doug's phone marks a break in the carefully maintained façade of polite conversation that had heretofore existed during the party, and Kathy insists that Beatriz go to bed. In Kathy's daughter's room, Beatriz leaves a voicemail for her friend Naroli in which she wonders if the mangroves are still there as they were in the Mexico of her childhood memories. She mentions the goat a second time: "a man murdered my goat." In this pronounce-ment, Beatriz's rhetoric shifts: the perpetrator is less specific, "a man" as opposed to "my neighbor," and the act is now "murder" instead of "killing." She searches online for information about Doug, convinced that he is the developer who destroyed her village, but she discovers that he is not. She returns to the party and sings a song in Spanish for the guests before confronting Doug again: "If you had been *that man*, I would have thought that fate brought us together" (my emphasis). He says, "many men do what I do," to which she responds, "one man, many men." She returns to his killing of the rhino, saying, "you think killing is hard? Try healing something. That is hard. You can break something in two seconds, but it can take a lifetime to fix it." Doug counters that "the world doesn't need your feelings. It needs jobs. It needs what I do." When she tells him that the world is dying and that its death will touch him, that he cannot hide from it, he laughs and says, "the world is dying. Accept it and enjoy yourself." Beatriz again says, "I know I know you," yet she remains uncertain how.

At this point, Kathy's husband Grant (David Warshofsky), furious with Beatriz, calls a tow truck and after it arrives, Beatriz suddenly runs back into the house, grabs a letter opener, and fantasizes about killing Doug, only to drop the letter opener in front of him before turning to leave. In the truck, the driver asks Beatriz if she is alright, and her final words are "that man killed my goat." "That man" is, of course, Doug Strutt, but "that man" is also her unnamed neighbor, as well as "a man," effectively, *any* man like Strutt, any man driven by capitalist greed and imperialist desire to conquer: "one man, many men." She does know him. Her life has been determined by him, by men like him, by a type, a homogenous category of undifferentiated and indifferent men. That the goat is named Geronimo is, of course, significant: Geronimo "was the last American Indian warrior to formally surrender to the United States" (Landry) after three decades of fighting to maintain his homeland in what is now Arizona. Geronimo was a refugee in his homeland, forced into the confinement of reservation land by that same category of man, those responsible for the decimation of the Apache and other native peoples in the project of Manifest Destiny. The goat is the exiled native person, the refugee, the woman; all are connected in their various displacements orchestrated by that man, those many men.

Beatriz orders the driver to pull over, and she runs into the surf, and the film ends with the image of surfacing, the camera coming up through the water and emerging in the mangrove swamp in which the story begins. What do we make of a film where the protagonist, a compassionate humanist and ecofeminist immigrant, walks into the sea and presumably drowns, dies like the refugees in the meat truck in Austria? Reviewers generally praised the film's first half as well as both Hayek's and the rest of the cast members' performances, and they consistently compare Strutt to real estate mogul (whose sons kill apex predators in Africa) Donald Trump, but by and large, they panned the film's ending. Oliver Jones writes that the ending "strikes out not once but twice" and Emily Yoshida asserts that "the ambiguous ending will be infuriating for some, and while I didn't need Arteta and White to go out with fireworks . . . something more character-driven might have felt more satisfying." Susan Wloszczyna is slightly more kind, noting that the end leaves us hanging, "which seems about right when we don't know which way the tweet wind will blow day after day." My ecofeminist vegan reading is somewhat different. Beatriz recognizes that Doug Strutt is the man who killed her goat, not literally, but in the sense that his actions are the product of the same mentality that allows her neighbor to kill the animal just because it annoyed him. Doug is allegorical, a stand-in for the greed and entitlement that enable rich white men to take without concern for the people from whom they are stealing and displacing, to justify the killing of big game animals as something profoundly primal, and to eat other animals without so much as a second thought. During dinner, the camera lands for a moment on the bloodred slab of meat that Doug cuts into and eats, overdetermining his status as a carnivore. Doug is Charles or David Koch, or Donald Trump, or any number of other obscenely wealthy *any* men who conquer and take and take. To him, Beatriz is a commodity (he thinks she's the help), an annoyance, a drain on the system. She has come here and taken a job from a rightful citizen, at least in the eyes of a man who claims to want to create jobs for others.

But by walking into the ocean and drowning—if that is in fact what she does—she refuses to be commodified; when she first asks if she knows Doug, he jokes, asking her if she ever danced in Vegas. She is nothing more than a body, a sexualized *piece of meat* to him, but by committing suicide, she regains control of a narrative that is consistently told about women, about immigrants, and about animals by Doug and by men like him. In her telling, she is not a body in a meat truck, a commodity traded among smugglers and displaced by violence and environmental degradation, even as those things do cause her to flee her homeland. Beatriz claims at one point, "you have unfinished business with someone and in the next life, they come back in a different form," and such a belief allows Beatriz's walk into the sea to be read as a transition, not as an ending: it will take more than this lifetime to counter the harm that the Doug Strutts of the world are doing to the planet and its creatures, and Beatriz knows that she and these "many men" have unfinished business.

Furthermore, Beatriz's ethical veganism is a confrontation that looms large over a film that is all about consumption, about a single allegorical dinner, and that position situates her as a woman fully aware of the interconnected and enmeshed politics that her veganism, as well as other confrontations that she performs throughout the film—throwing Doug's phone at him, returning to sing a song in Spanish to the guests who clearly cannot understand the lyrics, and refusing to engage in polite conversation—can be deconstructed to render Beatriz in control and an incredibly wealthy man "another kind of cancer," as Beatriz calls him, one that she cannot heal. Her final statement that "that man killed my goat" flips the narrative and turns the named men who destroy the environment, its animals, and its humans into a homogenous menace, even as it individualizes the immigrant Beatriz; it creates an exact reversal of the story that renders immigrants criminals, animals, and meat. At the end of the film, the viewer enters the film again, this time not as Beatriz but as an outsider looking into her world, as the camera breaks the surface of the water and we see the shoreline again from a first-person perspective. This time, the camera scans the shore and approaches a girl in a boat. Her back is to the viewer, but it is clear that this is Beatriz, looking for Geronimo.

WORKS CITED

Adams, Carol J. *The Sexual Politics of Meat: A Feminist-Vegetarian Critical Theory*. New York: Continuum, 1990.

Attridge, Derek. 2010. *Reading and Responsibility: Deconstruction's Traces*. Edinburgh: Edinburgh University Press.

Arteta, Miguel, dir. *Beatriz at Dinner*. Performances by Selma Hayek, John Lithgow, and Connie Britton. British Columbia, CA: Bron Studios, 2017.

Bennett, Laura. "An 'Enlightened' Mike White wants to Change TV." *New Republic*, January 17, 2013. https://newrepublic.com/article/111959/can-mike-white-change-television-tk.

Cacciola, Scott, and Victor Mather. "Larry Nassar Sentencing: 'I Just Signed your Death Warrant.'" *The New York Times*, January 24, 2018. https://www.nytimes.com/2018/01/24/sports/larry-nassar-sentencing.html.

Franklin, Sarah. "Staying with the Manifesto: An Interview with Donna Haraway." *Theory, Culture & Society* 34, no. 4 (2017): 49–63.

Gruen, Lori, and Kari Weil. "Introduction." *Hypatia* 27, no. 3 (2012): 492–93.

Honey, Martha. *Ecotourism and Sustainable Development: Who Owns Paradise?* Washington, DC: Island Press. 1999

Jenkins, Stephanie. "Returning the Ethical and Political to Animal Studies." *Hypatia* 27, no. 3 (2012): 504–09.

Jones, Oliver. "Beatriz at Dinner" Boasts Dynamite Performances, but About that Ending . . . *Observer*, 9 June 2017. http://observer.com/2017/06/beatriz-at-dinner-movie-review-salma-hayek/.

Landry, Alyssa. "Native History: Geronimo Is Last Native Warrior to Surrender." *Indian Country Today*, 4 September 2013. https://indiancountrymedianetwork.com/history/events/native-history-geronimo-is-last-native-warrior-to-surrender/.

Lawson, Richard. "Dark, Hopelessly Humane *Beatriz at Dinner* is the Perfect Film for the Trump Era" *Vanity Fair*, 24 January 2017. https://www.vanityfair.com/hollywood/2017/01/beatriz-at-dinner-sundance-review.

McKay, Robert. "What Kind of Literary Animal Studies Do We Want, or Need?" *MFS*. 60, no. 3, (2014): 636–44.

Murrian, Samuel R. "*Beatriz at Dinner* Screenwriter Reveals His Inspiration and How Trump's Election Helped the Movie." *Parade*, 5 June 2017. https://parade.com/575305/samuelmurrian/beatriz-at-dinner-screenwriter-reveals-his-inspiration-and-how-trumps-election-helped-the-movie/.

Olsen, Mark. "Mike White and Miguel Arteta serve up Trump-era allegory in *Beatriz at Dinner*." *Los Angeles Times*, 26 January 2017. http://www.latimes.com/entertainment/movies/la-et-mn-sundance-beatriz-at-dinner-feature-20170126-story.html.

Plotczyk, Lorelei. "Photos: Found the Vegans at the Women's March!" *Eat Plants/Drink Beer*, 24 January 2017. http://www.eatplantsdrinkbeer.com/readup/2017/1/23/vegans-at-womens-march.

Vidal, John. "The Tribes Paying the Brutal Price of Conservation." *Guardian*, 28 August 2016. https://www.theguardian.com/global-development/2016/aug/28/exiles-human-cost-of-conservation-indigenous-peoples-eco-tourism.

Warkentin, Traci. "Must Every Animal Studies Scholar by Vegan?" *Hypatia* 27, no. 3, (2012): 499–504.

Wloszczyna, Susan. "*Beatriz at Dinner*." Roger Ebert.com 9 June 2017, http://www.rogerebert.com/reviews/beatriz-at-dinner-2017.

Wolfe, Cary. "Human, All Too Human: 'Animal Studies' and the Humanities." *PMLA*. 124, no. 2 (2009): 564–75.

Wright, Laura. *Wilderness into Civilized Shapes: Reading the Postcolonial Environment.* Athens: University of Georgia Press, 2010.

Yoshida, Emily. "*Beatriz at Dinner* is an *Enlightened* Sequel for the Trump Era." *Vulture*, June 7, 2017. http://www.vulture.com/2017/06/beatriz-at-dinner-movie-review.html.

END NOTES

1. I could cite any number of examples of the #metoo movement, but to my mind the most compelling is the case of Larry Nasser, the former doctor for the American gymnastics team, who was sentenced to 40 to 175 years in prison on January 24, 2017 for multiple sex crimes: "capping an extraordinary seven-day hearing that drew more than 150 young women to publicly confront him and speak of their abuse, Judge Rosemarie Aquilina, who had opened her courtroom to the young women, including several prominent Olympic athletes, bluntly made clear that Dr. Nassar, fifty-four, was likely to die in prison. 'I just signed your death warrant,' she said as she imposed the sentence" (Cacciola and Mather).

2. For images of vegan feminist signs at the Women's March of 2017, check out this blogpost http://www.eatplantsdrinkbeer.com/readup/2017/1/23/vegans-at-womens-march.

3. I have written about the history of big game hunting in *Wilderness into Civilized Shapes: Reading the Postcolonial Environment*.

Index

About the Editor and Contributors

Laura Wright is Professor of English at Western Carolina University, where she specializes in postcolonial literatures and theory, ecocriticism, and animal studies. Her monographs include *Writing Out of All the Camps: J. M. Coetzee's Narratives of Displacement* (Routledge, 2006 and 2009), *Wilderness into Civilized Shapes: Reading the Postcolonial Environment* (University of Georgia Press, 2010), and *The Vegan Studies Project: Food, Animals, and Gender in the Age of Terror* (University of Georgia Press, 2015). She has been funded by the National Science Foundation for her work titled InTeGrate Cli-Fi, dedicated to the role that literature can play in our understanding of climate science. https://serc.carleton.edu/integrate/teaching_materials/climate_fact/index.html

∼

Dr. Kadri Aavik is an Associate Professor of Gender Studies at Tallinn University, Estonia, and a postdoctoral researcher at the University of Helsinki, Finland. Her recent research includes work in the emergent fields of critical animal studies and vegan studies. She has studied the animal advocacy movement and its links to other social justice movements in the post-socialist space, the reluctance of mainstream feminists to embrace animal justice and veganism, institutional resistance to veganism, on the example of medical encounters in Estonia, and the role of national dietary guidelines in promoting human use of other animals.

∼

Carol J. Adams is the author of *The Sexual Politics of Meat,* now in a twenty-fifth anniversary edition, *Burger,* in Bloomsbury's Object Lessons Series, *Protest Kitchen: Fight Injustice, Save the Planet, and Fuel Your Resistance One Meal at a Time* and many other books. She has written for *The New York Times,* the *Washington Post, Ms. Magazine, The Christian Century, Tikkun,* and *Truthdig,* among others. She lives in Dallas with her partner and two rescue dogs. www.caroljadams.com.

∼

Margarita Carretero-González is Senior Lecturer in English Literature at the English and German Department of the University of Granada (Spain) and a member of the research groups "Studies in English-language Narratives" (University of Granada) and GIECO—Research Group on Ecocriticism (Franklin Institute-UAH). She has published nationally and internationally on ecocriticism and ecofeminism, fantasy fiction, narratives by women, and intertextual relationships between literature and other artistic discourses. Margarita is member of the Advisory Board of *Ecozon@: European Journal of Literature, Culture and Environment*, Consultant Editor of the *Journal of Animal Ethics*, and Fellow of the Oxford Centre for Animal Ethics. Her most recent work is a collection of essays on *Spanish Thinking about Animals*, currently being reviewed for publication by Michigan State University Press.

Shanti Chu is an Assistant Professor of Philosophy at the College of Lake County where she directs the LGBTQ+ Resource Center, the Philosophy Club, and co-facilitates a feminist discussion group. She holds an MA in Philosophy from Miami University. Her courses and research focus on feminist theories of embodiment, postcolonial theory, and political philosophy. Shanti has presented her philosophical work at political philosophy conferences, and her article on recognition will be published in *Philosophy for Girls*. She is focused on making philosophy palatable through her two blogs: one on ethical, affordable, and vegetarian eating in Chicago, chiveg.com, and a Tumblr blog on race, culture, and gender. She was recently featured in *VoyageChicago*: an online publication featuring creative individuals.

Dr. Natalie M. Dorfeld is currently an Associate Professor of English in the School of Arts and Communication at Florida Institute of Technology. Her work has been featured in *The Chronicle of Higher Education, Inside Higher Ed, Working Papers in Composition and TESOL, Journal of Excellence in College Teaching*, and *CEA MAGazine*. Additionally, she serves on the editorial board of *Forum: Issues About Part-Time and Contingent Faculty,* which focuses on adjunct professors working in the humanities. She is a lifelong animal lover, conservationist, and vegetarian since the age of fifteen.

೧

D. Gilson is the author of *Jesus Freak* (with Will Stockton, Bloomsbury 2018); *I Will Say This Exactly One Time: Essays* (Sibling Rivalry 2015); and *Brit Lit* (Sibling Rivalry 2013). He is an Assistant Professor of English at Texas Tech University, and his work has appeared in *Threepenny Review, POETRY*, and *The Rumpus*.

೧

Tom Hertweck holds a PhD in Literature & Environment from the University of Nevada, Reno, where he teaches courses in American literary and cultural studies, film, and food studies. He is the editor of *Food on Film: Bringing Something New to the Table* (Rowman & Littlefield), founding book review and special issues editor of *Territories: A Trans-Cultural Journal of Regional Studies* (University of California), and coeditor of the book series of *Cultural Ecologies of Food in the 21st Century* with the University of Nevada Press.

೧

Christopher Kocela is Associate Professor of English at Georgia State University where he teaches contemporary U.S literature, theory, and popular culture. He is the author of *Fetishism and Its Discontents in Post-1960 American Fiction* and his essays and articles have appeared in the journals *Postmodern Culture, Genders, Comparative Literature and Culture, LIT*, and in critical studies on the work of Thomas Pynchon and David Foster Wallace. His current research examines intersections between Eastern thought (especially Buddhism) and the depiction of racial and gender difference in contemporary U.S novels.

೧

Alex Lockwood, PhD, is a writer, educator, and activist working in the fields of Critical Animal Studies, media, creative writing, and the environmental humanities. His hybrid memoir/study of the body in animal advocacy, *The Pig in Thin Air*, was published by Lantern Books in 2016. He has published widely on Rachel Carson and her importance for nature writing, and his environmentally themed debut novel *The Chernobyl Privileges* is scheduled for publication by Roundfire Books in March 2019. He lives in Newcastle, UK, and speaks on veganism, especially in relation to men and masculinities.

∼

Ryan J. A. Phillips is a PhD Candidate in Ryerson University's Communication and Culture program, where his work focuses on the rhetoric and political economy of alternative food and sports media.

∼

Caitlin E. Stobie is a Bonamy Dobrée doctoral candidate and assistant lecturer at the University of Leeds, where she is co-founder of the Leeds Animal Studies Network. Her work has appeared, or is forthcoming, in a special cluster on vegan studies and ecocriticism in *ISLE: Interdisciplinary Studies in Literature and Environment*, *Green Letters*, and *Scrutiny2: Issues in English Studies in Southern Africa*. Additionally, she coedits *EPIZOOTICS!*, an online literary journal focusing on ecocritical responses to the anthropocene and the posthuman. Her collaborative ecopoetic project *Read These Leaves* is featured in the ASLE-UKI's 2017 exhibition *In the Open* at SIA Gallery, Sheffield (UK).

∼

Alexa Weik von Mossner is Associate Professor of American Studies at the University of Klagenfurt in Austria. Her research explores the theoretical intersections of cognitive science, affective narratology, and environmental literature and film. She is the author of *Cosmopolitan Minds: Literature, Emotion, and the Transnational Imagination* (University of Texas Press 2014) and *Affective Ecologies: Empathy, Emotion, and Environmental Narrative* (Ohio State University Press 2017), and the editor of *Moving Environments: Affect, Emotion, Ecology, and Film* (Wilfrid Laurier University Press 2014). Her new research project, "Feeding the Senses," investigates how media depictions and narrativizations of food engage audiences on the sensual and emotional level.

John Yunker writes plays, short stories, and novels about the conflicted and evolving relationships between humans and animals. He is a co-founder of Ashland Creek Press, author of the novel *The Tourist Trail*, and editor of two fiction anthologies, *Among Animals* and *Among Animals 2*. His plays have been produced and staged at such venues as Centre Stage New Plays Festival, Oregon Contemporary Theatre, and the ATHE (Association for Theatre in Higher Education) conference. His teleplay *Sanctuary* was performed at the 2017 Compassion Arts Festival in New York, and his short stories have been published in *Phoebe, Qu, Flyway, Antennae*, and other journals. He is editor of the forthcoming anthology from Ashland Creek Press: *Writing for Animals: New Perspectives for Writers and Instructors to Educate and Inspire*.